A SOURCE BOOK OF ROMAN HISTORY

BY

DANA CARLETON MUNRO, A.M.

UNIVERSITY OF WISCONSIN

"Yours, Roman, be the lesson to govern the nations as their lord; this is your destined culture, to impose the settled rule of peace, to spare the humbled, and to crush the proud."

— *Vergil's Æneid*, Bk. VI, ll. 851–853 (CONINGTON).

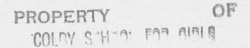
D. C. HEATH & CO., PUBLISHERS

BOSTON   NEW YORK   CHICAGO

PREFACE

THE extracts in this volume are intended to be used in connection with the text-book. No attempt has been made to tell a continuous story. It has seemed wise to choose a few general topics, and for these to furnish enough material for satisfactory work. It is needless to say that with such a wealth of sources the task of selection has been difficult. Of the passages originally selected for inclusion, less than one-quarter could be printed in this volume.

Easily accessible translations have been used wherever it was possible. In the appendix I have indicated after the name of each author the translation used. Where no name is given, the extracts were translated either by Mr. R. F. Scholz or by myself. In using the translations I have made a few slight changes in wording and punctuation. I have usually retained any important notes given in the translations.

The illustrations are intended merely to suggest that pictures form a very important class of sources. In the appendix brief statements are given as to the provenance and description of these pictures. Most of our text-books are well illustrated, and their pictures should be utilized as far as possible for class-room exercises. No " fancy-pictures " should be so used ; only representations of actual remains, of statuary, or of Roman drawings. The students should describe what the picture represents and its historic importance.

The references to secondary works include the most common treatises and text-books ;[1] occasionally a foreign work has been

---

[1] Botsford's *Story of Rome* was not published in time to be included among these references. It should be consulted by teachers.

added because of its exceptional value for that particular subject. It is hoped that the additional references to sources will aid pupils to work in the school library, which ought to include some of the translations noted. In a "manual for teachers," soon to be published, I shall offer some additional suggestions as to the manner in which this book may be used.

Mr. Richard F. Scholz, Fellow in European History in this University, has aided me greatly in the preparation of this work. He has prepared the references to sources and to secondary works, most of the biographical notices and descriptions of illustrations, and some of the translations. His accurate knowledge and painstaking care have been of the greatest service. I wish also to thank the various publishers for permission to use the translations and illustrations. I hope that the extracts in this book may lead some schools to purchase the complete translations. I must also express my gratitude to Professor Earl Barnes for many helpful suggestions.

DANA CARLETON MUNRO.

UNIVERSITY OF WISCONSIN.

CONTENTS

ILLUSTRATIONS

A SOURCE BOOK OF
ROMAN HISTORY

SOURCE BOOK

OF

ROMAN HISTORY

I. ITALY — ROME.   SOURCES AND CREDIBILITY OF EARLY ROMAN HISTORY

Italy : the Land and the People

Allen: *History of the Roman People*, ch. 1 ; Botsford : *A History of Rome*, ch. 1 ; Duruy: *History of Rome*, Vol. I, Introduction, pp. i–cxliii ; Freeman: *Historical Geography of Europe*, Vol. I (text), pp. 7–9, 43–49 ; How and Leigh: *History of Rome*, ch. 1, 2 ; Ihne : *Early Rome*, ch. 1 ; Kiepert : *Manual of Ancient Geography*, pp. 209–247 ; Leighton : *History of Rome*, Introduction, ch. 1, 2 ; Liddell : *History of Rome*, Introduction ; Michelet : *History of the Roman Republic*, ch. 2 ; Mommsen : *History of Rome*, Vol. I, Bk. I, ch. 1–3, 8–10 ; Morey : *Outlines of Roman History*, ch. 1 ; Myers : *Rome : Its Rise and Fall*, ch. 1 ; Pelham : *Outlines of Roman History*, pp. 14 ff. ; Robinson : *Short History of Rome*, ch. 2 ; Seignobos : *History of the Roman People* (translated by Fairley), ch. 1, pp. 1–14 ; Shuckburgh : *History of Rome*, ch. 2, 3 ; Tozer : *Classical Geography*, ch. 9, 10 ; West : *Ancient History*, ch. 1, pp. 249–254 ; Wolfson : *Essentials in Ancient History*, ch. 18, pp. 218–221.

Credibility of Early History

Abbott : *Roman Political Institutions*, par. 5, 14, 24 ; Allen, ch. 2, pp. 13, 14 ; Botsford, ch. 2, *passim* (p. 31) ; Duruy, ch. 1, pp. 59–63 ; How and Leigh, pp. 34–37 ; Ihne, ch. 4 ; Leighton, ch. 3 ; Lewis, Geo. C. : *The Credibility of Early Roman History*, 2 vols. ; Liddell, ch. 5 ; Michelet, pp. 403–424 ; Mommsen, Vol. I, pp. 316 ff. ; Morey, p. 22 ; Myers, pp. 46–48 ;

Pais: *Storia di Roma*, 2 vols.; Pelham, Bk. I, ch. 1, 2; Robinson, ch. 3, *passim*, pp. 28–30; Seeley: *Livy*, Bk. xiii, Introduction; Seignobos, pp. 33–35; Shuckburgh, pp. 54–60; West, ch. 1, pp. 256–259; Wolfson, pp. 222–225.

1. The Advantages of Italy

Dionysius: *Roman Antiquities*, Book I, chapters 36 and 37

. . . If countries of this size, not only in Europe, but throughout the whole earth, are compared with one another, Italy is, in my opinion, the best. . . . For that country which is fully supplied with all the most necessary products and is as little as possible dependent upon the importation of foreign goods, I consider the best. It is, so to speak, full of all delights and advantages. For to what grain fields is the so-called Campania inferior? There, indeed, I saw fields that were threefold productive, where a summer harvest followed the winter harvest, and an autumn harvest ripened after the summer harvest. What olive lands surpass the Messapian, Daunian, Sabine, and many others? What vineyards are better than the Tuscan, Alban, and Falernian? . . . and besides the cultivated land there is a great deal of waste land suitable for pasturing sheep, goats, horses, and cows. . . . Most wonderful of all are the forests on the steep heights, in the woodland valleys, and on the uncultivated hills whence is obtained much excellent wood for shipbuilding, and much also that is usable for other purposes.

And of all these no one is difficult to obtain, none too distant to be of use to men; but everything is easy to work and close at hand, on account of the abundance of rivers which flow through the whole coast district and facilitate the transportation and exchange of the products of the land. Also in this country there are in many places warm springs suitable for the pleasantest baths and which are excellent for healing chronic diseases. Furthermore, there are all kinds of metals, a great extent of hunting ground, many kinds of sea-food, and a thousand other things, some useful, some worthy of admiration. But the most delightful of all is the air, which in the various seasons is so temperate that the growth of fruit or the rearing of animals suffers neither from excessive heat nor too great cold.

2. The Position of Rome

Cicero: *On the Commonwealth*, Book II, parts of chapters 3, 4, 5, and 6

The position of the city, moreover, . . . he [Romulus] chose with incredible good fortune; for he did not draw near to the seacoast. . . . He felt and saw that maritime sites were not the most favorable for those cities which were founded with the hope of long-continued existence and power; first because maritime cities were exposed not only to many attacks but also to hidden dangers. . . . In maritime cities, moreover, there is also a certain corruption and revolution in manners; for there is a mixture of new languages and customs, and not only foreign wares but also foreign fashions are imported, so that none of the national institutions can remain in their integrity. . . . The sea also supplies to cities many pernicious incentives to luxury in the objects which are captured or imported. . . . But in spite of these vices there is one great advantage, and one that is general, namely, that new inhabitants are able to come to the city and that the citizens are able to export to other countries the products of their territory and whatever else they may wish.

How could Romulus, therefore, more successfully obtain the advantages and shun the dangers of maritime sites, than by placing the city on the bank of an inexhaustible and quiet river with a broad channel to the sea, so that the city might receive from the sea what it needed and return its own superabundance? . . . A city placed in any other part of Italy could not maintain firmly so great a power with as much ease.

Moreover, who is so negligent of the natural fortifications of the city itself that he does not have them fixed in his mind and clearly known? The plan and direction of the wall was so fixed by the wisdom of Romulus and the later kings that the city is bounded on all sides by steep and precipitous hills. . . . He also chose a spot which abounded in springs and which was healthful, although in a pestilential region.

3. Uncertainty of Early History

a. Livy, Book VI, chapter 1

The deeds of the Romans, from the foundation of the city of Rome to the capture of the same city, first under kings, then under consuls and dictators, decemvirs, and consular tribunes, their wars abroad, their dissensions at home, I have described in five books. The facts were obscure by reason of their great antiquity, like objects which from their great distance are seen with difficulty, and also because in those times written records, which are the only faithful guardians of the memory of events, were few and rare. Besides, even such records as were contained in the commentaries of the pontiffs, and other monuments, public and private, perished for the most part at the burning of the city. . . .

b. Dionysius, Book I, chapter 72

Moreover, among the writers there is great doubt not only as to the date when the city was founded, but also as to who the founders were. . . .

c. Plutarch: *Life of Numa*, chapter 1

There is even a lively dispute concerning the date when King Numa lived, although family pedigrees seem to go back with sufficient accuracy to his time. But a certain Clodius, in a book which he called *Strictures on Chronology*, states that the ancient records were destroyed when the Gauls burned the city, and that those which are now in existence were forged in favor of certain men who wished to thrust themselves into most noble families and clans to which they were in no way related.

d. Livy, Book VIII, chapter 40

. . . I am inclined to think that history has been much corrupted by means of funeral panegyrics and false inscriptions on statues; each family striving by false representations to appropriate to itself the fame of warlike exploits and public honors. From this cause, certainly, both the actions of individuals and the public records of events have been confused. Nor is there extant any writer, contemporary with those events, on whose authority we can rely.

e. The Battle of Sentinum. Livy, Book X, chapter 30[1]

. . . The glory of the day on which they fought at Sentinum was great, even when truly estimated; but some have gone beyond credibility by their exaggerations, who assert in their writings, that there were in the army of the enemy forty thousand three hundred and thirty foot, six thousand horse, and one thousand chariots, that is, including the Etrurians and Umbrians, who [they affirm] were present in the engagements: and, to magnify likewise the number of Roman forces, they add to the consuls another general, Lucius Volumnius, proconsul, and his army to the legions of the consul. In the greater number of annals, that victory is ascribed entirely to the two consuls. . . .

f. Funeral Laudations. Cicero: *Brutus*, chapter 16

. . . For it was customary, in most families of note, to preserve their images, their trophies of honor, and their memoirs, either to adorn a funeral when any of the family deceased, or to perpetuate the fame of their ancestors, or prove their own nobility. But the truth of history has been much corrupted by these encomiastic essays; for many circumstances were recorded in them which never existed, such as false triumphs, a pretended succession of consulships, and false alliances and elevations, when men of inferior rank were confounded with a noble family of the same name. . . .

[1] Cf. Livy, Bk. IX, ch. 44.

II. RELIGION

Allen, pp. 22–28, *et passim;* Boissier, G.: *La Religion Romaine;* Botsford, ch. 2, pp. 27–29, *et passim;* Coulanges, F. de: *The Ancient City*, Bk. I, ch. 1–4; Duruy, Vol. I, ch. 3; Vol. V, pp. 690–754, *et passim;* Granger, F. G.: *The Worship of the Romans;* How and Leigh, pp. 288–293, *et passim;* Ihne: *History of Rome*, Vol. IV, ch. 13; Inge: *Society in Rome under the Cæsars*, ch. 1; Leighton, ch. 4; Mommsen, Bk. I, ch. 12, *et passim;* Morey, pp. 31–33, 215, 227; Myers, ch. 3, pp. 25–38; Pelham, *passim;* Robinson, pp. 19, 20; Seignobos, ch. 4, *et passim;* Shuckburgh, *passim;* West, pp. 266–268, *et passim;* Wolfson, pp. 226, 242, 336 ff.

4. Things Subject to Divine Dominion

Gaius, II, paragraphs 3–6

3. Subject to divine dominion are things sacred and things religious.

4. Sacred things are those consecrated to the gods above; religious those devoted to the gods below.

5. Sacred things can only become so with the authority of the people of Rome, by consecration in pursuance of a law or a decree of the senate.

6. A religious thing becomes so by private will, when an individual buries a dead body in his own ground, if the burial is his proper business.

5. Cause of Roman Greatness

Polybius, Book VI, chapter 56 (in part) [1]

. . . But the most important difference for the better which the Roman commonwealth appears to me to display is in their

[1] Cf. Polybius, 18, 35; 32, 11.

religious beliefs. For I conceive that what in other nations is looked upon as a reproach, I mean a scrupulous fear of the gods, is the very thing which keeps the Roman commonwealth together. To such an extraordinary height is this carried among them, both in private and public business, that nothing could exceed it.

6. No Images

Augustine: *City of God*, Book IV, chapter 31 [1]

. . . He [Varro] says, also, that the ancient Romans, for more than a hundred and seventy years, worshipped the gods without an image. "And if this custom," he says, "could have remained till now, the gods would have been more purely worshipped." . . .

7. Numa's Institution of Religion

Livy, Book I, chapter 20

Then he turned his attention to the appointment of priests, although he performed very many sacred rites himself, especially those which now belong to the *flamen* of Jupiter. But because he thought that in a warlike city there would be more kings like Romulus than like Numa, and that they would go to war in person, he appointed a residentiary priest as *flamen* to Jupiter, that the sacred functions of the royal office might not be neglected, and he distinguished him by a fine robe, and a royal curule chair. To him he added two other *flamines*, one for Mars, the other for Quirinus. He also selected virgins for Vesta, a priesthood derived from Alba, and not foreign to the family of the founder. That they might be constant attendants in the temple, he appointed them salaries out of the public treasury; and by enjoining virginity, and other religious observances, he made them sacred and venerable. He also selected twelve *Salii* for Mars *Gradivus*, and gave them the distinction of an embroidered tunic,

[1] Cf. Plutarch: *Numa*, ch. 8.

and over the tunic a brazen covering for the breast. He commanded them to carry the celestial shields called *Ancilia*, and to go through the city singing songs, with leaping and solemn dancing. Then he chose out of the number of the fathers Numa Marcius, son of Marcus, as pontiff, and consigned to him an entire system of religious rites written out and sealed [showing] with what victims, upon what days, and in what temples the sacred rites were to be performed ; and from what funds the money was to be taken for these expenses. He also placed all the other religious rites, public and private, under the cognizance of the pontiff, in order that there might be some one whom the people should come to consult, lest any confusion in the divine worship might be occasioned by neglecting the ceremonies of their country, and introducing foreign ones. [He ordained] that the same pontiff should instruct the people not only in the celestial ceremonies, but also in the fitting funeral solemnities, and in placating the Manes, and what prodigies sent by lightning or by any other phenomenon were to be attended to and expiated. To elicit such knowledge from the divine mind, he dedicated an altar on the Aventine to Jupiter *Elicius*, and consulted the god by auguries as to what should be regarded.

8. Multitude of Gods

a. Petronius: *Satires*, chapter 17

For our country is so peopled with divinities that you can find a god more easily than a man.

b. Cicero: *On the Nature of the Gods*, Book II, chapter 2

The voices of the Fauns have been often heard, and deities have appeared in forms so visible, that they have compelled every one who is not senseless or hardened in impiety to confess the presence of the gods.

9. Religious Formalism

a. Cicero: *On the Responses of the Soothsayers*, chapter 11

. . . Shall we say that, if a morris-dancer stops, or a flute-player has on a sudden ceased to play, or if a boy with both father and mother alive has ceased to touch the ground, or has lost his hold of the sacred car, or of the reins, or if an ædile has used the wrong word or made the slightest mistake, then the games have not been duly celebrated, and those mistakes are forced to be expiated and the minds of the immortal gods are appeased by their repetition. . . .

b. Livy, Book XLI, chapter 16

The Latin festival was celebrated on the third day before the nones of May; and because, on the offering of one of the victims, the magistrate of Lanuvium had not prayed for the Roman People, the Quirites, religious scruples were felt. When the matter was laid before the senate, and they referred it to the college of pontiffs, the latter determined that the Latin festival had not been duly performed, and must be repeated. . . .

10. Farmer's Calendar

C. I. L., Vol. VI, p. 637

The Month
of May
XXXI days,
The nones fall on the 7th day.
The day has $14\frac{1}{2}$ hours.
The night has $9\frac{1}{2}$ hours.
The sun is in the sign of Taurus.
The month is under the protection of Apollo.
The corn is weeded.
The sheep are shorn.
The wool is washed.

Young steers are put under the yoke.
The vetch of the meadows
is cut.
The lustration of the crops
is made.
Sacrifices to Mercury
and Flora.

FIG. 2. — FARMER'S CALENDAR

Schreiber, plate 62, fig. 3

11. Religious Laws

Cicero : *On the Laws*, Book II, chapters 8–9

Let men approach the gods with purity ; let men appear before them in the spirit of devotion ; let men remove riches from
their temples — whoever doth otherwise shall suffer the vengeance
of heaven. Let no one have private gods ; neither new gods nor
strange gods. unless publicly acknowledged, are to be worshipped
privately ; let the temples which our fathers have constructed in
the cities be upheld ; let the people maintain the groves in the
country, and the abodes of the Lares ; let men preserve the customs of their fathers and of their family ; let the gods who have

always been accounted celestial be worshipped, and those likewise who have merited celestial honors by their illustrious actions, such as Hercules, Bacchus, Æsculapius, Castor, Pollux, and Quirinus. Let due honor be likewise paid to those virtues by which man is exalted to heaven — as Intelligence, Valor, Piety, Fidelity ; and let temples be consecrated to their honor ; with regard to the vices, let no sacred sacrifice be paid to them.

Let men put aside all contentions of every kind on the sacred festivals, and let servants enjoy them, their toils being remitted, for therefore they were appointed at certain seasons. Let the priests duly render the public thank-offering to heaven, with herbs and fruits, on the sacrificial day. Also, on the appointed holidays, let them offer up the cream of milk, and the sucklings ; and lest the priests should commit any mistakes in these sacrifices, or the reason of these sacrifices, let them carefully observe the calendar, and the revolutions of the stars. Let them provide those particular victims which are most appropriate and agreeable to each particular deity. . . .

Let there be two classes of these priests, one to preside over ceremonials and sacrifices, and the other to interpret the obscure predictions of the prophets and diviners, whenever the senate and the people require it. . . .

As to alliances, peace, war, truces, and the rights of ambassadors, let the two Fetiales be the appropriate judges, and let them determine all questions relating to military affairs. Let them report all prodigies and portents to the Etruscans and soothsayers, if the senate orders it; and let the chiefs of Etruria explain their system. Then will they learn what deities it behooves them to propitiate. . . .

Let there be no nocturnal sacrifices performed by women, except those which they offer according to custom on behalf of the people ; and let none be initiated in the mysteries except by the usual forms consecrated to Ceres, according to the Grecian ceremonials. . . .

Let men temper the public hilarity with song, and harp, and flute at the public games, as far as can be done without the games of the race-course and the wrestling-matches, and let them unite these amusements with the honors of the gods. Let them retain whatever is best and purest in the ancient form of worship. . . .

Let the rights of the deities of the dead be considered sacred. Let those who have passed into the world of souls be considered as deified; but let men diminish the unnecessary expense and sorrow which is lavished on them.

12. Authority of Augurs

Cicero: *On the Laws*, Book II, chapter 12

One of the greatest and most important offices in the Commonwealth is that of the augurs, conjoined as it is with the highest authority. I do not say this because I am an augur myself, but because we are bound to be of this opinion. For what can be more important, in respect of official dignity, than the power of dismissing the assemblies of the people, and the councils, though convoked by the chief rulers, or of annulling their enactments? What power, I say, can be more absolute than that by which even a single augur can adjourn any political proceeding to another day? What can be more transcendent than that authority which may command even consuls to lay down their office? What more sacred than their power of granting or refusing permission to form treaties and compacts? or their power of abrogating laws which have not been legitimately enacted? . . . What can be more honorable than the fact that there is no edict of the magistrates, relating either to domestic or foreign affairs, which can be ratified without the augur's authority?

415 A.U.C.   ### 13. Form of Self-devotion   B.C. 339

Livy, Book VIII, chapter 9

In this state of trepidation the consul Decius cries out with a loud voice to Marcus Valerius, "Valerius, we have need of the aid of the gods. Come, as public pontiff of the Roman people, dictate to me the words in which I may devote myself for the legions." The pontiff directed him to take the gown called *prætexta*, and with his head covered and his hand thrust out under the gown to the chin, standing upon a spear placed under his feet, to say these words : " Janus, Jupiter, father Mars, Quirinus, Bellona, ye Lares, ye Gods *Novensiles*, ye Gods *Indigetes*, ye Divinities, under whose power we and our enemies are, and ye *Dii Manes*, I pray you, I adore you, I ask your favor, that you would prosperously grant strength and victory to the Roman people, the Quirites ; and that ye may affect the enemies of the Roman people, the Quirites, with terror, dismay, and death. In such manner as I have expressed in words, so do I devote the legions and auxiliaries of the enemy, together with myself, to the *Dii Manes* and to Earth for the republic of the Quirites, for the army, legions, auxiliaries of the Roman people, the Quirites."

14, a. Ritual for the Feast of Spectres (*Lemuria*)[1]

Ovid : *Fasti*, Book V, lines 429, *et seq.*

In the depth of night when quietness is given for sleep, when we hear no more the baying of the dogs nor the cry of the birds, the man who is faithful to the rites of old, and fears the gods, rises from his couch. He is barefoot. Lest the unsubstantial shadow should steal upon him, he snaps his fingers. Thrice he washes his hands from all stain in spring water. He turns and takes the black beans in his mouth. Then he casts them over his shoulder, and while he does this he says, " These I offer, and with these beans I redeem myself and my house." So he speaks nine times, and does not look behind him. The shadow is thought to pick up the beans and to follow unseen. Again he touches the water, and rattles the copper from the mine, and he implores the shadow to go forth from his roof. After saying nine times, " Come forth, spirits of my fathers," he looks back, and accounts the rite duly performed.

[1] Cf. comment on the illustration, No. 18 (Altar of the Lares).

14, b. Sacrifices for the Penates

Horace: *Odes*, III, 23 (in part)

The victim mark'd for sacrifice, that feeds
On snow-capp'd Algidus, in leafy lane
Of oak and ilex, or on Alba's meads,
With its rich blood the pontiff's axe may stain;

Thy little gods for humbler tribute call,
Than blood of many victims; twine for them
Of rosemary a simple coronal,
And the lush myrtle's frail and fragrant stem.

The costliest sacrifice that wealth can make
From the incensed Penates less commands
A soft response, than doth the poorest cake,
If on the altar laid with spotless hands.

15. Lots (*Sortes*) [1]

"You can't put what's crooked straight."   "Don't be such a
fool as to believe them."   "Take care lest what is uncertain becomes
a fact."   "Don't let what's true become false by judging falsely."
"It's a very fine horse, but not one for *you* to ride."   "Ask boldly
and cheerfully, and you will succeed."   "Don't despise what you are
running away from, what you are tossing aside, I mean what is
being offered you."   "Why ask too late? you ask for something that
has no existence."   "We are not liars, as you said; you ask questions like a fool."   "I often help very many, but when I have done
so I get no thanks."

16. Sibylline Books

Cicero: *On Divination*, Book II, chapter 54

We Romans preserve with solicitude the verses which the Sibyl
is reported to have uttered when in an ecstasy, — the interpreter

[1] Translated by J. Wordsworth, in *Fragments and Specimens of Early Latin*,
page 493.

of which is by common report believed to have uttered recently
certain falsities in the senate, to the effect that he whom we did
really treat as king should also be called king, if we would be
safe. If such a prediction is indeed contained in the books of
the Sibyl, to what particular person or period does it refer? For,
whoever was the author of these Sibylline oracles, they are very
ingeniously composed; since, as all specific definition of person
and period is omitted, they in some way or other appear to pre-
dict everything that happens. Besides this, the Sibylline oracles
are involved in such profound obscurity, that the same verses
might seem at different times to refer to different subjects. . . .

. . . Now, in the verses of the Sibyl, the whole of the paragraph
on each subject is contained in the initial letters of every verse of
that same paragraph. This is evidently the artifice of a practised
writer, not of one in a frenzy; and rather of a diligent mind than
of an insane one. Therefore, let us consider the Sibyl as so distinct and isolated a character, that, according to the ordinance
of our ancestors, the Sibylline books shall not even be read except
by decree of the senate and be used rather for the putting down
than the taking up of religious fancies. And let us so arrange
matters with the priests under whose custody they remain, that
they may prophesy anything rather than a king from these mysterious volumes; for neither gods nor men any longer tolerate
the notion of restoring kingly government at Rome.

17. Cato's Opinion of Divination

Cicero: *On Divination*, Book II, chapter 24

There is an old saying of Cato, familiar enough to everybody,
that "he wondered that when one soothsayer met another, he
could help laughing." For of all the events predicted by them,
how very few actually happen? And when one of them does take
place, where is the proof that it does not take place by mere
accident?

18. Neglect of the Auspices

Cicero: *On the Nature of the Gods*, Book II, chapter 3

. . . Will not the temerity of P. Claudius, in the first Punic war, affect us? who, when the poultry were let out of the coop and would not feed, ordered them to be thrown into the water, and, joking even upon the gods, said, with a sneer, "Let them drink, since they will not eat"; which piece of ridicule, being followed by a victory over his fleet, cost him many tears, and brought great calamity on the Roman people. Did not his colleague Junius, in the same war, lose his fleet in a tempest by disregarding the auspices? Claudius therefore was condemned by the people; and Junius killed himself. Cœlius says that P. Flaminius,[1] from his neglect of religion, fell at

FIG. 3. — COOP WITH SACRED CHICKENS

Schreiber, plate 19, fig. 13

Thrasimenus; a loss which the public severely felt. By these instances of calamity we may be assured that Rome owes her grandeur and success to the conduct of those who were tenacious of their religious duties; and if we compare ourselves to our neighbors, we shall find that we are infinitely distinguished above foreign nations by our zeal for religious ceremonies, though in other things we may be only equal to them, and in other respects even inferior to them. . . .

[1] Cf. Cicero: *On Divination*, I, 35

19. Prodigies

Pliny: *Natural History*, Book II, chapter 57 (56)

Besides these, we learn from certain monuments, that from the lower part of the atmosphere it rained milk and blood, in the consulship of M. Acilius and C. Porcius, and frequently at other times. This was the case with respect to flesh, in the consulship of P. Volumnius and Servius Sulpicius, and it is said, that what was not devoured by the birds did not become putrid. It also rained iron among the Lucanians, the year before Crassus was slain by the Parthians, as well as all the Lucanian soldiers, of whom there was a great number in this army. The substance which fell had very much the appearance of sponge; the augurs warned the people against wounds that might come from above. In the consulship of L. Paulus and C. Marcellus it rained wool, round the castle of Carissanum, near which place, a year after, T. Annius Milo was killed. It is recorded, among the transactions of that year, that when he was pleading his own cause, there was a shower of baked tiles.

539 A.U.C.   ## 20. Foreign Rites and Superstitions   B.C. 215

a. Livy, Book XXV, chapter 1

. . . In proportion as the war was protracted, and the sentiments no less than the circumstances of men fluctuated accordingly as events flowed prosperously or otherwise, the citizens were seized with such a passion for superstitious observances, and those for the most part introduced from foreign countries, that either the people or the gods appeared to have undergone a sudden change. And now the Roman rites were growing into disuse, not only in private, and within doors, but in public also; in the forum and Capitol there were crowds of women sacrificing, and offering up prayers to the gods, in modes unusual in that country. A low order of sacrificers and soothsayers had enslaved men's understandings, and the numbers of these were increased by the coun-

try people, whom want and terror had driven into the city from
the fields which had lain uncultivated during a protracted war,
and had suffered from the incursions of the enemy, and by the
profitable trading in the ignorance of others which they carried on
like an allowed and customary trade.   At first, good men gave
utterance in private to the indignation they felt at these proceedings ; but afterwards the thing came before the fathers, and formed
a matter of public complaint.   The ædiles and triumvirs, appointed for the execution of criminals, were severely reprimanded
by the senate for not preventing these irregularities ; but when
they attempted to remove the crowd of persons thus employed
from the forum, and to overthrow their preparations for their
sacred rites, they narrowly escaped personal injury.   It being now
evident that the evil was too powerful to be checked by inferior
magistrates, the senate commissioned Marcus Atilius, the city
prætor, to rid the people of these superstitions.   He called an
assembly, in which he read the decree of the senate, and gave
notice, that all persons who had any books of divination, or forms
of prayer, or any written system of sacrificing, should lay all the
aforesaid books and writings before him before the calends of
April ; and that no person should sacrifice in any public or consecrated place according to new or foreign rites.

568 A.U.C.   B.C. 186
b. Livy, Book XXXIX, chapters 8, 9, 17–18

8. . . . The making inquisition concerning clandestine meetings
was decreed to both consuls.   A Greek of mean condition came,
first into Etruria, not with one of the many trades which his nation, of all others most skilful in the cultivation of mind and body,
has introduced among us, but a low operator in sacrifices, and a
soothsayer ; nor was he one who, by open religious rites, and by
publicly professing his calling and teaching, imbued the minds of
his followers with terror, but a priest of secret and nocturnal rites.
These mysterious rites were, at first, imparted to a few, but afterwards communicated to great numbers, both men and women.

To their religious performances were added the pleasures of wine
and feasting, to allure a greater number of proselytes. . . . From
this store-house of villainy proceeded false witnesses, counterfeit
seals, false evidences, and pretended discoveries. From the same
place, too, proceeded poison and secret murders, so that in some
cases, even the bodies could not be found for burial. Many of
their audacious deeds were brought about by treachery, but most
of them by force ; it served to conceal the violence, that on account of the loud shouting, and the noise of drums and cymbals,
none of the cries uttered by the persons suffering violation or murder could be heard abroad.

9. The infection of this mischief, like that from the contagion
of disease, spread from Etruria to Rome. . . .

17. . . . Above seven thousand men and women are said to
have taken the oath of the association. . . .

18. . . . With regard to the future, the senate passed a decree, . . . that no Bacchanalian rites should be celebrated in
Rome or in Italy : " and ordering that, in case any person should
believe some such kind of worship incumbent on him, and necessary ; and that he could not, without offence to religion, and incurring guilt, omit it, he should represent this to the city prætor,
and the prætor should lay the business before the senate. If permission were granted by the senate, when not less than one hundred members were present, then he might perform those rites,
provided that no more than five persons should be present at the
sacrifice, and that they should have no common stock of money,
nor any president of the ceremonies, nor priest."

21. Religious Revival under Augustus

Suetonius : *Life of Augustus*, chapter 31

The office of Pontifex Maximus, of which he could not decently
deprive Lepidus as long as he lived, he assumed as soon as he
was dead. He then caused all prophetical books, both in Latin

and Greek, the authors of which were either unknown, or of no great authority, to be brought in; and the whole collection, amounting to upwards of two thousand volumes, he committed to the flames, preserving only the Sibylline oracles; but not even those, without a strict examination, to ascertain which were genuine. . . . He restored the calendar, which had been corrected by Julius Cæsar, but through negligence had again fallen into confusion, to its former regularity; and upon that occasion, called the month *Sextilis*, by his own name, August, rather than September, in which he was born; . . . He increased the number, dignity, and revenues of the priests, and especially those of the Vestal Virgins. . . . He likewise revived some old religious customs, which had become obsolete; as the augury of public health, the office of high priest of Jupiter, the religious solemnity of the *Lupercalia*, with the Secular, and Compitalian games. . . . He ordered the household gods to be decked twice a year with spring and summer flowers, in the Compitalian festival. . . .

22. Worship of the Emperor

a. Tacitus: *Annals*, Book I, chapter 78

A request from the Spaniards that they might erect a temple to Augustus in the colony of Tarraco was granted, and a precedent thus given for all the provinces. . . .

b. Tacitus: *Annals*, Book IV, chapter 36

. . . Next, the people of Cyzicus were accused of publicly neglecting the established worship of the Divine Augustus, and also of acts of violence to Roman citizens. They were deprived of the franchise which they had earned during the war with Mithradates. . . .

23. Sacrifices

Suetonius: *Life of Caligula*, chapter 14

Immediately on his [Caligula's] entering the city, . . . the whole government and administration of affairs was placed in his hands;

so much to the joy and satisfaction of the public, that, in less than three months after, above 160,000 victims are said to have been offered in sacrifice.   Upon his going, a few days afterwards, to the nearest islands on the coast of Campania, vows were made for his safe return. . . .   And when he fell ill, the people hung about the Palatium all night long ; some vowed, in public handbills, to risk their lives in the combats of the amphitheatre, and others to lay them down for his recovery. . . .

FIG. 4. — SUOVETAURILIA
Baumeister, fig. 1799

24. Loss of Religious Beliefs

Petronius : *Satires*, XLIV

. . . So help me gracious, I think all this trouble comes from the gods, for now-a-days nobody believes in Heaven and nobody cares a straw for Jove ; but every Jack of them shuts his eyes and just keeps thinking about his own affairs. . . .   That's why the gods are stealthily dogging us to-day.   It's because we haven't any more religion. . . .

Additional References to Sources

Sacredness of oath, Livy, III, 20; Religious formality, Cicero: *On the Nature of the Gods*, II, 4; Auspices given to Romulus, Livy, I, 7; Cicero: *On Divination*, I, 48; Auspices at the election of Numa, Livy, I, 18; Augury of Attus Naevius, Livy, I, 36; Hymn of the Arval Brethren, translated in J. Wordsworth's *Fragments*, p. 391; True religion, Seneca: *Epistles*, 95, 50; 115, 5; Cicero: *On the Laws*, II, 10; Euhemerism, Augustine: *City of God*, IV, 27; Self-devotion, Livy, VIII, 10; Prodigies, Livy, XXV, 1; I, 31; XXIX, 14; XXVIII, 11; XXVII, 37; Extraordinary sacrifice (209 B.C.), Livy, XXII, 57; Seneca, *On Benefits*, III, 27, 1; Ammianus Marcellinus, XXV, 4, 17; Haruspices, Cicero: *On the Responses of the Sooth-sayers*, IX ff.; Tacitus: *Annals*, XI, 15; Ceremonies at the founding of a colony, Cicero: *Philippics*, II, 40; Ceremonies upon the making of a treaty, Livy, I, 24; Ceremonies upon a declaration of war, Livy, I, 32; Decay of religion, Juvenal, XIII; Attitude of the cultured Roman toward immortality (death), Pliny: *Natural History*, VII, 56 (55); Manner of burial, Pliny: *Natural History*, VII, 55 (54); Spurious books of Numa, Livy, XL, 29; Divination, Cicero: *On Divination*, I, 2; *On the Laws*, II, 13; Introduction of the *Magna Mater*, Livy, XXIX, 14; A religious procession, Livy, XXVII, 37; Auspices taken with chickens, Livy, X, 40; A sacred spring declared, — full legal formula and ritual, Livy, XXII, 10; A "strike" of the flute-players needed for sacrifice, Livy, IX, 30; Religious conservatism, Livy, IX, 29; Neglect of religion (under J. Cæsar), Cicero: *On the Nature of the Gods*, II, 3; Worship of the emperor, Tacitus: *Annals*, I, 57, 73; The Augustales, Tacitus: *Annals*, I, 54.

III. THE ROMAN ARMY

Allen, pp. 20, 32, 68–70, 170, *et passim;* Botsford, pp. 33, 45–48, 162, *et passim;* Duruy, Vol. I, ch. 11, *et passim;* How and Leigh, pp. 45, 46, 135–142, *et passim;* Leighton, ch. 55, pp. 365–383; Mommsen, Bk. I, ch. 6; Bk. II, ch. 8, *et passim;* Morey, pp. 42, 94–99, 220, 298; Myers, pp. 51, 53, 54, 229; Pelham, pp. 36, 39, 105 ff., 461–465; Robinson, pp. 32, 95, 223, *et passim;* Seignobos, ch. 7, *et passim;* Shuckburgh, pp. 84, 130, 131, 214–218, *et passim;* West, pp. 270–272, 310–312, *et passim;* Wolfson, pp. 230–236, 410 f., *et passim.*

25. The Roman Army (Punic Wars)

Polybius, Book VI, chapters 19–26, 37–39, 42

19. After electing the consuls they proceed to elect military tribunes, — fourteen from those who had five years', and ten from those who had ten years' service. All citizens must serve ten years in the cavalry or twenty years in the infantry before the forty-sixth year of their age, except those rated below four hundred asses. The latter are employed in the navy; but if any great public necessity arises they are obliged to serve as infantry also for twenty campaigns: and no one can hold an office in the state until he has completed ten years of military service. . . .

When the consuls are about to enrol the army, they give public notice of the day on which all Roman citizens of military age must appear. This is done every year. When the day has arrived, and the citizens fit for service are come to Rome and have assembled on the Capitoline, the fourteen junior tribunes divide themselves, in the order in which they were appointed by the people or by the imperators, into four divisions, because the primary division of the forces thus raised is into four legions. . . .

20. This division and assignment of the tribunes having been settled in such a way that all four legions have an equal number of officers, the tribunes of the several legions take up a separate position and draw lots for the tribes one by one ; and summon the tribe on whom it from time to time falls. From this tribe they select four young men as nearly like each other in age and physical strength as possible. These four are brought forward, and the tribunes of the first legion pick out one of them, those of the second another, those of the third another, and the fourth have to take the last. When the next four are selected the tribunes of the second legion have the first choice, and those of the first the last. With the next four the tribunes of the third legion have the first choice, those of the second the last ; and so on in regular rotation : of which the result is that each legion gets men of much the same standard. But when they have selected the number prescribed, — which is four thousand two hundred infantry for each legion, or at times of special danger five thousand, — they next used to pass men for the cavalry, in old times after the four thousand two hundred infantry ; but now they do it before them, the selection having been made by the censor on the basis of wealth ; and they enrol three hundred for each legion.

21. The roll having been completed in this manner, the tribunes belonging to the several legions muster their men; and selecting one of the whole body that they think most suitable for the purpose, they cause him to take an oath that he will obey his officers and do their orders to the best of his ability. And all the others come up and take the oath separately, merely affirming that they will do the same as the first man.

At the same time the consuls send orders to the magistrates of the allied cities in Italy, from which they determine that allied troops are to serve : declaring the number required, and the day and place at which the men selected must appear. The cities then enrol their troops with much the same ceremonies as to selection and administration of the oath, and appoint a commander and a paymaster.

The military tribunes at Rome, after the administering of the oath to their men, and giving out the day and place at which they are to appear without arms, for the present dismiss them. When they arrive on the appointed day, they first select the youngest and poorest to form the *velites*, the next to them the *hastati*, while those who are in the prime of life they select as *principes*, and the oldest of all as *triarii*. For in the Roman army these divisions, distinct not only as to their ages and nomenclature, but also as to the manner in which they are armed, exist in each legion. The division is made in such proportions that the senior men, called *triarii*, should number six hundred, the *principes* twelve hundred, the *hastati* twelve hundred, and that all the rest as the youngest should be reckoned among the *velites*. And if the whole number of the legion is more than four thousand, they vary the numbers of these divisions proportionally, except those of the *triarii*, which is always the same.

22. The youngest soldiers or *velites* are ordered to carry a sword, spears, and target. . . .

The second rank, the *hastati*, are ordered to have the complete panoply. This to a Roman means, first, a large shield. . . . With the shield they also carry a sword hanging down by their right thigh, which is called a Spanish sword. . . . In addition to these they have two *pila*, a brass helmet, and greaves. Some of the *pila* are thick, some fine. . . . Besides these each man is decorated with a plume of feathers, with three purple or black feathers standing upright, about a cubit long. . . . The common soldiers also receive a brass plate, a span square, which they put upon their breast and call a breastpiece, and so complete their panoply. Those who are rated above a hundred thousand asses, instead of these breastpieces wear, with the rest of their armor, coats of mail. The *principes* and *triarii* are armed in the same way as the *hastati*, except that instead of *pila* they carry long spears (*hastæ*).

24. The *principes*, *hastati*, and *triarii*, each elect ten centurions according to merit, and then a second ten each. All these sixty have the title of centurion alike, of whom the first man chosen is a member of the council of war. And they in their turn select a rear-rank officer each who is called *optio*. Next, in conjunction with the centurions, they divide the several orders (omitting the *velites*) into ten companies each, and appoint to each company two centurions and two *optiones;* the *velites* are divided equally among all the companies; these companies are called orders or maniples, or *vexilla*, and their officers are called centurions or *ordinum ductores*. Each maniple selects two of its strongest and best born men as standard-bearers. . . . When the two centurions are both on the field, the first elected commands the right of the maniple, the second the left: if both are not there, the one who is commands the whole. . . .

FIG. 5. — A ROMAN STANDARD-BEARER

Schreiber, plate 39, fig. 7

25. Similarly they divide the cavalry into ten squadrons, and from each they select three officers (*decuriones*), who each select a subaltern (*optio*). The *decurio* first elected commands the squadron, the other two have the rank of *decuriones:* a name indeed which applies to all alike. If the first *decurio* is not on

the field, the second takes command of the squadron. The armor
of the cavalry is very like that in Greece. In old times they did
not wear the *lorica*, but fought in their tunics. . . . They used
to have shields of bull's hide, . . . which were useless at close
quarters because they were flexible rather than firm. . . . Wherefore, as experience showed them the uselessness of these, they
lost no time in changing to the Greek fashion of arms : the
advantages of which were, first, that men were able to deliver
the first stroke of their lance-head with a good aim and effect,
because the shaft from the nature of its construction was steady
and not quivering ; and, secondly, that they were able, by revers-
ing the lance, to use the spike at the butt-end for a steady and
effective blow. And the same may be said about the Greek
shields : for, whether used to ward off a blow or to thrust against
the enemy, they neither give nor bend. When the Romans learnt
these facts about the Greek arms they were not long in copying
them ; for no nation has ever surpassed them in readiness to
adopt new fashions from other people, and to imitate what they
see is better in others than in themselves.

26. Having made this distribution of their men and given
orders for their being armed, as I have described, the military
tribunes dismiss them to their homes. But when the day has
arrived on which they were all bound by their oath to appear at
the place named by the consuls (for each consul generally ap-
points a separate place for his own legions, each having assigned
to him two legions and a moiety of the allies), all whose names
were placed on the roll appear without fail : no excuse being
accepted in the case of those who have taken the oath, except a
prohibitory omen or absolute impossibility. The allies muster
along with the citizens, and are distributed and managed by the
officers appointed by the consuls, who have the title of *præfecti
sociis* and are twelve in number. These officers select for the
consuls from the whole infantry and cavalry of the allies such as
are most fitted for actual service, and these are called *extraor-*

dinarii. The whole number of the infantry of the *socii* generally equals that of the legions, but the cavalry is treble that of the citizens. Of these they select a third of the cavalry, and a fifth of the infantry to serve as *extraordinarii.* The rest they divide into two parts, one of which is called the right, the other the left wing (*alæ*). . . .

37. . . . The man who is found guilty [of neglecting guard-duty] is punished by the *fustuarium ;* the nature of which is this. The tribune takes a cudgel and merely touches the condemned man ; whereupon all the soldiers fall upon him with cudgels and stones. Generally speaking, men thus punished are killed on the spot ; but if by any chance, after running the gauntlet, they manage to escape from the camp, they have no hope of ultimately surviving even so. They may not return to their own country, nor would any one venture to receive such an one into his house. Therefore those who have once fallen into this misfortune are utterly and finally ruined. . . . The punishment of the *fustuarium* is assigned also to any one committing theft in the camp, or bearing false witness : as also to any one who in full manhood is detected in shameful immorality : or to any one who has been thrice punished for the same offence. All these things are punished as crimes. But such as the following are reckoned as cowardly and dishonorable in a soldier : for a man to make a false report to the tribunes of his valor in order to get reward ; or for men who have been told off to an ambuscade to quit the place assigned them from fear ; and also for a man to throw away any of his arms from fear, on the actual field of battle. Consequently it sometimes happens that men confront certain death at their stations, because, from their fear of the punishment awaiting them at home, they refuse to quit their post : while others, who have lost shield or spear or any other arm on the field, throw themselves upon the foe, in hopes of recovering what they have lost, or of escaping by death from certain disgrace and the insults of their relations.

38. But if it ever happens that a number of men are involved in these same acts : if, for instance, some entire maniples have quitted their ground in the presence of the enemy, it is deemed impossible to subject all to the *fustuarium* or to military execution ; but a solution of the difficulty has been found at once adequate to the maintenance of discipline and calculated to strike terror. The tribune assembles the legion, calls the defaulters to the front, and, after administering a sharp rebuke, selects five or eight or twenty out of them by lot, so that those selected should be about a tenth of those who have been guilty of the act of cowardice. Those selected are punished with the *fustuarium* without mercy ; the rest are put on rations of barley instead of wheat, and are ordered to take up their quarters outside the *vallum* and the protection of the camp. As all are equally in danger of having the lot fall on them, and as all alike who escape that, are made a conspicuous example of by having their rations of barley, the best possible means are thus taken to inspire fear for the future, and to correct the mischief which has actually occurred. . . .

39. The pay of the foot soldier is $5\frac{1}{3}$ asses a day ; of the centurion $10\frac{2}{3}$; of the cavalry 16. The infantry receive a ration of wheat equal to about $\frac{2}{3}$ of an Attic *medimnus* a month, and the cavalry 7 *medimni* of barley, and 2 of wheat ; of the allies the infantry receive the same, the cavalry $1\frac{1}{3}$ *medimnus* of wheat, and 5 of barley. This is a free gift to the allies ; but in the cases of the Romans, the quæstor stops out of their pay the price of their corn and clothes, or any additional arms they may require at a fixed rate.

42. It is because the first object of the Romans in the matter of encampment is facility, that they seem to me to differ diametrically from Greek military men in this respect. Greeks, in choosing a place for a camp, think primarily of security from the natural strength of the position. . . . The Romans, on the other hand, prefer to undergo the fatigue of digging, and of the other labors

of circumvallation, for the sake of the facility in arrangement, and to secure a plan of encampment which shall be one and the same, and familiar to all.[1]

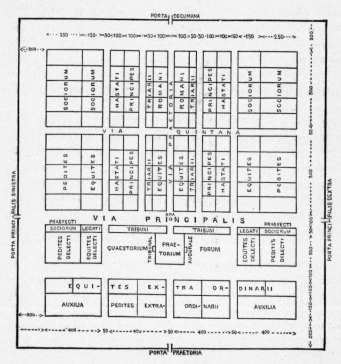

FIG. 6. — A ROMAN CAMP

Marquardt, Vol. VI, p. 404

26. Advantage of Native Army

Polybius, Book VI, chapter 52

. . . In regard to military service on land, the Romans train themselves to a much higher pitch than the Carthaginians.

[1] For a detailed description of the Roman camp, see Polybius, Bk. VI, ch. 27–31.

The former bestow their whole attention upon this department: whereas the Carthaginians wholly neglect their infantry, though they do take some slight interest in the cavalry. The reason of this is that they employ foreign mercenaries, the Romans, native and citizen levies. It is in this point that the latter polity is preferable to the former. They have their hopes of freedom ever resting on the courage of mercenary troops : the Romans on the valor of their own citizens, and the aid of their allies. The result is that even if the Romans have suffered a defeat at first, they renew the war with undiminished forces, which the Carthaginians cannot do. For, as the Romans are fighting for country and children, it is impossible for them to relax the fury of their struggle ; but they persist with obstinate resolution until they have overcome their enemies. What has happened in regard to their navy is an instance in point. In skill the Romans are much behind the Carthaginians, as I have already said ; yet the upshot of the whole naval war has been a decided triumph for the Romans, owing to the valor of their men. . . .

27. Flexibility of the Roman Order

Polybius, Book XVIII, chapter 32

. . . The Macedonian phalanx is difficult, and sometimes impossible to handle, because the men cannot act either in squads or separately. The Roman order on the other hand is flexible ; for every Roman, once armed and on the field, is equally well equipped for every place, time, or appearance of the enemy. He is, moreover, quite ready and needs to make no change, whether he is required to fight in the main body, or in a detachment, or in a single maniple, or even by himself. Therefore, as the individual members of the Roman force are so much more serviceable, their plans are also much more often attended by success than those of others. . . .

28. Marius's Reforms

Sallust: *Jugurthine War*, LXXXVI

. . . He himself [Marius] proceeded to enlist soldiers, not after
the ancient method, or from the classes, but taking all that were
willing to join him, and the greater part from the lowest ranks.
Some said this was done from a scarcity of better men, and others
from the consul's desire to pay court to the poorer class, because
it was by that order of men that he had been honored and pro-
moted ; and, indeed, to a man grasping at power, the most needy
are the most serviceable persons, to whom their property (as they
have none) is not an object of care, and to whom everything
lucrative appears honorable.[1] . . .

29. Demoralization of the Army (under Sulla)

Sallust: *Catiline*, XI

. . . But after Lucius Sulla, having recovered the government
by force of arms, proceeded, after a fair commencement, to a
pernicious termination, all became robbers and plunderers ; some
set their affections on houses, others on lands ; his victorious
troops knew neither restraint nor moderation, but inflicted on the
citizens disgraceful and inhuman outrages. Their rapacity was
increased by the circumstance that Sulla, in order to secure the
attachment of the forces which he had commanded in Asia, had
treated them, contrary to the practice of our ancestors, with extraordinary indulgence, and exemption from discipline ; and pleasant
and luxurious quarters had easily, during seasons of idleness, ener-
vated the minds of the soldiery. Then the armies of the Roman
people first became habituated to licentiousness and intemperance,
and began to admire statues, pictures, and sculptured vases ; to
seize such objects alike in public edifices and private dwellings ;
to spoil temples ; and to cast off respect for everything, sacred

[1] Cf. Plutarch : *Marius*, 13.

and profane. Such troops, accordingly, when once they obtained the mastery, left nothing to the vanquished. . . .

30. The Veterans of Sulla[1]

Cicero: *Against L. Catiline* II, paragraph 9

. . . There is a third class, already touched by age, but still vigorous from constant exercise ; of which class is Manlius himself, whom Catiline is now succeeding. These are men of those colonies which Sulla established at Fæsule, which I know to be composed, on the whole, of excellent citizens and brave men ; but yet there are colonists, who, from becoming possessed of unexpected and sudden wealth, boast themselves extravagantly and insolently ; these men, while they build like rich men, while they delight in farms, in litters, in vast families of slaves, in luxurious banquets, have incurred such great debts, that, if they would be saved, they must raise Sulla from the dead ; and they have even excited some countrymen, poor and needy men, to entertain the same hopes of plunder as themselves. . . .

713 A.U.C.   ### 31. Spirit of the Army   B.C. 41

Appian: *Civil Wars*, Book V, paragraph 17

. . . The cause [of the prevailing insubordination] was that generals, for the most part, as is usually the case in civil wars, were not regularly chosen ; that their armies were not drawn from the enrolment according to the custom of the fathers, nor for the benefit of their country ; that they did not serve the public so much as they did the individuals who brought them together ; and that they served these not by the force of law, but by reason of private promises ; not against the common enemy, but against private foes ; not against foreigners, but against fellow-citizens, their equals in rank. All these things impaired military discipline,

[1] Cf. Sallust: *Catiline*, XXVIII (at end) ; Livy: *Epitome*, LXXXIX.

and the soldiers thought that they were not so much serving in
the army as lending assistance, by their own favor and judgment,
to leaders who needed them for their own personal ends.   Deser-
tion, which had formerly been unpardonable, was now rewarded
with gifts, and whole armies resorted to it. . . .   Understanding
these facts, the generals tolerated this behavior, for they knew
that their authority over their armies depended on donatives
rather than on law.

718 A.U.C.   **32. Slaves in the Armies**   B.C. 36

Appian: *Civil Wars,* Book V, paragraph 131

. . . He [Octavius] sent sealed letters to all the armies, with
instructions to open them all on a designated day and to execute
the orders contained therein.   These orders related to the slaves
who had run away during the civil dissensions and joined the
armies, for whom Pompeius had asked freedom, which the senate
and the treaty had granted.   These were all arrested on the same
day and brought to Rome, and Octavius returned them to their
Roman or Italian masters, or to the heirs of the same.   He also
gave back those belonging to Sicilian masters.   Those whom
nobody claimed he caused to be put to death in the cities from
which they had absconded.

33. Privileges of Soldiers (under the Empire)

Juvenal: *Satires*, XVI, 7 ff.

Let us treat, in the first place, of advantages in which all
share ; of which not the least important is this, that no civilian
must dare to strike you.   Nay, even though he be himself the
party beaten, he must dissemble his wrath, and not dare to show
the prætor the teeth he has had knocked out, and the black
bruises on his face with its livid swellings, and all that is left of
his eye, which the physician can give him no hopes of saving.
. . . You could with greater ease suborn a false witness against a

civilian, than one who would speak the truth against the fortune and the dignity of the man-at-arms.

34. Rewards Paid to the Army

Appian: *Civil War*, Book V, paragraph 128

Fortune became jealous of his [Octavius's] great prosperity. His army revolted, especially his own troops. They demanded to be discharged from the service and that rewards should be given them. . . . They said that they would not go to war again until they had received the prizes and honors of the previous wars. He said that he would not postpone the honors. So he distributed many prizes, and gave to the legions additional crowns, and to the centurions and tribunes purple-bordered garments and the dignity of chief councillors in their native towns. While he was distributing other awards of this kind, the tribune Ofilius exclaimed that crowns and purple garments were playthings for boys, that the rewards for soldiers were lands and money. The multitude cried out, "Well said"; whereupon Octavius descended from the platform in anger. . . .

35. Land Allotments and Pensions (under Augustus)

Monumentum Ancyranum, chapter 16

For the lands which in my fourth consulship, and afterwards in the consulship of Marcus Crassus and Cnæus Lentulus, the augur, I assigned to soldiers, I paid money to the municipia. The sum which I paid for Italian farms was about six hundred million sesterces, and that for land in the provinces was about two hundred and sixty millions.[1] Of all those who have established colonies of soldiers in Italy or in the provinces I am the first and

---

[1] Six hundred million sesterces equal $30,000,000. Cf. Dio, LI. 3, 4; Suet. Aug. 17. "This was in 724. There were 120,000 veterans to be provided for. Cf. c. 15. Six hundred million sesterces was the compensation for the lands given to these men, an average of 5000 sesterces ($250) for each holding." (Fairley: *Mon. Ancyr.*)

only one within the memory of my age to do this. And afterward in the consulship of Tiberius Nero and Cnæus Piso, and also in that of . . . I gave gratuities in money to the soldiers whom I sent back to their municipia at the expiration of their terms of service, and for this purpose I freely spent four hundred million sesterces.[1]

36. The Army under Augustus

Suetonius: *Life of Augustus*, chapter 49

With respect to the army, he distributed the legions and auxiliary troops throughout the several provinces. He stationed a fleet at Misenum, and another at Ravenna, for the protection of the Upper and Lower Seas.[2] A certain number of forces were selected to occupy the posts in the city, and partly for his own body-guard; but he dismissed the Spanish guard, which he retained about him till the fall of Antony; and also the Germans, whom he had amongst his guards, until the defeat of Varus. Yet he never permitted a greater force than three cohorts in the city, and had no [prætorian] camps. The rest he quartered in the neighborhood of the nearest towns, in winter and summer camps. All the troops throughout the empire he reduced to one fixed model with regard to pay and their pensions; determining these according to their rank in the army, the time they had served, and their private means; so that after their discharge they might not be tempted by age or necessities to join the agitators for a revolution. For the purpose of providing a fund always ready to meet their pay and pensions, he instituted a military exchequer, and appropriated new taxes to that object. . . .

37. Mutiny of the Army in Pannonia   A.D. 14

Tacitus: *Annals*, Book I, chapter 6

"When," he [Percennius, who had once been a leader of one of the theatrical factions] says, "will you dare to demand relief, if you

---

[1] "The dates are 747, 748, 750, 751, and 752 A.U.C. The amount is $20,000,000."
[2] The Adriatic and Tuscan Seas.

do not go with your prayers or arms to a new and yet tottering throne? We have blundered enough by our tameness for so many years, in having to endure thirty or forty campaigns till we grow old, most of us with bodies maimed by wounds. Even dismissal is not the end of our service, but, quartered under a legion's standard, we toil through the same hardships under another title. . . . Assuredly military service itself is burdensome and unprofitable ; ten asses[1] a day is the value set on life and limb ; out of this, clothing, arms, tents, as well as the mercy of centurions and exemptions from duty, have to be purchased. But indeed of floggings and wounds, of hard winters, wearisome summers, of terrible war, or barren peace, there is no end. Our only relief can come from military life being entered on under fixed conditions, from receiving each the pay of a denarius,[2] and from the sixteenth year terminating our service. We must be retained no longer under a standard, but in the same camp a compensation in money must be paid us. Do the prætorian cohorts, which have just got their two denarii per man, which after sixteen years are restored to their homes, encounter more perils? We do not disparage the guards of the capital ; still, here amid barbarous tribes, we have to face the enemy from our tents."

38. The Prætorians at the Death of Nero A.D. 68

Tacitus : *History*, Book I, chapter 5

The soldiery of the capital, who were imbued with the spirit of an old allegiance to the Cæsars, and who had been led to desert Nero by intrigues and influences from without rather than by their own feelings, were inclined for change, when they found that the donative promised in Galba's name was withheld, and reflected that for great services and great rewards there was not the same room in peace as in war, and that the favor of an emperor created by the legions must be alrcady preoccupied. They were further

---

[1] About fifteen cents.　　　　[2] About twenty cents.

excited by the treason of Nymphidius Sabinus, their prefect, who himself aimed at the throne. . . . The strictness once so commended, and celebrated in the praises of the army, was galling to the troops who rebelled against the old discipline, and who had been accustomed by fourteen years' service under Nero to love the vices of their emperors, as much as they had once respected their virtues. . . .

39. Rebellion in Army   A.D. 69

Tacitus: *History*, Book I, chapter 12

A few days after the first of January, there arrived from *Belgica* despatches of Pompeius Propinquus, the procurator, to this effect : that the legions of Upper Germany had broken through the obligation of their military oath, and were demanding another emperor, but conceded the power of choice to the senate and people of Rome, in the hope that a more lenient view might be taken of their revolt. . . .

553 A.U.C.   40. A Roman Triumph   B.C. 201

Appian : *Foreign Wars*, Book VIII, paragraph 66

The form of the triumph (which the Romans continue to employ) was as follows : All who were in the procession wore crowns. Trumpeters led the advance and wagons laden with spoils. Towers were borne along representing the captured cities, and pictures showing the exploits of war ; then gold and silver coin and bullion, and whatever else they had captured of that kind; then came the crowns that had been given to the general as a reward for his bravery by cities, by allies, or by the army itself. White oxen came next, and after them elephants and the captive Carthaginian and Numidian chiefs. Lictors clad in purple tunics preceded the general ; also a chorus of musicians and pipers, in imitation of an Etruscan procession, wearing belts and golden crowns, and they marched evenly with song and dance. . . . One of these, in the middle of the procession, wearing a purple cloak and golden bracelets and necklace, caused laughter by making various gesticulations, as though he were insulting the enemy. Next came a lot of incense bearers, and after them the general himself on a chariot embellished with various designs, wearing a crown of gold and precious stones, and dressed, according to the fashion of the country, in a purple toga embroidered with golden stars. He bore a sceptre of ivory,

FIG. 7. — A TESTUDO (From the Column of Trajan)
Baumeister, fig. 571

and a laurel branch, which is always the Roman symbol of victory. Riding in the same chariot with him were boys and girls, and on horses on either side of him, young men, his own relatives. Then followed those who had served him in the war as secretaries, aids, and armor-bearers. After these came the army arranged in companies and cohorts, all of them crowned and carrying laurel branches, the bravest of them bearing their military prizes. They praised some of their captains, derided others, and reproached others; for in a triumph everybody is free, and is allowed to say what he pleases. When Scipio arrived at the Capitol the procession came to an end, and he entertained his friends at a banquet in the temple.

ROMAN TRIUMPHS. — Livy, III, 29 (Cincinnatus); Livy, 34, 52; Plutarch: *Flaminius*, 14 (Flaminius); Livy, 45, 39, and Plutarch: *Æmilius Paulus* (Æmilius Paulus); Plutarch: *Lucullus*, 36 (Lucullus); Appian: *Foreign Wars*, XII, par. 116, *et seq.* (Pompey); Dio Cassius, 43, 19 (Cæsar). Citizen-soldiers receive pay, Livy, IV, 59. A soldier's career (Speech of Spurius Ligustinus), Livy, XLII, 34. Gladiators enlisted in the army, Appian: *Civil Wars*, III, 49.

IV. MONARCHICAL INSTITUTIONS. THE CONSTITUTION OF THE REPUBLIC. LAWS OF THE EARLY REPUBLIC

The Constitution. Early Laws

Abbott, ch. 2–11; Allen, *passim;* Botsford, ch. 2, pp. 24–27; ch. 4, 6–8, *passim;* Botsford: *Roman Assemblies;* Duruy, Vol. I, ch. 6, 8, 12, 13, 17, 22; Vol. II, ch. 36–39, *et passim;* Fowler, ch. 4, 7; Greenidge: *Roman Public Life,* ch. 1–6; How and Leigh, ch. 4, 5, 6, 8, 12, 17, 28, 44, *et passim;* Ihne: *Early Rome,* ch. 10–14, 18, 19; Ihne: *History of Rome,* Vol. IV, ch. 1–3; Leighton, ch. 14, *et passim;* Mommsen, Bk. I, ch. 5, 6, 11; Bk. II, ch. 1, 2, 3; Bk. III, ch. 11, *et passim;* Morey, ch. 3, 5–9, 13, 18–22, *et passim;* Morey: *Outlines of Roman Law,* periods i, ii; Myers, *passim;* Pelham, pp. 158–173, *et passim;* Robinson, *passim;* Seignobos, ch. 3, 5, 12, *et passim;* Shuckburgh, ch. 8, 13, 16, 26, 35, *et passim;* Taylor: *Constitutional and Political History of Rome,* ch. 1–5, 7, 8; Tighe: *The Development of the Roman Constitution;* West, pp. 304–308, *et passim;* Wolfson, ch. 18, pp. 228–231, ch. 20.

41. Institutions of the Regal Period

Dionysius, Book II, chapters 7–10, 12

7. First of all I shall speak of the form of polity, which I regard of all other political forms as the most self-sufficient, both in peace and in war. . . . Having divided the whole multitude into three groups, he [Romulus] appointed the most illustrious leader of each one of the divisions. Then again dividing each one of the three groups into ten sections, he appointed an equal number of the bravest leaders of these also. He called the larger groups tribes, the smaller, *curiæ,* by which names they are called to-day. . . . The leaders of the tribes . . . the Romans call tribunes; those in

41

command of the *curiæ*, . . . they call *curiones*. The *curiæ* were also subdivided by him into *decuriæ*, and a leader, called in our tongue *decurio*, commanded each *decuria*. When all were apportioned and arranged in tribes and *curiæ*, then dividing the land into thirty equal portions, he allotted one to each *curia*, reserving however sufficient land for the support of the sacred rites and for temples, and in addition, some for the public use. . . .

8. Another division . . . was made, pertaining to benefits and honors, on the basis of worth. He separated the men of distinguished birth, of well-known virtue, men of means as times were then, who had children, from the obscure and common and needy. Those of inferior station, he called plebeians . . . ; the better class, *patres* (fathers), whether on account of their being older than the rest, or because they had children, or because of their illustrious birth, or for all these reasons. . . . The most trustworthy historians who write about the Roman State affirm that for these reasons those men are called *patres*, and their descendants patricians. Those, on the other hand, who, out of private motives of envy and animosity, reproach the city with its obscure origin, say that these were so called not for these reasons, but because they alone could give proof of the legal status of the father, while the rest were fugitives and not able to name free-born fathers. And as a proof of this they cite the fact that whenever the kings decided to call a meeting of the *patres*, heralds summoned them by their own name and that of their father ; but all the plebeians were called to the assembly by certain servants, blowing on ox-horns. But neither is the summons by heralds a proof of the noble birth of the patricians, nor is the sound of the *bucina* an indication of the ignoble origin of the plebeians ; but the one is a matter of honor, the other of speed. For it is impossible in a short time to call together the whole multitude by name.

9. When Romulus had separated the better from the lower class, he next prescribed and fixed by law the duties of each : the patricians were intrusted with the care of the sacred rites, with

the offices, with justice, and they were to share the administration of the Commonwealth with Romulus himself, remaining in charge of the works in the city ; the plebeians were to be released from all these duties, as being inexperienced in them and without the necessary leisure on account of their lack of money ; they were to till the fields, tend the flocks and cattle, and work at the money-making trades. That no seditions might arise, as in other states, where those in authority treated with scorn those lowly born, or the vulgar and needy envied their distinguished superiors, he made the patricians responsible for the care of the plebeians, permitting each one of the plebeians to choose as his guardian (patron) whomsoever he wished. . . . Romulus ordered the matter under the [cover of a] fair name, calling the guardianship of the poor and needy *patronatus*, and he added duties suited to each, in this way bringing about a humane and politic union of the two classes.

10. The *ius patronatus* . . . was of this nature. It was necessary for the patricians to interpret the law for their clients, who were totally ignorant of it, to look after their interests whether present or not, doing all that a father would do for his children both in money-matters and in cases of contracts, to undertake the cases of their clients who had suffered injustice in the matter of contracts, and to conduct their case against their accusers, — in a word, — to the best of their ability to insure to their clients complete freedom from both private and public business. The clients in turn must assist their patrons in providing a dowry for their daughters, if the fathers were in want of money, and to pay the ransom to the enemy, if any one of their patrons or their children chanced to be taken prisoners, to pay the expenses of unsuccessful [private] law-suits and [public] fines out of their own money, not in the way of a loan, but out of gratitude, to share the expenses of the magistracies, the priesthoods, and the other public duties, — as if related to their patrons by blood. Neither of them is justified by divine or human law in accusing the other, or giving testi-

mony or voting against one another, or in being enrolled among each other's enemies. If any one is convicted of any offence of this sort, he is amenable to the law of treason, which was sanctioned by Romulus. If convicted, any one is permitted to slay the offender, as a sacrifice to *Dis* [Zeus infernal]. . . . These unions of patrons and clients remained for many generations, differing in no way from the relations of kinsmen, binding even children's children. It was a matter of great praise for those of noble houses to have as many clients as possible, and to preserve the hereditary relationships handed down by their fathers, and through their own virtue to acquire others. There was the most extraordinary rivalry between both in manifesting their goodwill, each striving not to be behindhand in conferring favors; the clients thinking it worthy to assist their patrons to the best of their ability, the patrons in turn taking pains in no way to show ill-will to their clients, and accepting no gift of money. Such was their self-control, measuring happiness by virtue, not by fortune. . . .

12. Now when Romulus had ordered these matters, he next determined to create senators, with whom he intended to share the administration of the Commonwealth, choosing a hundred men from the ranks of the patricians, in the following manner. He himself selected one from all as the best man to whom he ought to intrust the administration of the city, whenever he himself led the army out beyond the limits [of the city]. He ordered each of the tribes to choose three men, wise in years and preëminent in birth. After these nine [were chosen], he next ordered each *curia* to select three patricians especially qualified. Then, adding these ninety chosen by the *curiæ* to the nine selected by the tribes, and appointing the one he himself had chosen to the headship of these, he filled out the number of one hundred senators. This council (*senatus*), if you interpret the word from the Greek, (γεροντία), signifies the council of old men, and is so called by the Romans up to the present day. . . .

176? A.U.C. **42. Constitution of Servius Tullius** B.C. 578?

Livy, Book I, chapters 42–44

42. . . . He then set about a work of peace of the utmost importance; that, as Numa had been the author of religious institutions, so posterity might celebrate Servius as the founder of all distinction among the members of the State, and of those orders by which a limitation is established between the degrees of rank and fortune. For he instituted the census, a most salutary measure for an empire destined to become so great, according to which the services of war and peace were to be performed, not by every person (indiscriminately) as formerly, but in proportion to the amount of property. Then he formed, according to the census, the classes and centuries, and the arrangement as it now exists, eminently suited either to peace or war.

43. Of those who had an estate of a hundred thousand asses or more, he made eighty centuries, forty of seniors and forty of juniors. All these were called the first class; the seniors were to be in readiness to guard the city, the juniors to carry on war abroad. The arms enjoined them were a helmet, a round shield, greaves, and a coat of mail, all of brass; these were for the defence of their body; their weapons of offence were a spear and a sword. To this class were added two centuries of mechanics, who were to serve without arms; the duty imposed upon them was to carry the military engines. The second class comprehended all whose estate was from seventy-five to a hundred thousand asses, and of these, seniors and juniors, twenty centuries were enrolled. The arms enjoined them were a buckler instead of a shield, and except a coat of mail, all the rest were the same. He appointed the property of the third class to amount to fifty thousand asses; the number of centuries was the same, and formed with the same distinction of age, nor was there any change in their arms, only greaves were taken from them. In the fourth class, the property was twenty-five thousand asses, the same number of centuries

was formed ; the arms were changed, nothing was given them but a spear and a long javelin. The fifth class was increased, thirty centuries were formed ; these carried slings and stones for throwing. Among them were reckoned the horn-blowers, and the trumpeters, distributed into three centuries. This whole class was rated at eleven thousand asses. Property lower than this comprehended all the rest of the citizens, and of them one century was made up which was exempted from serving in war. Having thus divided and armed the infantry, he levied twelve centuries of knights from among the chief men of the State. Likewise out of the three centuries appointed by Romulus he formed other six under the same names which they had received at their first institution. Ten thousand asses were given them out of the public revenue, for the buying of horses, and widows were assigned them, who were to pay two thousand asses yearly for the support of the horses. All these burdens were taken off the poor and laid on the rich. Then an additional honor was conferred upon them ; for the suffrage was not now granted promiscuously to all, as it had been established by Romulus, and observed by his successors, to every man with the same privilege and the same right ; but gradations were established, so that no one might seem excluded from the right of voting, and yet the whole power might reside in the chief men of the State. For the knights were first called, and then the eighty centuries of the first class ; and if they happened to differ, which was seldom the case, those of the second were called : and they seldom ever descended so low as to come to the lowest class. . . .

44. The census being now completed, which he had expedited by the terror of a law passed on those not rated, with threats of imprisonment and death, he issued a proclamation that all the Roman citizens, horse and foot, should attend at the dawn of day in the Campus Martius, each in his century. There he drew up his army and performed a lustration of it by the sacrifices called *suovetaurilia*,[1] and that was called the closing of the *lustrum*, because that

---

[1] Cf. illustration, Fig. 4, p. 21, and comment in Appendix II.

was the conclusion of the census. Eighty thousand citizens are said to have been rated in that survey. Fabius Pictor, the oldest of our historians, adds, that such was the number of those who were able to bear arms. To accommodate that number the city seemed to require enlargement. He adds two hills, the Quirinal and Viminal; then in continuation he enlarges the Esquiline, and takes up his own residence there, in order that respectability might attach to the place. He surrounds the city with a rampart, a moat, and a wall; thus he enlarges the pomœrium.

43. The Roman Constitution (Punic Wars)

Polybius, Book VI, chapters 11-17

TRIPLE ELEMENTS IN THE ROMAN CONSTITUTION

As for the Roman constitution, it had three elements, each of them possessing sovereign powers: and their respective share of power in the whole State had been regulated with such a scrupulous regard to equality and equilibrium that no one could say for certain, not even a native, whether the constitution as a whole were an aristocracy or a democracy or despotism. And no wonder: for if we confine our observation to the power of the consuls, we should be inclined to regard it as despotic; if on that of the senate, as aristocratic; and if finally one look at the power possessed by the people it would seem a clear case of democracy. What the exact powers of these several parts were, and still, with slight modifications, are, I will now state.

THE CONSULS

The consuls, before leading out the legions, remain in Rome and are supreme masters of the administration. All other magistrates, except the tribunes, are under them and take their orders. They introduce foreign ambassadors to the senate; bring matters requiring deliberation before it; and see to the execution of its decrees. If, again, there are any matters of state which require the authorization of the people, it is their business to see to them, to summon the popular meetings, to bring the proposals before them and to carry out the decrees of the majority. In the preparations for war also, and, in a word, in the entire administration of a campaign, they have all but absolute power. It is competent to them to impose on the allies such levies as they think good, to appoint the military tribunes, to make up the roll for soldiers, and to select those that are suitable. Besides, they have absolute power of inflicting punishment on all who are under their command while on active service ; and they have authority to expend as much of the public money as they choose, being accompanied by a quæstor, who is entirely at their orders. A survey of these powers would, in fact, justify our describing the constitution as despotic, — a clear case of royal government. Nor will it affect the truth of my description, if any of the institutions I have described are changed in our time, or in that of our posterity ; and the same remarks apply to what follows.

THE SENATE

The senate has first of all the control of the treasury, and regulates the receipts and disbursements alike. For the quæstors cannot issue any public money for the various departments of the State without a decree of the senate, except for the service of the consuls. The senate controls also what is by far the largest and most important expenditure, that, namely, which is made by the censors every *lustrum* for the repair or construction of public buildings ; this money cannot be obtained by the censors except by the grant of the senate. Similarly all crimes committed in Italy requiring a public investigation, such as treason, conspiracy, poisoning, or wilful murder, are in the hands of the senate. Besides, if any individual or state among the Italian allies requires a controversy to be settled, a penalty to be assessed, help or protection to be afforded, — all this is the province of the senate. Or again, outside of Italy, if it is necessary to send an embassy to reconcile warring communities, or to remind them of their duty, or sometimes to impose requisitions upon them, or to receive their submission, or finally to proclaim war against them, — this too is the business of the senate. With such business the people have nothing to do. Consequently, if one were staying at Rome when the consuls were not in town, one would imagine the constitution to be a complete aristocracy : and this has been the idea entertained by many Greeks, and by many kings as well, from the fact that nearly all the business they had with Rome was settled by the senate.

THE PEOPLE

After this one would naturally be inclined to ask what part is left for the people in the constitution, when the senate has these various functions, especially the control of the receipts and expenditures of the exchequer; and when the consuls, again, have absolute power over the details of military preparation, and an absolute authority in the field? There is, however, a part left the people, and it is a most important one. For the people is the sole fountain of honor and of punishment; and it is by these two things and these alone that dynasties and constitutions, and, in a word, human society are held together; for where the distinction between them is not sharply drawn, both in theory and practice, there no undertaking can be properly administered, — as indeed we might expect when good and bad are held in exactly the same honor. The people then are the only court to decide matters of life and death ; and even in cases where the penalty is money, if the sum to be assessed is sufficiently serious, and especially when the accused have held the high magistracies. And in regard to this arrangement there is one point deserving especial commendation and record. Men who are on trial for their lives at Rome, while sentence is in process of being voted, — if even one of the tribes whose votes are needed to ratify the sentence has not voted, — have the privilege at Rome of openly departing and condemning themselves to a voluntary exile. Such men are safe at Naples or Præneste or at Tibur, and at other towns with which this arrangement has been duly ratified on oath.

Again, it is the people who bestow offices on the deserving, which are the most honorable rewards of virtue. It has also the absolute power of passing and repealing laws ; and most important of all, it is the people who deliberate on the question of peace or war. And when provisional terms are made for alliance, suspension of hostilities, or treaties, it is the people who ratify them or the reverse.

These considerations again would lead one to say that the power in the State was the people's, and that the constitution was a democracy.

MUTUAL RELATION OF THE THREE. — CONSUL DEPENDENT ON SENATE AND PEOPLE

Such, then, is the distribution of power between the several parts of the State. I must now show how each of these several parts can, when it chooses, oppose or support the others.

The consul, then, when he has started on an expedition with the powers I have described, is to all appearance absolute in the administration of the business in hand ; still he has need of the support both of people and of senate, and without them is quite unable to bring the matter to a successful conclusion. For it is plain that he must have supplies sent to his legions from time to time ; but without a decree of the senate they can be supplied neither with corn, nor clothes, nor pay, so that all the plans of a commander must be futile if the senate is resolved either to shrink from danger or hamper his plans. And again, whether a consul shall bring any undertaking to a conclusion or no depends entirely upon the senate ; for it has absolute authority at the end of a year to send another consul to supersede him, or to continue the existing one in his command. Again, even to the successes of the generals, the senate has the power to add distinction and glory, and on the other hand to obscure their merits and lower their credit. For these high achievements are brought in tangible form before the eyes of the citizens by what are called "triumphs." But these triumphs the commanders cannot celebrate with proper pomp, or in some cases celebrate at all, unless the senate concurs and grants the necessary money. As for the people, the consuls are preëminently obliged to court their favor, however distant from home may be the field of their operations; for it is the people, as I have said before, that ratifies, or refuses to ratify, terms of peace and treaties; but most of all because when laying down their office they have to give account of their administration before it. Therefore in no case is it safe for the consuls to neglect either the senate or the good-will of the people.

THE SENATE CONTROLLED BY THE PEOPLE

As to the senate, which possesses the immense power I have described, in the first place it is obliged, in public affairs, to take the multitude into account and respect the wishes of the people; and it cannot put into execution the penalty for offences against the republic which are punishable by death, unless the people first ratify its decrees. Similarly, even in matters which directly affect the senators, — for instance, in the case of a law diminishing the senate's traditional authority, or depriving senators of certain dignities and offices, or even actually cutting down their property, — even in such cases the people have the sole power of passing or rejecting the law. But most important of all is the fact that, if the tribunes interpose their veto, the senate not only is unable to pass a decree, but cannot even hold a meeting at all, whether formal or informal. Now, the tribunes are always bound to carry out the decree of the people, and above all things to have regard to their wishes: therefore, for all these reasons the senate stands in awe of the multitude, and cannot neglect the feelings of the people.

THE PEOPLE DEPENDENT ON THE SENATE AND CONSUL

In like manner the people on its part is far from being independent of the senate, and is bound to take its wishes into account, both collectively and individually. For contracts, too numerous to count, are given out by the censors in all parts of Italy for the repairs or construction of public buildings; there is also the collection of revenue from many rivers, harbors, gardens, mines, and land, — everything, in a word, that comes under the control of the Roman government: and in all these the people at large are engaged; so that there is scarcely a man, so to speak, who is not interested either as a contractor or as being employed in the works. For some purchase the contracts from the censors themselves; and others go partners with them; while others again go security for these contractors, or actually pledge their property to the treasury for them. Now over all these transactions the senate has absolute control. It can grant an extension of time; and in case of unforeseen accident can relieve the contractors from a portion of their obligation, or release them from it altogether, if they are absolutely unable to fulfil it. And there are many details in which the senate can inflict great hardships, or, on the other hand, grant great indulgences to the contractors; for in every case the appeal is to it. But the most important point of all is that the judges are taken from its members in the majority of trials, whether public or private, in which the charges are heavy. Consequently all citizens are much at its mercy, and being alarmed at the uncertainty as to when they may need its aid, are cautious about resisting or actively opposing its will. And for a similar reason men do not rashly resist the wishes of the consuls, because one and all may become subject to their absolute authority on a campaign.

44. Penalties under Romulus

Cicero: *On the Commonwealth*, Book II, chapter 9

The judicial punishments were mostly fines of sheep and oxen ; for the property of the people at that time consisted in their fields and cattle, and this circumstance has given rise to the expressions which still designate real and personal wealth. Thus the people were kept in order rather by mulctations than by bodily inflictions.

45. Early Laws

a. Cicero: *On the Commonwealth*, Book II, chapter 31

It was the same man, who in this respect preëminently deserved the name of Publicola, who carried in favor of the people the first law received in the comitia centuriata, that no magistrate should sentence to death or scourging a Roman citizen who appealed from his authority to the people. And the pontifical books attest that the right of appeal had existed, even against the decision of the kings. Our augural books affirm the same thing. And the Twelve Tables prove, by a multitude of laws, that there was a right of appeal from every judgment and penalty.

283? A.U.C.   b. The Publilian Law   B.C. 471?

Livy, Book II, chapters 56 and 57[1]

56. . . . He [Volero] proposed a law to the people that plebeian magistrates should be elected at the comitia by tribes. A matter of no trifling moment was now being brought forward, under an aspect at first sight by no means alarming ; but one which in reality deprived the patricians of all power to elect whatever tribunes they pleased by the suffrages of their clients. The patricians used all their energies in resisting this proposition, which was most pleasing to the commons ; and though none of the col-

[1] Cf. Livy, IV, 60.

lege could be induced by the influence of either of the consuls or of the chief members of the senate to enter a protest against it, the only means of resistance which now existed, yet the matter, important as it was by its own weight, is spun out by contention till the following year. The commons reëlect Volero as tribune. The senators, considering that the question would be carried to the very extreme of a struggle, elect to the consulate Appius Claudius, the son of Appius, who was both hated by and hated the commons, ever since the contests between them and his father. . . .

57. . . . Overcome, however, by the unanimous feeling of the senators, he [Appius Claudius] desisted : the law is carried without opposition. . . .

299? A.U.C.   B.C. 455?
c. Cicero : *On the Commonwealth*, Book II, chapter 35

. . . About fifty-four years after the first consulate, Spurius Tarpeius and Aulus Aternius very much gratified the people by proposing in the comitia centuriata, the substitution of fines instead of corporal punishments. Twenty years afterwards, Lucius Papirius and Publius Pinarius, the censors, having by a strict levy of fines confiscated to the State the entire flocks and herds of many private individuals, a light tax on the cattle was substituted for the law of fines, in the consulship of Caius Julius and Publius Papirius.

46. The Twelve Tables

a. Some Fragments

TABLE III

1. A judgment debtor by prætor's verdict shall have thirty days, grace.

2. At their expiration, *the plaintiff* shall serve a formal summons on *the defendant* by hand-touch, and take him forcibly before the prætor.

3. If *the debtor* does not satisfy the judgment, or if no one stands trial in his stead before the prætor, *the plaintiff* shall detain him by force, binding him by shackles or fetters of at least fifteen pounds weight; heavier at discretion of *plaintiff*.

4. The *plaintiff* shall maintain him at his own home, if he chooses; if not, the *custodian* of the debtor shall furnish him a pound of meal per day; more at his own discretion.

6. On the third market day, the *creditors* shall make a division of the property. If they take more or less *than their debt*, no guilt shall attach to them.

7. The right of possession (*by usucaption*) shall never pass to a foreigner.

TABLE IV

2. If a son shall be thrice sold by his father, he shall be free from the *patria potestas*.

TABLE VIII

2. If any one shall have maimed another, and does not compromise with him, there shall be retaliation in kind.

3. If with a hand or club he break a bone of a free man, he shall be fined three hundred asses; if of a slave, he shall be fined one hundred and fifty asses.

4. If he does a lesser injury, twenty-five asses.

TABLE X

4. Women shall not scar their faces, nor indulge in excessive demonstrations of grief for the dead.

b. Cicero: *On the Commonwealth,* Book IV (at end)

Our laws of the Twelve Tables, on the contrary, — so careful to attach capital punishment to a very few crimes only, — have included in this class of capital offences the offence of composing or publicly reciting verses of libel, slander, and defamation, in order to cast dishonor and infamy on a fellow-citizen.

47. Valerio-Horatian Laws

Livy, Book III, chapter 55

Then through an interrex Lucius Valerius and Marcus Horatius were elected consuls, who immediately entered on their office; whose consulship was popular without any actual injury to the patricians, though not without their displeasure; for whatever provision was made for securing the liberty of the commons, that they considered to be a diminution made in their own power. First of all, when it was as it were a point in controversy, whether patricians were bound by regulations enacted in an assembly of the commons, they proposed a law in the assembly of the centuries, that whatever the commons ordered collectively, should bind the entire people; by which law a most keen-edged weapon was given to motions introduced by tribunes. Then another law made by a consul concerning the right of appeal, a singular security to liberty, and subverted by the decemviral power, they not only restore, but guard it also for the time to come, by enacting a new law, " that no one should appoint any magistrate without a right of appeal; if any person should so elect, it would be lawful and right that he be put to death; and that such killing should not be deemed a capital offence." And when they had sufficiently secured the commons by the right of appeal on the one hand, by tribunitian aid on the other, they renewed for the tribunes themselves [the privilege] that they should be held sacred and inviolable, the memory of which matter had now been almost lost, reviving certain ceremonies which had been long disused; and they rendered them inviolable both by the religious institution, as well as by a law, enacting that " whoever should offer injury to tribunes of the people, ædiles, judges, decemvirs, his person should be devoted to Jupiter, and his property be sold at the temple of Ceres, Liber, and Libera." . . .

309? A.U.C.   **48. Lex Canuleia**   B.C. 445 ?

Livy, Book IV, chapter 6

. . . And now . . . there was no end of the contentions, until
the patricians . . . agreed that the law regarding intermarriage
should be passed, judging that by these means most probably the
tribunes would either give up altogether or postpone till after the
war the question concerning the plebeian consuls. . . .

377–387 A.U.C.   B.C. 377–367
49. Struggle of Plebeians for Equal Privileges

Livy, Book VI, chapters 34, 35, and 42

34. In proportion as all matters were more tranquil abroad in
consequence of their success in war this year, so much did the
violence of the patricians and the distresses of the commons in
the city increase every day; as the ability to pay was prevented
by the very fact that it was necessary to pay. Accordingly, when
nothing could now be paid out of their property, being cast in
suits and assigned over to custody, they satisfied their creditors
by their character and persons, and punishment was substituted
for payment. Wherefore not only the lowest but even the leading men in the commons had sunk so low in spirit, that no enter-
prising and adventurous man had courage not only to stand for
the military tribuneship among the patricians (for which privileges
they had strained all their energies), but not even to take on them
and sue for plebeian magistracies ; and the patricians seemed to
have forever recovered the possession of an honor that had been
only usurped by the commons for a few years. . . .

35. There appeared a favorable opportunity for making innovations on account of the immense load of debt, no alleviation of
which evil the commons could hope for unless their own party
were placed in the highest authority. To [bring about] that object

[they saw] that they should exert themselves; that the plebeians, by endeavoring and persevering, had already gained a step towards it, whence, if they struggled forward, they might reach the summit, and be on a level with the patricians, in honor as well as in merit. For the present it was resolved that plebeian tribunes should be created, in which office they might open for themselves a way to other honors. And Caius Licinius and Lucius Sextius, being elected tribunes, proposed laws all against the power of the patricians, and for the interests of the commons: one regarding the debt, that, whatever had been paid in interest being deducted from the principal, the remainder should be paid off in three years by equal instalments; the other concerning the limitation of land, that no one should possess more than five hundred acres of land; a third, that there should be no election of military tribunes, and that one at least of the consuls should be elected from the commons; all matters of great importance, and such as could not be attained without the greatest struggles. A contest therefore for all those objects, of which there is ever an inordinate desire among men, viz., land, money, and honors, being now proposed, the patricians became terrified and dismayed, and finding no other remedy in their public and private consultations except the protest, which had been tried in many previous contests, they gained over their colleagues to oppose the bills of the tribunes. When they saw the tribes summoned by Licinius and Sextius to announce their votes, surrounded by bands of patricians, they neither suffered the bills to be read, nor any other usual form for taking the votes of the commons to be gone through. And now assemblies being frequently convened to no purpose, when the propositions were now considered as rejected: "It is very well," says Sextius; "since it is determined that a protest should possess so much power, by that same weapon will we protect the people. Come, patricians, proclaim an assembly for the election of military tribunes; I will take care that that word, I FORBID IT, [veto] which you listen to our colleagues chanting with so much pleasure shall not be very delightful to you." Nor did the threats fall ineffectual : no elections were held, except those of ædiles and plebeian tribunes. Licinius and Sextius, being reëlected plebeian tribunes, suffered not any curule magistrates to be appointed, and this total absence of magistrates continued in the city for the space of five years, the people reëlecting the two tribunes, and these preventing the election of military tribunes. . . .

42. The speech of Appius merely had this effect, that the time for passing the propositions was deferred. The same tribunes, Sextius and Licinius, being reëlected for the tenth time, succeeded in passing a law, that of the decemvirs for religious matters one-half should be elected from the commons. Five patricians were elected, and five out of the plebeians ; and by that step the way appeared open to the consulship. The commons, content with this victory, yielded to the patricians, that, all mention of consuls being omitted for the present, military tribunes should be elected. . . . Scarcely had he [Marcus Furius] as yet finished the war [with the Gauls], when a more violent disturbance awaited him at home ; and by great struggles the dictator and the senate were overpowered, so that the measures of the tribunes were admitted ; and the elections of the consuls were held in spite of the resistance of the nobility, at which Lucius Sextius was made consul, the first of plebeian rank. And not even was that an end of the contests. Because the patricians refused to give their approbation, the affair came very near a secession of the people, and other terrible threats of civil contests : when, however, the dissensions were accommodated on certain terms through the interference of the dictator ; and concessions to the commons were made by the nobility regarding the plebeian consuls ; by the commons to the nobility, with respect to one prætor to be elected out of the patricians, to administer justice in the city. . . .

387 A.U.C.   **50.** The Licinian Laws   B.C. 367

Appian: *Civil Wars*, Book I, paragraph 8

For these reasons the people became troubled lest they should no longer have sufficient allies of the Italian stock, and lest the government itself should be endangered by such a vast number of slaves. Not perceiving any remedy, as it was not easy, nor exactly just, to deprive men of so many possessions they had held so long, including their own trees, buildings, and fixtures, a law was once passed with difficulty at the instance of the tribunes, that nobody should hold more than five hundred *jugera* of this land, or pasture on it more than one hundred cattle or five hundred sheep. To insure the observance of this law it was provided also that there should be a certain number of freemen employed on the farms, whose business it should be to watch and report what was going on. Those who held possessions of lands under the law were required to take an oath to obey the law, and penalties were fixed for violating it, and it was supposed that the remaining land would soon be divided among the poor in small parcels. But there was not the smallest consideration shown for the law or the oaths. The few who seemed to pay some respect to them conveyed their lands to their relations fraudulently, but the greater part disregarded it altogether.

415 A.U.C.   **51.** Laws of Publilius Philo   B.C. 339

Livy, Book VIII, chapter 12

. . . When the senate . . . ordered a dictator to be nominated against the Latins, who were again in arms, Æmilius, to whom the *fasces* then belonged, nominated his colleague dictator; by him Junius Brutus was constituted master of the horse. The dictatorship was popular, both in consequence of his discourses containing invectives against the patricians, and because he passed three laws, most advantageous to the commons, and injurious to the

nobility: one, that the orders of the commons should be binding
on all the Romans; another, that the patricians should, before the
suffrages commenced, declare their approbation of the laws which
should be passed in the assemblies of the centuries; the third,
that one at least of the censors should be elected from the commons, as they had already gone so far as that it was lawful that
both the consuls should be plebeians. . . .

450 A.U.C.   **52. Action of Cneius Flavius**   B.C. 304

Livy, Book IX, chapter 46

. . . He made public the rules of proceeding in judicial causes,
hitherto shut up in the closets of the pontiffs; and hung up to
public view, round the forum, the calendar on white tablets, that
all might know when business could be transacted in the
courts. . . .

467 A.U.C.   **53. Lex Hortensia**   B.C. 287

Pliny: *Natural History*, XVI, 15 (10) [1]

. . . Hortensius, the dictator, on the secession of the plebeians
to the Janiculum, passed a law . . . that what the plebeians had
enacted should be binding upon every Roman citizen.

54. General Laws

Cicero: *On the Laws*, Book III, chapters 3-4

3. "Let all authorities be just, and let them be honestly
obeyed by the people with modesty and without opposition. Let
the magistrate restrain the disobedient and mischievous citizen, by
fine, imprisonment, and corporal chastisement; unless some equal
or greater power, or the people forbid it; for there should be an
appeal thereto. If the magistrate shall have decided, and inflicted
a penalty, let there be a public appeal to the people respecting
the penalty and fine imposed.

[1] Cf. Livy: *Epitome*, XI.

"With respect to the army, and the general that commands it by martial law, there should be no appeal from his authority. And whatever he who conducts the war commands, shall be absolute law, and ratified as such.

"As to the minor magistrates, let there be such a distribution of their legal duties, that each may more effectively superintend his own department of justice. In the army, let those who are appointed command, and let them have tribunes. In the city, let men be appointed as superintendents of the public treasury. Let some devote their attention to the prison discipline, and capital punishments. Let others supervise the public coinage of gold, and silver, and copper. Let others judge of suits and arbitrations; and let others carry the orders of the senate into execution.

"Let there likewise be ædiles, curators of the city, the provisions, and the public games, and let these offices be the first steps to higher promotions of honor.

"Let the censors take a census of the people, according to age, offspring, family, and property. Let them have the inspection of the temples, the streets, the aqueducts, the rates, and the customs. Let them distribute the citizens according to their tribes; after that let them divide them with reference to their fortunes, ages, and ranks. Let them keep a register of the families of those of the equestrian and plebeian orders. Let them impose a tax on celibates. Let them guard the morals of the people. Let them permit no scandal in the senate. Let the number of such censors be two. Let their magistracy continue five years. Let the other magistrates be annual, but the offices themselves should be perpetual. . . .

"Let two magistrates be invested with sovereign authority; from their presiding, judging, and counselling, let them be called prætors, judges, or consuls. Let them have supreme authority over the army, and let them be subject to none; for the safety of the people is the supreme law; and no one should succeed to this magistracy till it has been held ten years — regulating the duration by an annual law.

"When a considerable war is undertaken, or discord is likely to ensue among the citizens, let a single supreme magistrate be appointed, who shall unite in his own person the authority of both consuls, if the senate so decrees, for six months only. And when such a magistrate has been proclaimed under favorable auspices, let him be the master of the people. Let him have for a colleague, with equal powers with himself, a knight whomsoever he may choose to appoint, as a judge of the law. And when such a dictator or master of the people is created, the other magistracies shall be suppressed.

"Let the auspices be observed by the senate, and let them authorize persons of their own body to elect the consuls in the comitia, according to the established ceremonials.

"Let the commanders, generals, and lieutenants leave the city whenever the senate decrees or the people orders that they shall do so. Let them properly prosecute all just wars. Let them spare our allies, and restrain themselves and their subordinates. . . .

"Let the ten officers whom the people elect to protect them against oppression be their tribunes ; and let all their prohibitions and adjudications be established, and their persons considered inviolable, so that tribunes may never be wanting to the people.

"Let all magistrates possess their auspices and jurisdictions, and let the senate be composed of these legitimate authorities. Let its ordinances be absolute, and let its enactments be written and ratified, unless an equal or greater authority disannul them. Let the order of the senators be free from reproach and scandal, and let them be an example of virtue to all. . . .

4. "If any question occur out of the established jurisdiction of the magistrates, let another magistrate be appointed by the people, whose jurisdiction shall expressly extend thereto. . . . Let the tribunes of the people likewise have free access to the senate, and advocate the interests of the people in all their deliberations. Let a just moderation predominate in the opinions and declarations of those who would thus act as mediators

between the senate and the people. Let a senator who does not
attend the senate, either show cause of his non-attendance, or
submit to an appropriate fine. Let a senator speak in his turn,
with all moderation, and let him be thoroughly acquainted with
the interests of the people.

. . . "Let those who act observe the auspices; obey the public augur; and carry into effect all proclamations, taking care
that they are exhibited in the treasury, and generally known."

55. Elections (under the Republic)

Pliny: *Letters*, Book III, chapter 20

. . . I have been told by some who remember those times that
the method observed in their assemblies was this: the name of
the individual who offered himself for any office being called out,
a profound silence ensued, when, after he had spoken for himself,
and given an account to the senate of his life and behavior generally, he called witnesses in support of his character. These were
either the person under whom he had served in the army, or to
whom he had been quæstor, or both (if the case admitted of it),
to whom he also joined some of those friends who espoused his
interest. They said what they had to say in his favor, in few but
impressive words; and this had far more influence than the
modern method of humble solicitation. Sometimes the candidate would object either to the birth, or age, or character of his
competitor; to which the senate would listen with a severe and
impartial attention: and thus merit was generally preferred to
interest. . . .

Other Laws of the Republic

Lex Valeria: Cicero: *Commonwealth*, II, 31; Decemvirate: Cicero: *Com-
monwealth*, II, 36 ff.; Livy, III, 33–59; Lex Ogulnia: Livy, X, 6–9; Lex Fla-
minia Agraria: Cicero: *On Invention*, II, 17; *On Old Age*, ch. 4; Polybius,
II, 21; Lex Claudia: Livy, XXI, 63; Leges Sumptuariæ, Livy, XXXIV, 1–8;
Lex Villia Annalis: Cicero: *Philippics*, V, 17; Livy, XL, 44; Lex Calpurnia:
Cicero: *Brutus*, ch. 27; *Offices*, II, 21; Lex Agraria Ti. Gracchi: Appian:

Civil·Wars, I, 9; Livy: *Epitome,* LVIII; Velleius, II, 2, 3; Lex Sempronia Frumentaria: Cicero: *For Sestius,* ch. 48; *Offices,* II, 72; Livy: *Epitome,* LX; Leges Semproniæ de Provocatione: Cicero: *For Rabirius,* ch. 4; *Against Catiline,* IV, 5; *For Cluentius,* ch. 55; Plutarch: *C. Gracchus,* 4; Lex Sempronia Iudiciaria: Appian: *Civil Wars,* I, 22; Cicero: *Against Verres,* I, 15; Livy: *Epitome,* LX; Tacitus: *Annals,* XII, 60; Velleius, II, 32; Lex Julia: Cicero: *For Balbus,* ch. 8; Lex Plautia Papiria: Cicero: *For Archias,* ch. 4; Leges Corneliæ de Magistratibus: Appian: *Civil Wars,* I, 100; Cæsar: *Civil War,* I, 32; Cicero: *Philippics,* XI, ch. 5; Tacitus: *Annals,* XI, 22; Lex Cornelia Tribunicia: Appian: *Civil Wars,* I, 100; Cæsar: *Civil War,* I, 5, 7; Cicero: *Laws,* III, 9; Livy: *Epitome,* LXXXIX; Leges Corneliæ Iudiciariæ: Cicero: *Against Piso,* ch. 21; *For Cluentius,* ch. 53, 54; Tacitus: *Annals,* XI, 22; XII, 60; Velleius, II, 32; Lex Gabinia: Cicero: *Manilian Law,* ch. 17 ff.: Plutarch: *Pompey,* 25; Velleius, II, 31; Lex Manilia: Cicero: *Manilian Law;* Plutarch: *Pompey,* 30; Velleius, II, 33; Lex Julia Agraria: Cicero: *To Atticus,* II, 18; Suetonius: *Julius Cæsar,* 20; Velleius, II, 44; Lex Vatinia: Suetonius: *J. Cæsar,* 22; Lex Titia: Appian: *Civil Wars,* IV, par. 7.

V. EARLY HISTORY

Abbott, ch. 1–5; Allen, ch. 2–7; Botsford, ch. 2–4; Duruy, Vol. I, ch. 1–18; Fowler: *The City-State of the Greeks and Romans*, ch. 1–3; Freeman: *Story of Sicily*, ch. 13; How and Leigh, ch. 4–16; Ihne, ch. 3, 5, 8–14, 18–21; Leighton, ch. 2–15; Mommsen, Bk. I, ch. 3, 4, 7; Bk. II, ch. 1–7; Montesquieu: *Grandeur and Decadence of the Romans*, ch. 1–4; Morey, ch. 1–13; Myers, ch. 2, 4, 5, 6; Pelham, Bk. I, II; Robinson, ch. 1, 2–9; Seignobos, ch. 2, 3, 5, 6; Shuckburgh, ch. 1, 4–15; Taylor: *Constitutional and Political History of Rome*, ch. 1, 6; West, Part IV, ch. 2, 3, 4, 5; Wolfson, ch. 19, 20, 21.

38? A.U.C.   **56. Death of Romulus**   B.C. 716?

Livy, Book I, chapter 16

After he had performed these immortal achievements, while he was holding an assembly of the people for reviewing his army, near the Goat's Pool, a storm arose suddenly, with great thunder and lightning, and enveloped the king in a cloud so dense that it concealed him entirely from the assembly. And Romulus was never seen again on earth. When at length the terror was over, and fine clear weather had succeeded the darkened sky, the Roman youth saw the royal seat empty, and though they readily believed the fathers who had stood nearest him, and who said that he had been snatched on high by the blast, yet, struck as it were with the fear of orphanage, they kept silence in sorrow for some time. Then, a few having begun, all order that Romulus shall be saluted as a god sprung from a god, the king, and parent of the Roman city; they implore his favor with prayers,

that he might always wish by his favor to preserve his offspring.
I believe that even then there were some who silently thought
that the king had been torn in pieces by the hands of the fathers ;
for this rumor also spread, but very obscurely. Their admiration
of the man, and their momentary consternation gave importance
to the other report. By the cunning, moreover, of one man, the
report obtained additional credit. For while the city was anxious
for lack of the king and incensed against the fathers, Proculus
Julius, a person of weight, according to tradition, in any matter
however important, proceeds into the assembly : " O Quirites ! "
he says, " Romulus, the father of this city, at daybreak to-day
suddenly descending from heaven, presented himself before me.
While I stood confused with awe, and was about to venerate him,
praying him to allow me to see him face to face, he said : ' Go tell
the Romans that the gods so will, that my Rome shall be the
capitol of the world. Therefore let them cultivate the art of war,
and let them know and hand down to posterity, that no human
power can withstand the Roman arms." Having said this, he as-
cended on high. It is surprising how much credit was shown
to that man announcing these things, and how greatly the longing
for Romulus on the part of the people and army was assuaged by
the belief in his immortality.

87 ? A.U.C. **57. New Citizens from Alba** B.C. 667 ?

Livy, Book I, chapter 30

In the meantime Rome grew from the ruins of Alba. The
number of citizens is doubled. The Cœlian mount is added to
the city, and in order that it might be inhabited more populously,
Tullus selects that situation for his palace and dwells there. The
princes of the Albans he enrols among the fathers, that that branch
of the State also might increase, the Julii, Servilii, Quinctii, Geganii,
Curiatii, Clœlii ; and as a temple for the order augmented by him
he built a senate-house, which was called *Hostilia* even down to

the age of our fathers. And that every rank might acquire some additional strength from the new people, he formed ten troops of horsemen from among the Albans : he likewise recruited the old, and raised new legions from the same source.

Livy, Book II, chapters 1 and 2

1. . . . But the origin of liberty you may date from this period, rather because the consular authority was made annual, than that any diminution was made from the kingly prerogative. The first consuls had all their privileges and ensigns of authority, only care was taken that the terror might not appear doubled, by both having the fasces at the same time. Brutus, who had not been a more zealous assertor of liberty than he was afterwards its guardian, was, with the consent of his colleague, first attended by the fasces. First of all he bound over the people, whilst still enraptured with their newly acquired liberty, by an oath that they would suffer no one to be king in Rome, lest afterwards they might be perverted by the importunities or bribes of the royal family. Next in order, that the fulness of the house might produce more of strength in the senate, he filled up the number of the senators, diminished by the king's murders, to the amount of three hundred, having elected the principal men of the equestrian rank; and from thence it is said the custom was derived of summoning into the senate both those who were *patres* and those who were *conscripti*.[1] Forsooth they styled those who were elected into the new senate *conscripti*. It is wonderful how much that contributed to the concord of the State, and to attach the affection of the commons to the patricians.

2. Then attention was paid to religious matters, and as some part of the public worship had been performed by the kings in

[1] All were called *Patres conscripti. Scil. Patres et Conscripti*, the conjunction being omitted.

person, that they might not be missed in any respect, they elect
a king of the sacrifices. This office they made subject to the
pontiff, that honor being added to the name might be no infringe-
ment on their liberty, which was now their
principal care. And I know not whether by
fencing it on every side to excess, even in
the most trivial matters, they may not have
exceeded bounds.

246? A.U.C.   **59. Horatius**   B.C. 508?

Livy, Book II, chapter 10

Some parts seemed secured by the walls,
others by the interposition of the Tiber.
The Sublician bridge well-nigh afforded a
passage to the enemy, had there not been
one man, Horatius Cocles, (that defence the
fortune of Rome had on that day,) who,
happening to be posted on guard at the
bridge, when he saw the Janiculum taken
by a sudden assault, and that the enemy
were pouring down from thence in full
speed, and that his own party, in terror and
confusion, were abandoning their arms and ranks, laying hold
of them one by one, standing in their way, and appealing to the
faith of gods and men, declared, "That their flight would avail
them nothing if they deserted their post; if they passed the
bridge and left it behind them, there would soon be more of
the enemy in the Palatium and Capitol than in the Janiculum;
for that reason he advised and charged them to demolish the
bridge, by their sword, by fire, or by any means whatever; that
he would stand the shock of the enemy as far as could be
done by one man." He then advanced to the first entrance of
the bridge, and being easily distinguished among those who

FIG. 8. — A ROMAN
SACRIFICING

Schreiber, plate 85, fig. 11

showed their back in retreating from the fight, facing about to engage the foe hand to hand, by his surprising bravery he terrified the enemy. Two, indeed, a sense of shame kept with him, Sp. Lartius and T. Herminius, men eminent for their birth, and renowned for their gallant exploits. With them he for a short time stood the first storm of the danger, and the severest brunt of the battle. But as they who demolished the bridge called upon them to retire, he obliged them also to withdraw to a place of safety on a small portion of the bridge still left. Then casting his stern eyes round all the officers of the Etrurians in a threatening manner, he sometimes challenged them singly, sometimes reproached them all; "the slaves of haughty tyrants, who, regardless of their own freedom, came to oppress the liberty of others." They hesitated for a considerable time, looking round one at the other, to commence the fight; shame then put the army in motion, and a shout being raised, they hurl their weapons from all sides on their single adversary; and when they all stuck in the shield held before him, and he with no less obstinacy kept possession of the bridge with firm step, they now endeavored to thrust him down from it by one push, when at once the crash of the falling bridge, at the same time a shout of the Romans raised for joy at having completed their purpose, checked their ardor with sudden panic. Then Cocles says, "Holy father Tiberinus, I pray that thou wouldst receive these arms, and this thy soldier, in thy propitious stream." Armed as he was, he leaped into the Tiber, and, amid showers of darts hurled on him, swam across safe to his party, having dared an act which is likely to obtain more fame than credit with posterity. The State was grateful towards such valor; a statue was erected to him in the comitium, and as much land was given to him as he ploughed around in one day. The zeal of private individuals also was conspicuous among the public honors. For, amid the great scarcity, each person contributed something to him according to his supply at home, depriving himself of his support.

60. History of the Early Republic

Cicero: *On the Commonwealth*, Book II, chapters 33-37

33. . . . For when the excessive debts of the citizens had thrown the State into disorder, the people first retired to Mount *Sacer*, and next occupied Mount Aventine. . . .

34. . . . When the plebeians were oppressed by the weight of the expenses occasioned by public misfortunes, a cure and remedy were sought for the sake of public security. The senate, however, having forgot their former decision, gave an advantage to the democracy; for, by the creation of two tribunes to appease the sedition of the people, the power and authority of the senate were diminished; which, however, still remained dignified and august, inasmuch as it was still composed of the wisest and bravest men, who protected their country both with their arms and with their counsels; whose authority was exceedingly strong and flourishing, because in honor they were as much before their fellow-citizens as they were inferior in luxuriousness, and, as a general rule, not superior to them in wealth. And their public virtues were the more agreeable to the people, because even in private matters they were ready to serve every citizen, by their exertions, their counsels, and their liberality.

35. Such was the situation of the Commonwealth, when the quæstor impeached Spurius Cassius of being so much emboldened by the excessive favor of the people, as to endeavor to make himself master of monarchical power. And, as you have heard, his own father, having said that he had found that his son was really guilty of this crime, condemned him to death at the instance of the people. . . .

36. But, some years previous to this, at a period when the senate possessed the supreme influence, and the people were submissive and obedient, a new system was adopted. At that time both the consuls and tribunes of the people abdicated their magistracies, and the decemvirs were appointed, who were invested with great authority,

from which there was no appeal whatever, so as to exercise the chief
domination, and to compile the laws. After having composed,
with much wisdom and equity, the Ten Tables of laws, they
nominated as their successors in the ensuing year other decemvirs,
whose good faith and justice do not deserve equal praise. . . .

37. A third year followed under the authority of the same decemvirs, and still they were not disposed to appoint their successors. In a situation of the Commonwealth like this, which, as I
have often repeated, could not be durable, because it had not an
equal operation with respect to all the ranks of the citizens, the
whole public power was lodged in the hands of the chiefs and
decemvirs of the highest nobility, without the counterbalancing
authority of the tribunes of the people, without the sanction of
any other magistracies, and without appeal to the people in the
case of a sentence of death or scourging.

Thus, out of the injustice of these men, there was suddenly produced a great revolution, which changed the entire condition of
the government ; for they added two tables of very tyrannical laws,
and though matrimonial alliances had always been permitted, even
with foreigners, they forbade, by the most abominable and inhuman
edict, that any marriages should take place between the nobles and
the commons — an order which was afterwards abrogated by the
decree of Canuleius. Besides, they introduced into all their political measures, corruption, cruelty, and avarice. And indeed the
story is well known, and celebrated in many literary compositions,
that a certain Decimus Virginius was obliged, on account of the
libidinous violence of one of these decemvirs, to stab his virgin
daughter in the midst of the forum.

364 A.U.C.   **61. Gauls at Rome**   B.C. 390

Livy, Book V, chapter 47

Whilst these things were going on at Veii, in the meanwhile
the citadel and Capitol of Rome were in great danger. For the

Gauls either having perceived the track of a human foot where the messenger from Veii had passed, or having of themselves remarked the easy ascent by the rock at the temple of Carmentis, on a moonlight night, after they had at first sent forward an unarmed person, to make a trial of the way, delivering their arms, whenever any difficulty occurred, alternately supported and supporting each other, and drawing each other up, according as the ground required, they reached the summit in such silence that they not only escaped the notice of the sentinels, but of the dogs also, an animal extremely wakeful with respect to noises by night. The notice of the geese they did not escape, which, as being sacred to Juno, were spared, though they were in the greatest scarcity of food. Which circumstance was the cause of their preservation. For Marcus Manlius, who three years before had been consul, a man distinguished in war, being roused from sleep by their cackling and the clapping of their wings, snatched up his arms, and at the same time calling the others to do the same, proceeds to the spot; and whilst the others are thrown into confusion, he struck with the boss of his shield and tumbled down a Gaul, who had already got footing on the summit; and when the fall of this man as he tumbled threw down those who were next him, he slew others, who in their consternation had thrown away their arms, and caught hold of the rocks to which they clung. And now the others also having assembled, beat down the enemy by javelins and stones, and the entire band, having lost their footing, were hurled down the precipice in promiscuous ruin. The alarm then subsiding, the remainder of the night was given up to repose (as far as could be done considering the disturbed state of their minds), when the danger, even though passed, still kept them in a state of anxiety. Day having appeared, the soldiers were summoned by sound of trumpet to attend the tribunes in assembly, when recompense was to be made both to merit and to demerit; Manlius was first of all commended for his bravery and presented with gifts, not only by the military tribunes, but with the consent of the soldiers, for they all carried to his house, which was in the citadel, a contribution of half a pound of corn and half a pint of wine : a matter trifling in the relation, but the [prevailing] scarcity had rendered it a strong proof of esteem, when each man, depriving himself of his own food, contributed in honor of one man a portion subtracted from his body and from his necessary requirements. Then the guards of that place where the enemy had climbed up unobserved were summoned ; and when Quintus Sulpicius declared openly that he would punish all according to the usage of military discipline, being deterred by the consentient shout of the soldiers who threw the blame on one sentinel, he spared the rest. The man who was manifestly guilty of the crime, he threw down from the rock, with the approbation of all. From this time forth the guards on both sides became more vigilant ; on the part of the Gauls, because a rumor spread that messengers passed between Veii and Rome, and on that of the Romans, from the recollection of the danger which occurred during the night.

433 A.U.C.   **62. Defeat at the Caudine Forks**   B.C. 321

Livy, Book IX, chapters 2–6

2. There were two roads leading to Luceria, one along the coast of the upper sea, wide and open ; but, as it was the safer, so it was proportionately longer ; the other, which was shorter, through the Caudine forks. The nature of the place is this : there are two deep glens, narrow and covered with wood, connected together by mountains ranging on both sides from one to the other ; between these lies a plain of considerable extent enclosed in the middle, abounding in grass and water, and through the middle of which the passage runs : but before you can arrive at it, the first defile must be passed, while the only way back is through the road by which you entered it ; or if in case of resolving to proceed forward, you must go by the other glen, which is still more narrow and difficult. Into this plain the Romans, having marched down

their troops by one of those passes through the cleft of a rock, when they advanced onward to the other defile, found it blocked up by trees thrown across, and a mound of huge stones lying in their way. When the stratagem of the enemy now became apparent, there is seen at the same time a body of troops on the eminence over the glen. Hastening back, then, they proceed to retrace the road by which they had entered; they found that also shut up by such another fence and men in arms. . . .

3. Night came on them while lamenting their situation, rather than consulting; whilst they urged expedients, each according to his temper, one crying out: " Let us go over those fences of the roads," others, "over the steeps, through the woods, any way where arms can be carried. Let us be but permitted to come to the enemy, whom we have been used to conquer now near thirty years. All places will be level and plain to a Roman, fighting against the perfidious Samnite." Another would say : " Whither or by what way can we go? Do we expect to remove the mountains from their foundations? While these cliffs hang over us, by what road will you reach the enemy? Whether armed or unarmed, brave or dastardly, we are all, without distinction, captured and vanquished. The enemy will not even show us a weapon by which we might die with honor. He will finish the war, without moving from his seat." In such discourse, thinking of neither food nor rest, the night was passed. . . .

4. In the Roman camp also, when many fruitless efforts to force a passage had been made, and they were now destitute of every means of subsistence, forced by necessity, they send ambassadors, who were first to ask peace on equal terms; if they did not obtain this they were to challenge the enemy to battle. To this Pontius answered, that " the war was at an end ; and since, even in their present vanquished and captive state, they were not willing to acknowledge their situation, he would send them under the yoke unarmed, each with a single garment; that the other conditions of peace should be such as were just between the con-

querors and the conquered. If their troops would depart, and their colonies be withdrawn out of the territories of the Samnites, for the future the Romans and Samnites, under a treaty of equality, shall live according to their own respective laws. On these terms he was ready to negotiate with the consuls, and if any of these should not be accepted, he forbade the ambassadors to come to him again." When the result of this embassy was made known, such general lamentation suddenly arose, and such melancholy took possession of them that, had they been told that all were to die on the spot, they could not have felt deeper affliction. . . .

5. The consuls having gone to Pontius to confer with him, when he talked, in the strain of a conqueror, of a treaty, they declared that such could not be concluded without an order of the people, nor without the ministry of the heralds, and the other customary rites. Accordingly the Caudine peace was not ratified by settled treaty, as is commonly believed, and even asserted, by Claudius, but by conventional sureties. For what occasion would there be either for sureties or hostages in the former case, where the ratification is performed by the imprecation, "that whichever nation shall give occasion to the said terms being violated, may Jupiter strike that nation in like manner as the swine is struck by the heralds." . . . First, they were ordered to go out, beyond the rampart unarmed, and with single garments; then the hostages were surrendered and carried into custody. The lictors were next commanded to depart from the consuls, and the robes of the latter were stripped off. This excited such a degree of commiseration in the breasts of those very men, who a little before, pouring execrations upon them, had proposed that they should be delivered up and torn to pieces, that every one, forgetting his own condition, turned away his eyes from that degradation of so high a dignity as from a spectacle too horrid to behold.

6. First, the consuls, nearly half naked, were sent under the yoke; then each officer, according to his rank, was exposed to disgrace, and the legions successively. The enemy stood on each

side under arms, reviling and mocking them ; swords were pointed at most of them, several were wounded and some even slain, when their looks, rendered too fierce by the indignity to which they were subjected, gave offence to the conquerors. Thus were they led under the yoke ; and what was still more intolerable, under the eyes of the enemy.

Additional References to Sources

REGAL PERIOD

Cicero: *Commonwealth*, II, 1–23; Eutropius, I, 1–10; Florus, I. 1–9; Livy, I; Ovid: *Fasti*, IV, 800 ff.; Plutarch: *Romulus, Numa*. ETRUSCAN RULE IN LATIUM: Livy, 1, 2.

EARLY REPUBLIC

I. 509–390 B.C.: Eutropius, I, 9–19; Florus, I, 9; Livy, II–IV; Plutarch: *Poplicola, Coriolanus, Camillus;* Tacitus: *History*, III, 72. VOLSCI AND ÆQUI: Livy, IV, 26–29; VI, 2, 32. SIEGE OF VEII: Livy, IV, 32–V, 22 ; Plutarch: *Camillus*, 2–6. CAPTURE OF ROME BY THE GAULS: Appian: *Foreign Wars*, IV, 2–8; Eutropius, I, 20; Livy, V, 34–55; Polybius, II, 17–21 ; Plutarch: *Camillus*.

II. 390–275 B.C. FIRST SAMNITE WAR and THE LATIN WAR: Livy, VII, 29–VIII, 3; Eutropius, II, 1–8. SECOND SAMNITE WAR: Appian: *Foreign Wars*, IV, 2–7; Cicero: *Offices*, III, 109; Eutropius, II, 4; Florus, I, 11; Livy, VIII, 23–IX, 46. THIRD SAMNITE WAR: Eutropius, II, 9 ff.; Florus, I, 16 and 17 ; Livy, X, 11–47; *Epitome*, XI; Polybius, II, 19. TARENTUM AND THE WAR WITH PYRRHUS: Appian: *Foreign Wars*, III, 7–12; Eutropius, II, 11–14; Justin, XVI, 3; Livy: *Epitome*, XI–XV; Pausanias, I, ch. 11, 12; Plutarch: *Pyrrhus;* Polybius, I, 6, 7; II, 19, 20.

VI. THE CONQUEST OF THE MEDITERRANEAN.
THE PUNIC WARS

Punic Wars

Abbott, ch. 5 (*passim*); Allen, ch. 8, 9, 11 (pp. 100 ff.); Arnold, T., *History of Rome*, ch. 40, 43–47; Botsford, ch. 5, pp. 95–116, 123–126; Church, A. J., *Carthage* (*Story of Nations*); Dodge, T. A.: *Hannibal* (*Captains*); Duruy, Vol. I, ch. 19–25; Vol. II, ch. 32; Freeman: *Story of Sicily*, ch. 14; How: *Hannibal;* How and Leigh, ch. 18, 20–22, 24 (pp. 245–253); Ihne: *History of Rome*, Bk. IV, ch. 1, 3, 8, 9; Bk. V, ch. 5; Leighton, ch. 20, pp. 117–127; ch. 22–24, pp. 132–156; ch. 27, pp. 167–174; Mahan, A. T.: *The Influence of Sea Power on History*, pp. 14–21; Mommsen, Bk. III, ch. 1, 2, 4–7; Bk. IV, ch. 1 (pp. 237–260); Morey, ch. 14, 15, 17 (pp. 136–139); Morris, W. O.: *Hannibal* (*Heroes*); Myers, ch. 7, 9, 11 (pp. 200–205); Pelham, Bk. III (Introd.), ch. 1–p. 134; Robinson, ch. 10, pp. 106–117; ch. 12, 13, pp. 127–160; ch. 15, pp. 188–195; Seignobos, pp. 86–120, 133–135; Shuckburgh, ch. 17–22, 32, pp. 527–536; Smith: *Smaller History of Rome* (*revised by Greenidge*), ch. 10–14; Smith, R. B.: *Rome and Carthage* (*Epochs*); Smith, R. B.: *Carthage and the Carthaginians;* Taylor, ch. 7; West, par. 356–362, 366–375, 379–382; Wolfson, ch. 22, 23, 26 (pp. 326–330).

63. Beginning of Roman Empire

Polybius, Book I, chapters 1 and 3

1. . . . Can any one be so indifferent or idle as not to care to know by what means, and under what kind of polity, almost the whole inhabited world was conquered and brought under the dominion of the single city of Rome, and that too within a period of not quite fifty-three years?

3. . . . Now up to this time the world's history has been, so to speak, a series of disconnected transactions, as widely separated in

their origin and results as in their localities. But from this time forth history becomes a connected whole : the affairs of Italy and Libya are involved with those of Asia and Greece, and the tendency of all is to unity. This is why I have fixed upon this era as the starting point of my work. For it was their victory over the Carthaginians in this war, and their conviction that thereby the most difficult and most essential step towards universal empire had been taken, which encouraged the Romans for the first time to stretch out their hands upon the rest, and to cross with an army into Greece and Asia.

64. Roman Character

Polybius, Book I, chapter 37

. . . But it is a peculiarity of the Roman people as a whole to treat everything as a question of main strength ; to consider that they must of course accomplish whatever they have proposed to themselves ; and that nothing is impossible that they have once determined upon. The result of such self-confidence is that in many things they do succeed, while in some few they conspicuously fail, and especially at sea. On land it is against men only and their works that they have to direct their efforts : and as the forces against which they exert their strength do not differ intrinsically from their own, as a general rule they succeed ; while their failures are exceptional and rare. . . .

490 A.U.C.   ### 65. Building a Fleet   B.C. 264

Polybius, Book I, chapters 20–21.

20. . . . It was, then, because they saw that the war they had undertaken lingered to a weary length, that they first thought of getting a fleet built, consisting of a hundred quinqueremes and twenty triremes. But one part of their undertaking caused them much difficulty. Their shipbuilders were entirely unacquainted

with the construction of quinqueremes, because no one in Italy had at that time employed vessels of that description. There could be no more signal proof of the courage, or rather the extraordinary audacity of the Roman enterprise. Not only had they no resources for it of reasonable sufficiency; but without any resources for it at all, and without having ever entertained an idea of naval war, — for it was the first time they had thought of it, — they nevertheless handled the enterprise with such extraordinary audacity, that, without so much as a preliminary trial, they took upon themselves there and then to meet the Carthaginians at sea, on which they had for generations held undisputed supremacy. Proof of what I say, and of their surprising audacity, may be found in this.   When they first took in hand to send troops across to Messene they not only had no decked vessels but no war-ships at all, not so much as a single galley : but they borrowed quinqueremes and triremes from Tarentum and Locri, and even from Elea and Neapolis ; and having thus collected a fleet, boldly sent their men across upon it.   It was on this occasion that, the Carthaginians having put to sea in the Strait to attack them, a decked vessel of theirs charged so furiously that it ran aground, and falling into the hands of the Romans served them as a model on which they constructed their whole fleet.   And if this had not happened it is clear that they would have been completely hindered from carrying out their design by want of constructive knowledge.

21. Meanwhile, however, those who were charged with the shipbuilding were busied with the construction of the vessels; while others collected crews and were engaged in teaching them to row on dry land : which they contrived to do in the following manner.   They made the men sit on rowers' benches on dry land in the same order as they would sit on the benches in actual vessels : in the midst of them they stationed the *celeustes*, and trained them to get back and draw in their hands all together in time, and then to swing forward and throw them out again, and to begin and cease these movements at the word of the *celeustes*.

By the time these preparations were completed the ships were built. They therefore launched them, and, after a brief preliminary practice of real sea-rowing, started on their coasting voyage along the shore of Italy, in accordance with the consul's order. . . .

513 A.U.C.   **66. Battle of Ægusa**   B.C. 241

Polybius, Book I, chapters 61–62–63

61. When the Carthaginians saw that the Romans were intercepting their passage across, they lowered their masts, and after some words of mutual exhortation had been uttered in the several ships, closed with their opponents. But the respective state of equipment of the two sides was exactly the converse of what it had been in the battle of Drepana ; and the result of the battle was, therefore, naturally reversed also. The Romans had reformed their mode of shipbuilding, and had eased their vessels of all freight, except the provisions necessary for the battle : while their rowers having been thoroughly trained and got well together, performed their office in an altogether superior manner, and were backed up by marines who, being picked men from the legions, were all but invincible. The case with the Carthaginians was exactly the reverse. Their ships were heavily laden and therefore unmanageable in the engagement; while their rowers were entirely untrained, and merely put on board for the emergency ; and such marines as they had were raw recruits, who had never had any previous experience of any difficult or dangerous service. The fact is that the Carthaginian government never expected that the Romans would again attempt to dispute the supremacy at sea : they had, therefore, in contempt for them, neglected their navy. The result was that, as soon as they closed, their manifold disadvantages quickly decided the battle against them. They had fifty ships sunk, and seventy taken with their crews. The rest set their sails, and running before the wind, which luckily for them suddenly veered round at the nick of time to help them, got away again to

Holy Isle. The Roman consul sailed back to Lilybæum to join the army, and there occupied himself in making arrangements for the ships and men which he had captured; which was a business of considerable magnitude, for the prisoners made in the battle amounted to little short of ten thousand.

THE TREATY, B.C. 242

62. As far as strength of feeling and desire for victory was concerned this unexpected reverse did not diminish the readiness of the Carthaginians to carry on the war; but when they came to reckon up their resources they were at a complete standstill. On the one hand, they could not any longer send supplies to their forces in Sicily, because the enemy commanded the sea: on the other, to abandon and, as it were, to betray these, left them without men and without leaders to carry on the war. They therefore sent a despatch to Barcas with all speed, leaving the decision of the whole matter in his hands. Nor was their confidence misplaced. He acted the part of a gallant general and a sensible man. As long as there was any reasonable hope of success in the business he had in hand, nothing was too adventurous or too dangerous for him to attempt; and if any general ever did so, he put every chance of victory to the fullest proof. But when all his endeavors miscarried, and no reasonable expectation was left of saving his troops, he yielded to the inevitable, and sent ambassadors to treat of peace and terms of accommodation. And in this he showed great good sense and practical ability; for it is quite as much the duty of a leader to be able to see when it is time to give in, as when it is the time to win a victory. Lutatius was ready enough to listen to the proposal, because he was fully aware that the resources of Rome were at the lowest ebb from the strain of the war; and eventually it was his fortune to put an end to the contest by a treaty of which I here give the terms. *"Friendship is established between the Carthaginians and Romans on the following terms, provided always that they are ratified by*

the Roman people. The Carthaginians shall evacuate the whole of Sicily: they shall not make war upon Hiero, nor bear arms against the Syracusans or their allies. The Carthaginians shall give up to the Romans all prisoners without ransom. The Carthaginians shall pay to the Romans in twenty years 2200 Euboic talents of silver." [1]

63. When this treaty was sent to Rome the people refused to accept it, but sent ten commissioners to examine into the business. Upon their arrival they made no change in the general terms of the treaty, but they introduced some slight alterations in the direction of increased severity towards Carthage. Thus they reduced the time allowed for the payment of the indemnity by one-half; they added a thousand talents to the sum demanded; and extended the evacuation of Sicily to all islands lying between Sicily and Italy.

GREATNESS OF THE WAR

Such were the conditions on which the war was ended, after lasting twenty-four years continuously. It was at once the longest, most continuous, and most severely contested war known to us in history. Apart from the other battles fought and the preparations made, which I have described in my previous chapters, there were two sea fights, in one of which the combined numbers of the two fleets exceeded five hundred quinqueremes, in the other nearly approached seven hundred. In the course of the war, counting what were destroyed by shipwreck, the Romans lost seven hundred quinqueremes, the Carthaginians five hundred. Those therefore who have spoken with wonder of the sea-battles of an Antigonus, a Ptolemy, or a Demetrius, and the greatness of their fleets, would we may well believe have been overwhelmed with astonishment at the hugeness of these proportions if they had had to tell the story of this war. If, further, we take into consideration the superior size of the quinqueremes, compared with the triremes employed by the Persians against the Greeks,

[1] About £500,000.

and again by the Athenians and Lacedæmonians in their wars
with each other, we shall find that never in the whole history of
the world have such enormous forces contended for mastery at
sea.

These considerations will establish my original observation, and
show the falseness of the opinion entertained by certain Greeks.
It was *not* by mere chance or without knowing what they were
doing that the Romans struck their bold stroke for universal
supremacy and dominion, and justified their boldness by its success. No; it was the natural result of discipline gained in the
stern school of difficulty and danger.

67. Comparison of Rome and Carthage (Second Punic War)

Polybius, Book VI, chapters 51 and 52

51. . . . But about the period of its entering on the Hannibalian
war the political state of Carthage was on the decline,[1] that of Rome
improving. . . . In Carthage therefore the influence of the people in the policy of the State had already risen to be supreme,
while at Rome the senate was at the height of its power: and so,
as in the one measures were deliberated upon by the many, in the
other by the best men, the policy of the Romans in all public undertakings proved the stronger; on which account, though they
met with capital disasters, by force of prudent counsels they
finally conquered the Carthaginians in the war.

52. If we look, however, at separate details, for instance at the
provisions for carrying on a war, we shall find that whereas for a
naval expedition the Carthaginians are the better trained and prepared, — as it is only natural with a people with whom it has been
hereditary for many generations to practise this craft, and to follow
the seaman's trade above all nations in the world, — yet, in regard
to military service on land, the Romans train themselves to a much
higher pitch than the Carthaginians. . . .

[1] See Bosworth Smith: *Carthage*, etc., pp. 26 ff.

68. Hannibal Crossing the Alps

Polybius, Book III, chapters 54–56

54. . . . Next day he began the descent, in which he no longer met with any enemies, except some few secret pillagers ; but from the dangerous ground and the snow he lost almost as many men as on the ascent. For the path down was narrow and precipitous, and the snow made it impossible for the men to see where they were treading, while to step aside from the path, or to stumble, meant being hurled down the precipices. The troops, however, bore up against the fatigue, having now grown accustomed to such hardships ; but when they came to a place where the path was too narrow for the elephants or beasts of burden to pass, — and which, narrowed before by landslips extending about a stade and a half, had recently been made more so by another landslip, — then once more despondency and consternation fell upon the troops. Hannibal's first idea was to avoid this *mauvais pas* by a détour ; but this route, too, being made impossible by a snow-storm, he abandoned the idea.

55. The effect of the storm was peculiar and extraordinary. For the present fall of snow coming upon the top of that which was there before, and had remained from the last winter, it was found that the former, being fresh, was soft and offered no resistance to the foot ; but when the feet reached the lower frozen snow, they could no longer make any impression upon it, but the men found both their feet slipping from under them, as though they were on hard ground with a layer of mud on the top. And a still more serious difficulty followed : for not being able to get a foothold on the lower snow, when they fell and tried to get themselves up by their hands and knees, the men found themselves plunging downwards quicker and quicker, along with everything they laid hold of, the ground being a very steep decline. The beasts, however, when they fell did break through this lower snow as they struggled to rise, and having done so were obliged to re-

main there with their loads, as though they were frozen to it, both from the weight of these loads and the hardness of the old snow. Giving up, therefore, all hope of making this détour, he encamped upon the ridge after clearing away the snow upon it. He then set large parties of his men to work, and, with infinite toil, began constructing a road on the face of the precipice. One day's work sufficed to make a path practicable for beasts of burden and horses; and he accordingly took them across at once, and having pitched his camp at a spot below the snow line, he let them go in search of pasture; while he told off the Numidians in detachments to proceed with the making of the road; and after three days' difficult and painful labor he got his elephants across, though in a miserable condition from hunger. For the tops of the Alps, and the parts immediately below them, are completely treeless and bare of vegetation, because the snow lies there summer and winter; but about halfway down the slopes on both sides they produce trees and shrubs, and are, in fact, fit for human habitation.

56. So Hannibal mustered his forces and continued the descent; and on the third day after passing the precipitous path just described, he reached the plains. From the beginning of his march he had lost many men by the hands of the enemy, and in crossing rivers, and many more on the precipices and dangerous passes of the Alps; and not only men in this last way, but horses and beasts of burden in still greater numbers. The whole march from New Carthage had occupied five months, the actual passage of the Alps fifteen days; and he now boldly entered the valley of the Padus, and the territory of the Insubres, with such of his army as survived, consisting of twelve thousand Libyans and eight thousand Iberians, and not more than six thousand cavalry in all, as he himself distinctly states on the column erected on the promontory of Lacinium to record the numbers.

69. Hannibal's Policy towards Rome's Allies

Polybius, Book III, chapter 77

. . . Passing the winter in the Celtic territory, Hannibal kept his Roman prisoners in close confinement, supplying them very sparingly with food; while he treated their allies with great kindness from the first, and finally called them together and addressed them, alleging "that he had not come to fight against them, but against Rome in their behalf; and that, therefore, if they were wise, they would attach themselves to him : because he had come to restore freedom to the Italians, and to assist them to recover their cities and territory which they had severally lost to Rome." With these words he dismissed them without ransom to their own homes, wishing by this policy to attract the inhabitants of Italy to his cause, and to alienate their affections from Rome, and to awaken the resentment of all those who considered themselves to have suffered by the loss of harbors or cities under the Roman rule.

70. Fabian Policy

Polybius, Book III, chapters 89 and 90

89. When Hannibal learnt that Fabius had arrived, he determined to terrify the enemy by promptly attacking. He therefore led out his army, approached the Roman camp, and there drew up his men in order of battle; but when he had waited some time, and nobody came out to attack him, he drew off and retired to his own camp. For Fabius, having made up his mind to incur no danger and not to risk a battle, but to make the safety of his men his first and greatest object, kept resolutely to this purpose. . . .

90. He, then, during the following months, kept his army continually hovering in the neighborhood of the enemy, his superior knowledge of the country enabling him to occupy beforehand all the posts of vantage; and having supplies in abundance on his rear, he never allowed his soldiers to go on foraging expeditions,

or get separated, on any pretence, from the camp; but keeping them continually massed together and in close union, he watched for favorable opportunities of time and place; and by this method of proceeding, captured and killed a large number of the enemy, who in their contempt of him straggled from their camp in search of plunder. His object in these manœuvres was twofold, — to gradually diminish the limited numbers of the enemy; and to strengthen and renew by such successes in detail the spirits of his own men, which had been depressed, to begin with, by the general defeat of their armies. But nothing would induce him to agree to give the enemy a set battle. This policy, however, was by no means approved of by his master of the horse, Marcus. He joined in the general verdict, and decried Fabius in every one's hearing, as conducting his command in a cowardly and unenterprising spirit; and was himself eager to venture upon a decisive engagement.

538 A.U.C.   **71. The Old Roman Spirit**   B.C. 216

Polybius, Book III, chapter 118

. . . In spite of all, however, the senate left no means untried to save the State. It exhorted the people to fresh exertions, strengthened the city with guards, and deliberated on the crisis in a brave and manly spirit. And subsequent events made this manifest. For though the Romans were on that occasion [at Cannæ] indisputably beaten in the field, and had lost reputation for military prowess; by the peculiar excellence of their political constitution, and the prudence of their counsels, they not only recovered their supremacy over Italy, by eventually conquering the Carthaginians, but before very long became masters of the whole world. . . .

72. Treaties between Rome and Carthage [1]

Polybius, Book III, chapters 22, 24, 25, 27

22. The first treaty between Rome and Carthage was made in the year of Lucius Junius Brutus and Marcus Horatius, the first consuls appointed after the expulsion of the kings [B.C. 509–508]. . . . The treaty is as follows : —

"There shall be friendship between the Romans and their allies, and the Carthaginians and their allies, on these conditions : —

" Neither the Romans nor their allies are to sail beyond the Fair Promontory, unless driven by stress of weather or the fear of enemies. If any one of them be driven ashore, he shall not buy nor take aught for himself save what is needful for the repair of his ship and the service of the gods, and he shall depart within five days.

" Men landing for traffic shall strike no bargain save in the presence of a herald or town clerk. Whatever is sold in the presence of these, let the price be secured to the seller on the credit of the State — that is to say, if such sale be in Libya or Sardinia.

" If any Roman comes to the Carthaginian province in Sicily, he shall enjoy all rights enjoyed by others. The Carthaginians shall do no injury to the people of Ardea, Antium, Laurentium, Circeii, Tarracina, nor any other people of the Latins that are subject to Rome.

" From those townships even which are not subject to Rome they shall hold their hands ; and if they take one, shall deliver it unharmed to the Romans. They shall build no fort in Latium ; and if they enter the district in arms, they shall not stay a night therein." . . .

24. After this treaty there was a second [B.C. 306 ?] : . . .
"There shall be friendship between the Romans and their allies, and the Carthaginians, Tyrians, and township of Utica, on these terms :

[1] Cf. Mommsen, Appendix to Vol. III, pp. 523 ff.

The Romans shall not maraud, nor traffic, nor found a city east of the Fair Promontory, Mastia, Tarseium. If the Carthaginians take any city in Latium which is not subject to Rome, they may keep the prisoners and the goods, but shall deliver up the town. If the Carthaginians take any folk, between whom and Rome a peace has been made in writing, though they be not subject to them, they shall not bring them into any harbors of the Romans; if such an one be so brought ashore, and any Roman lay claim to him, he shall be released. In like manner shall the Romans be bound towards the Carthaginians.

"If a Roman take water or provisions from any district within the jurisdiction of Carthage, he shall not injure, while so doing, any between whom and Carthage there is peace and friendship. Neither shall a Carthaginian in like case. If any shall do so, he shall not be punished by private vengeance, but such action shall be a public misdemeanor.

"In Sardinia and Libya no Roman shall traffic nor found a city; he shall do no more than take in provisions and refit his ship. If a storm drive him upon those coasts, he shall depart within five days.

"In the Carthaginian province of Sicily and in Carthage he may transact business and sell whatsoever it is lawful for a citizen to do. In like manner also may a Carthaginian at Rome." . . .

25. A third treaty again was made by Rome at the time of the invasion of Pyrrhus into Sicily; before the Carthaginians undertook the war for the possession of Sicily [B.C. 279]. This treaty contains the same provisions as the two earlier treaties with these additional clauses : —

"If they make a treaty of alliance with Pyrrhus, the Romans or Carthaginians shall make it on such terms as not to preclude the one giving aid to the other, if that one's territory is attacked.

"If one or the other stand in need of help, the Carthaginians shall supply the ships, whether for transport or war; but each people shall supply the pay for its own men employed on them.

" The Carthaginians shall also give aid by sea to the Romans if need be ; but no one shall compel the crews to disembark against their will." . . .

27. At the end of the first Punic war [B.C. 241] another treaty was made, of which the chief provisions were these : " The Carthaginians shall evacuate Sicily and all islands lying between Italy and Sicily.

" The allies of neither of the parties to the treaty shall be attacked by the other.

" Neither party shall impose any contribution, nor erect any public building, nor enlist soldiers in the dominions of the other, nor make any compact of friendship with the allies of the other.

" The Carthaginians shall within ten years pay to the Romans two thousand two hundred talents, and a thousand on the spot, and shall restore all prisoners, without ransom, to the Romans."

Afterwards, at the end of the Mercenary war in Africa, the Romans went so far as to pass a decree for war with Carthage, but eventually made a treaty to the following effect : " The Carthaginians shall evacuate Sardinia, and pay an additional twelve hundred talents."

Finally, in addition to these treaties, came that negotiated with Hasdrubal in Iberia [B.C. 238], in which it was stipulated that " the Carthaginians should not cross the Iber with arms."

Such were the mutual obligations established between Rome and Carthage from the earliest times to that of Hannibal.

Sources : Foreign Wars, B.C. 264-146

FIRST PUNIC WAR.—Appian: *Foreign Wars*, V, par. 1, 2; VIII, ch. 1; Eutropius, II, 18-28; Florus, II, 2; Livy, XXX, 44; Livy: *Epitome*, XVI-XIX; Plutarch: *Marcellus;* Polybius, I, 7-63.

ILLYRIAN AND GALLIC WARS. — Appian: *Foreign Wars*, XI; Eutropius, II, 4-6; Florus, II, 3-5; Livy: *Epitome*, XX; Plutarch: *Marcellus*, III, IV; Polybius, II, 2-35.

SECOND PUNIC WAR. — Appian: *Foreign Wars*, VI, 2-38; VII, VIII, 4-66; Eutropius, III, 7-23; Florus, II, 6; Livy, XXI-XXX; C. Nepos: *Life of*

Hannibal; Plutarch: *Fabius Maximus* and *Marcellus;* Polybius, III–XV, *passim.*

FIRST MACEDONIAN WAR. — Appian: *Foreign Wars,* IX, 1 ff.; Florus, II, 7; Livy, XXII–XXIX, *passim;* Polybius, V, 101; VII, 9 ff.

SECOND MACEDONIAN WAR. — Appian: *Foreign Wars,* IX; Eutropius, IV, 1, 2; Florus, II, 12; Justin, XXX, 3, 4; Livy, XXXI–XXXIII, 30; Plutarch: *Titus Flamininus;* Polybius (*Fragments*), XV, 20–24; XVI, 1–13, 24–38; XVIII, 1–52; Velleius, II, 9.

WAR WITH ANTIOCHUS. — Appian: *Foreign Wars,* X. 1–37; Eutropius, IV, 3, 4; Josephus: *Antiquities of the Jews,* XII, 3, 3–4; Justin, XXXI, 1–8; Livy, XXXIII, 44–XXXVIII, *passim;* Plutarch: *Flamininus, Cato,* and *Philopœmen;* Polybius (*Fragments*), XVIII–XXI; Velleius, I, 10.

TO THE END OF THE THIRD MACEDONIAN WAR. — Appian: *Foreign Wars,* IX, X, 2 and 42–45; Eutropius, IV, 2–4; Florus, II, 12–14; Josephus: *Antiquities,* XII, 10 (on the Jewish Alliance); Justin, XXXII, 2–4; Livy, XXVIII, 42–XLV, *passim;* Plutarch: *Æmilius, Paulus,* and *Philopœmen;* Polybius, XXII, 8, 9, 15–18; XXIII, 1–4, 7–11, 14; XXIV, 1, 4; XXVII, 1–18; XXVIII–XXX; XXXVII.

WAR WITH ANDRISCUS. — Eutropius, 4, 6, 7, 13; Florus, 2, 14; Livy: *Epitome,* XLVIII, L, LIII; Pausanias, VII, 12, 9; Polybius, XXXVII, 2 and 9; Velleius, I, 11.

ACHÆAN WAR AND FALL OF CORINTH. — Eutropius, IV, 14 ; Florus, II, 16 ; Justin, XXXIV, 1, 2; Livy: *Epitome,* LI, LII; Pausanias, VII, 12–16; Polybius, XXXIX, 10–13; Velleius, I, 12.

THIRD PUNIC WAR. — Appian: *Foreign Wars,* VIII, 67–135; Eutropius, IV, 10–12; Florus, II, 15; Livy: *Epitome,* XLIX–LII; Polybius, XXXII, 2, 8–16; XXXVI; XXXVII, 1–3, 10; XXXVIII, 1, 2; XXXIX, 1–5; Velleius, I, 12.

VII. RESULTS OF FOREIGN WARS. MISRULE OF THE OPTIMATES

Abbott, ch. 5, 8–11; Allcroft and Masom: *Rome under the Oligarchs*, ch. 10, 11; Allen, ch. 7, pp. 100 ff.; 12, pp. 146–154; Arnold, W. T.: *The Roman System of Provincial Administration;* Botsford, ch. 6, pp. 129–143; Duruy, Vol. II, ch. 35–37; Fowler, ch. 8; How and Leigh, ch. 28–31; Ihne, Bk. VII, ch. 1; Leighton, ch. 29; Mommsen, Bk. III, ch. 11–14; Morey, ch. 18; Myers, ch. 12, pp. 207–211; Pelham, Bk. III, ch. 3, pp. 158–192; Robinson, ch. 17, pp. 201–206; Seignobos, ch. 11, 12; Shuckburgh, ch. 21, 26, 32; Taylor, ch. 7, 8; West, Pt. IV, ch. 8, par. 392–406; Wolfson, ch. 27.

566 A.U.C.   **73. Introduction of Foreign Luxuries**   B.C. 188

Livy, Book XXXIX, chapter 6

. . . Nor were the facts, which were reported to have happened in the province, far from the eyes of spectators, the only things that disgraced his [Cn. Manlius Vulso's] character; but still more so, those circumstances which were every day beheld in his soldiers; for by this army returning from Asia was the origin of foreign luxury imported into the city. These men first brought to Rome gilded couches, rich tapestry, with hangings and other works of the loom, and what were then deemed magnificent furniture, single-footed tables and buffets. At entertainments, likewise, were introduced female players on the harp and timbrel, with buffoons for the diversion of the guests. Their meats also began to be prepared with greater care and cost; while the cook, whom the ancients considered as the meanest of their slaves both in estimation and use, became highly valuable, and what had been considered as a servile office began to be considered an art. Nevertheless, those innovations which were then looked on as remarkable were scarcely even the seeds of the future luxury.

FIG. 9. — A ROMAN LITTER
Baumeister, fig. 1602

586 A.U.C.   **74. Effects of Foreign Wars**   B.C. 168

Polybius, Book XXXII, chapter 11

. . . This dissoluteness had as it were burst into flame at this period : in the first place, from the prevalent idea that, owing to the destruction of the Macedonian monarchy, universal dominion was now secured to them beyond dispute ; and, in the second place, from the immense difference made, both in public and private wealth and splendor, by the importation of the riches of Macedonia into Rome. . . .

75. Censorship of Cato

Livy, Book XXXIX, chapters 40-42, 44

40. . . . But M. Porcius far surpassed all of them, both plebeians and patricians of the highest ranks. So great powers of mind and energy of intellect were in this man, that, no matter how lowly the position in which he was born, he appeared capable of attaining to the highest rank. No one qualification for the management of business, either public or private, was wanting in him. He was equally skilled in affairs relating to town and country. Some have been advanced to the highest honors by their knowledge of the law, others by their eloquence, some by military renown ; but this man's genius was so versatile, and so well adapted to all things, that in whatever way engaged, it might be said, that nature formed him for that alone. In war, he was most courageous, distinguishing himself highly in many remarkable battles ; and, when he arrived at the highest posts, was likewise a most consummate commander. Then, in peace, if consulted on a point of law, he was the wisest counsellor ; if a cause was to be pleaded, the most eloquent advocate. Nor was he one of those whose oratory was striking only during their own lives, without leaving after them any monument of it. On the contrary, his eloquence still lives, and will long live, consecrated to memory by writings of every kind. His orations are many, spoken for himself, for others, and against others ; for he harassed his enemies, not only by supporting prosecutions against them, but by maintaining causes in opposition to them. Enmities in abundance gave him plenty of employment, and he never permitted them to lie dormant; nor was it easy to tell whether the nobility labored harder to keep him down, or he to oppose the nobility. His temper, no doubt, was austere, his language bitter and unboundedly free, but his mind was never conquered by his passions, his integrity was inflexible, and he looked with contempt on popularity and riches. In spare diet, in enduring toil and danger, his body and mind were

like iron ; so that even old age, which brings all things to dissolution, did not break his vigor.   In his eighty-sixth year he stood a trial, pleaded his own cause, and published his speech ; and in his ninetieth year he brought Servius Galba to trial before the people.

41. On this occasion, when he was a candidate for the censorship, as in all his previous career, the nobility endeavored to crush him. All the candidates, likewise, except Lucius Flaccus, who had been his colleague in the consulship, combined to disappoint him of the office, not merely with a view to their own success, in preference to him, nor because they felt indignant at the idea of seeing a man of no family censor, but because from one who had received offence from most of them, and who wished to retaliate, they anticipated a severe censorship, that would endanger the reputations of many. For, even while soliciting, he uttered frequent menaces, and upbraided them with using their interest against him, because they dreaded an impartial and courageous execution of the duty of censor ; at the same time, giving his interest to Lucius Valerius, he said, that " he was the only colleague, in conjunction with whom he could correct modern profligacy, and reëstablish the ancient morals." People were so inflamed by such discourses, that, in spite of the opposition made by the nobility, they not only made Marcus Porcius censor, but gave him for his colleague Lucius Valerius Flaccus. . . .

42. . . . The censors, M. Porcius and Lucius Valerius, while anxious curiosity was blended with fear, made their survey of the senate; they expelled seven from the senate, one of them a man of consular rank, highly distinguished by nobility of birth and honorable employments, — Lucius Quintius Flaminius. It is mentioned, as a practice instituted in the memory of our forefathers, that the censors should annex marks of censure to the names of such as they degraded from the senate. . . .

44. In the review of the knights, Lucius Scipio Asiaticus was degraded. In fixing the rates of taxation, also, the censor's conduct was harsh and severe to all ranks of men. People were

ordered to give account upon oath, of women's dress and ornaments, and carriages exceeding in value fifteen thousand asses;
and it was further ordered, that slaves, younger than twenty years,
which, since the last survey, had been sold for ten thousand asses
or more, should be estimated at ten times their value and that, on
all these articles, a tax should be laid of three denarii for each
thousand asses. The censors took away water which belonged to
the public, running or carried into any private building or field ;
and they demolished within thirty days all buildings or sheds, in
possession of private persons, that projected into public ground.
They then engaged contractors for executing national works, with
the money decreed for that purpose, — for paving cisterns with
stone, for cleansing the sewers where it was requisite, and forming
new ones on the Aventine, and in other quarters where hitherto
there had been none. Then, dividing their tasks, Flaccus built a
mole at Nepthunia, on the coast, and made a road through the
Formian mountains. Cato purchased for the use of the people
two halls, the Mænian and Titian, in the Lautumiæ, and four
shops, and built there a court of justice, which was called the
Porcian. They farmed out the several branches of the revenue at
the highest prices and bargained with the contractors for the performance of the public services on the lowest terms. When the
senate, overcome by the prayers and lamentations of the publicans,
ordered those bargains to be revoked, and new agreements to be
made, the censors, by an edict, excluded from competition the
persons who had eluded the former contract and farmed out all
the branches at prices very little reduced. This was a remarkable
censorship, and the origin of many deadly feuds; it rendered
Marcus Porcius, to whom all the harshness was attributed, uneasy
during the remainder of his life. . . .

593 A.U.C.   **76. Sumptuary Law**   B.C. 161

Speech of C. Titius for the *Lex Fannia* [1]

" They devote themselves to hazard, delicately perfumed, amid a
throng of their mistresses. When four o'clock comes they bid their
boy be called to go to the comitium and inquire what has been
done in the Forum, who have spoken in favor of the bill and who
against it, how many tribes have voted for it, how many against it ;
then they make their way to the court just in time to keep themselves from being summoned for non-appearance. . . . They
take their place sullenly on the tribunal and order the case to
come on. Those who are concerned make their statements, our
friend the judge requires the witnesses to be summoned, and
himself has a reason for retiring. When he returns, he says he
has heard everything, and asks for the documents : he looks into
the papers, and can scarce keep his eyes open for wine. The
jury withdraw to consider their verdict, and their talk is such as
this : ' Why should I trouble myself with these horrid bores?
Why should we not rather drink a bowl of mead and Greek wine,
and eat a fat thrush and a good fish with it, a genuine pike killed
between the two bridges?' "

594 A.U.C.   **77. Introduction of Greek Teachers**   B.C. 160

Polybius, Book XXXII, chapter 10

Polybius . . . said : . . . " as for learning, to which I see you
[Scipio Æmilianus] and your brother devoting yourselves at present with so much earnestness and zeal, you will find plenty of
people to help you both ; for I see that a large number of such
learned men from Greece are finding their way into Rome at the
present time. . . .

[1] Translated by J. Wordsworth, *Fragments*, etc., p. 630.

608 a.u.c.   **78. Results of the Fall of Carthage**   b.c. 146

Sallust: *Fragments*

But discord,[1] and avarice, and ambition, and other evils that usually spring from prosperity, were most increased after Carthage was destroyed.   For encroachments of the stronger on the weaker, and consequent separations of the people from the senate, with other domestic dissensions, had existed even from the very origin of the republic ; nor, on the expulsion of the kings, were equity and moderation observed any longer than till the dread of Tarquin, and

Fig. 10. — Romano-Carthaginian Aqueduct
Schreiber, plate 58, fig. 6

of a fierce war from Etruria, subsided ; after that time, the patricians began to tyrannize over the plebeians as over slaves ; to scourge and put them to death with authority like that of kings ; to dispossess them of their lands, and, excluding them from the government, to keep it entirely in their own hands.   The people, being greatly oppressed by these severities, and especially by the grievance of usury, and having also to contribute taxes and service for incessant wars, at last took up arms, and posted themselves on the Sacred and Aventine Mounts ; on which occasions they secured for themselves the right of electing tribunes, and other privileges.

[1] Compare Sallust: *Jugurtha*, c. 41; *Catiline*, c. 10.

To these disputes and contentions the second Punic war brought a termination.

When, after the terror of the Carthaginians was removed, the people were at liberty to resume their dissensions, innumerable disturbances, seditions, and subsequent civil wars arose, while a few powerful individuals, whose interest most of the other nobles had submitted to promote, sought, under the specious pretext of supporting the senate or the plebeians, to secure power for themselves; and men were esteemed or despised by them, not as they deserved well or ill of the republic (for all were equally corrupt); but whoever grew eminently wealthy, and better able to encroach on others, was styled, if he supported the present state of affairs, an excellent citizen. From this period the manners of our forefathers degenerated, not, as before, gradually, but with precipitation like that of a torrent; and the youth became so depraved with luxury and avarice, that they might be thought, with justice, to have been born powerless either to preserve their own property, or to suffer others to preserve theirs.

79. Jugurtha Bribes Influential Romans

Sallust: *Jugurthine War*, chapters 13, 15, 16, 27, 29, 32, 33, 35

13. Jugurtha, having thus accomplished his purposes, and reflecting, at leisure, on the crime, the murder of Hiempsal, which he had committed, began to feel a dread of the Roman people, against whose resentment he had no hopes of security but in the avarice of the nobility, and in his own wealth. A few days afterward, therefore, he despatched ambassadors to Rome, with a profusion of gold and silver, whom he directed, in the first place, to make an abundance of presents to his old friends, and then to procure him new ones; and not to hesitate, in short, to effect whatever could be done by bribery.

When these deputies had arrived at Rome, and had sent large presents, according to the prince's direction, to his intimate friends, and to others whose influence was at that time powerful, so remarkable a change ensued that Jugurtha, from being an object of the greatest odium, grew into great regard and favor with the nobility, who, partly allured with hope, and partly with actual largesses, endeavored, by soliciting the members of the senate individually, to prevent any severe measures from being adopted against him. When the ambassadors, accordingly, felt sure of success, the senate, on a fixed day, gave audience to both parties.

15. The partisans of the ambassadors, with a great many others, corrupted by their influence, expressed contempt for the statements of Adherbal, extolled with the highest encomiums the merits of Jugurtha, and exerted themselves as strenuously with their interest and their eloquence, in defence of the guilt and infamy of another, as they would have striven for their own honor. A few, however, on the other hand, to whom right and justice were of more estimation than wealth, gave their opinion that Adherbal should be assisted, and the murder of Hiempsal should be severely avenged. Of all these the most forward was Æmilius Scaurus, a man of noble birth and great energy, but factious, and ambitious of power, honor, and wealth ; yet an artful concealer of his vices. He, seeing that the bribery of Jugurtha was notorious and shameless, and fearing that, as in such cases often happens, its scandalous profusion might excite public odium, restrained himself from the indulgence of his ruling passion.

16. Yet that party gained the superiority in the senate, which preferred money and interest to justice. A decree was made " that ten commissioners should divide the kingdom, which Micipsa had possessed, between Jugurtha and Adherbal." Of this commission, the leading person was Lucius Opimius, a man of distinction and of great influence at that time in the senate, from having in his consulship on the death of Caius Gracchus and Marcus Fulvius Flaccus, prosecuted the victory of the nobility over the plebeians with great severity.

Jugurtha, though he had already counted Scaurus among his friends at Rome, yet received him with the most studied ceremony and by presents and promises, wrought on him so effectually that he preferred the prince's interest to his own character, honor, and all other considerations. The rest of the commissioners he assailed in a similar way and gained over most of them; by a few only integrity was more regarded than lucre. In the division of the kingdom, the part of Numidia which borders on Mauretania, and which is superior in fertility and population, was allotted to Jugurtha; of the other part, which, though better furnished with harbors and buildings, was more valuable in appearance than in reality, Adherbal became the possessor.

27. When this outrage was reported at Rome, and became a matter of discussion in the senate, the former partisans of Jugurtha applied themselves by interrupting the debates and protracting the time, sometimes exerting their interests, and sometimes quarrelling with particular members, to palliate the atrocity of the deed. And had not Caius Memmius, one of the tribunes of the people elect, convinced the people of Rome that an attempt was being made by the agency of a small faction to have the crimes of Jugurtha pardoned, it is certain that the public indignation against him would have passed off under the protraction of the debates, so powerful was party interest and the influence of Jugurtha's money.

29. But when Jugurtha began to tempt him [Calpurnius, the consul] with bribes, and to show the difficulties of the war which he had undertaken to conduct, his mind, corrupted with avarice, was easily altered. His accomplice, however, and manager in all his schemes, was Scaurus; who, though he had at first, when most of his party were corrupted, displayed violent hostility to Jugurtha, yet was afterwards seduced by a vast sum of money from integrity and honor to injustice and perfidy.

32. During the course of these proceedings at Rome, those whom Bestia had left in Numidia in command of the army, following the example of their general, had been guilty of many scanda-

lous transactions. Some, seduced by gold, had restored Jugurtha his elephants; others had sold him his deserters; others had ravished the lands of those at peace with us; so strong a spirit of rapacity, like the contagion of pestilence, had pervaded the breasts of all.

33. Jugurtha, accordingly, accompanied Cassius to Rome, but without any mark of royalty, and in the garb, as much as possible, of a suppliant; and though he felt great confidence on his own part, and was supported by all those through whose power or villainy he had accomplished his projects, he purchased, by a vast bribe, the aid of Caius Bæbius, a tribune of the people, by whose audacity he hoped to be protected against the law and against all harm.

35. A few days after, he himself departed, having been ordered by the senate to quit Italy. But, as he was going from Rome, he is said, after frequently looking back on it in silence, to have at last exclaimed, "That it was a venal city, and would soon perish if it could but find a purchaser!"

VIII. THE LAST CENTURY OF THE REPUBLIC

(*a*) THE BEGINNING OF THE REVOLUTION. THE GRACCHI. (*b*) THE
CIVIL WARS. MARIUS AND SULLA ; POMPEY AND CÆSAR

The Gracchi

Abbott, ch. 7, par. 85–87; Allen, ch. 12, pp. 154–165; Beesly, A. H.: *The Gracchi, Marius and Sulla* (*Epochs*); Botsford, ch. 7, pp. 151–160; Duruy, Vol. II, ch. 37; Greenidge, ch. 9, pp. 331–333; How and Leigh, ch. 33, 34, pp. 331–357; Ihne, Bk. VII, ch. 2, 3, 6, 7 ; Leighton, ch. 30, 31, pp. 199–214 ; Long: *Decline of the Roman Republic ;* Masom: *Decline of the Oligarchy ;* Merivale: *Fall of the Roman Republic*, ch. 1, pp. 1–31; Mommsen, Bk. IV, ch. 1–3; Morey, ch. 19; Myers, ch. 12, pp. 216–223; Nitzsch: *Die Gracchen ;* Pelham, Bk. IV, ch. 1, pp. 201–214; Robinson, ch. 17, pp. 201–218; Ramsay and Lanciani: *Manual of Roman Antiquities*, ch. 7; Seignobos, ch. 13, pp. 177–188; Shuckburgh, ch. 35 ; Taylor, ch. 9; West, par. 407–418; Wolfson, ch. 28.

80. The Period of the Revolution

Sallust: *Catiline*, chapters 41, 42

41. The prevalence of parties among the people, and of factions in the senate, and of all evil practices attendant on them, had its origin at Rome, a few years before, during a period of tranquillity, and amidst the abundance of all that mankind regard as desirable. For, before the destruction of Carthage, the senate and people managed the affairs of the republic with mutual moderation and forbearance ; there were no contests among the citizens for honor or ascendency ; but the dread of an enemy kept the State in order. When that fear, however, was removed from their minds, licentiousness and pride, evils which prosperity loves to foster, immediately

began to prevail; and thus peace, which they had so eagerly desired in adversity, proved, when they had obtained it, more grievous and fatal than adversity itself. The patricians carried their authority, and the people their liberty, to excess; every man took, snatched, and seized what he could. There was a complete division into two factions, and the republic was torn in pieces between them. Yet the nobility still maintained an ascendency by conspiring together; for the strength of the people, being disunited and dispersed among a multitude, was less able to exert itself. Things were accordingly directed, both at home and in the field, by the will of a small number of men, at whose disposal were the treasury, the provinces, offices, honors, and triumphs; while the people were oppressed with military service and with poverty, and the generals divided the spoils of war with a few of their friends. The parents and children of the soldiers,[1] meantime, if they chanced to dwell near a powerful neighbor, were driven from their homes. Thus avarice, leagued with power, disturbed, violated, and wasted everything, without moderation or restraint; disregarding alike reason and religion, and rushing headlong, as it were, to its own destruction. For whenever any arose among the nobility, who preferred true glory to unjust power, the State was immediately in a tumult, and civil discord spread with as much disturbance as attends a convulsion of the earth.

42. Thus when Tiberius and Caius Gracchus, whose forefathers had done much to increase the power of the State in the Punic and other wars, began to vindicate the liberty of the people, and to expose the misconduct of the few, the nobility, conscious of guilt, and seized with alarm, endeavored, sometimes by means of the allies and Latins, and sometimes by means of the equestrian order, whom the hope of coalition with the patricians had detached from the people, to put a stop to the proceedings of the Gracchi; and first they killed Tiberius, and a few years after Caius, who pursued the same measures as his brother, the one when he was

---

[1] Cf. Horace: *Odes*, II, 18.

tribune, the other when he was one of the triumvirate for settling colonies ; and with them they cut off Marcus Fulvius Flaccus.   In the Gracchi, indeed, it must be allowed that, from their ardor of victory, there was not sufficient prudence.   But to a reasonable man it is more agreeable to submit to injustice than triumph over it by improper means.   The nobility, however, using their victory with wanton extravagance, exterminated numbers of men by the sword or by exile, yet rather increased, for the time to come, the dread with which they were regarded, than their real power. . . .

81. The Gracchi

Plutarch : *Lives of Ti. and C. Gracchus* (Extracts)

. . . She [Cornelia] brought them up with such care, that though they were without dispute in natural endowments and dis-

positions the first among the Romans of their time, yet they seemed to owe their virtues even more to their education than to their birth. . . . Between these two noble youths, though there was a strong general likeness in their common love of fortitude and temperance, in their liberality, their eloquence, and their greatness of mind, yet in their actions and administrations of public affairs a considerable variation showed itself.   It will not be amiss, before we proceed. to mark the difference between them.

Tiberius, in the form and expression of his countenance and in his gesture and motion, was gentle and composed ; but Caius, earnest and vehement.   And so, in their public speeches to the people, the one spoke in a quiet, orderly manner, standing throughout on the same spot ; the other would walk about on the hustings, and in the heat of his orations pull his gown off

FIG. 11.— A ROMAN ORATOR

Baumeister, fig. 1921

his shoulders, and was the first of all the Romans that used such gestures. . . . Caius's oratory was impetuous and passionate, making everything tell to the utmost, whereas Tiberius was gentle, rather, and persuasive, awakening emotions of pity. His diction was pure, and carefully correct, while that of Caius was vehement and rich. So likewise in their way of living, and at their tables, Tiberius was frugal and plain ; Caius, compared with other men temperate and even austere, but contrasting with his brother in a fondness for new fashions and rarities. . . .

The same difference that appeared in their diction was observable also in their tempers. The one was mild and reasonable, the other rough and passionate, and to that degree, that often, in the midst of speaking, he was so hurried away by his passion, against his judgment, that his voice lost its tone, and he began to pass into mere abusive talking, spoiling his whole speech. . . . Such are the differences between the two brothers ; but their valor in war against their country's enemies, their justice in the government of its subjects, their care and industry in office, and their self-command in all that regarded their pleasures were equally remarkable in both. . . .

Of the land which the Romans gained by conquest from their neighbors, part they sold publicly, and turned the remainder into common ; this common land they assigned to such of the citizens as were poor and indigent, for which they were to pay only a small acknowledgment into the public treasury. But when the wealthy men began to offer larger rents, and drive the poorer people out, it was enacted by law that no person whatever should enjoy more than five hundred acres of ground. This act for some time checked the avarice of the richer, and was of great assistance to the poorer people, who retained under it their respective proportions of ground, as they had been formerly rented by them. Afterwards the rich men of the neighborhood contrived to get these lands again into their possession, under other people's names, and at last would not stick to claim most of them publicly in their own. The poor, who were thus deprived of their farms, were no longer either ready, as they had formerly been, to serve in war, or careful in the education of their children; insomuch that in a short time there were comparatively few free-men remaining in all Italy, which swarmed with workhouses full of foreign-born slaves. These the rich men employed in cultivating their ground, of which they dispossessed the citizens. Caius Lælius, the intimate friend of Scipio, undertook to reform this abuse; but meeting with opposition from men of authority, and fearing a disturbance, he soon desisted. . . .[1]

But Tiberius, being elected tribune of the people, entered upon that design without delay. . . . His brother Caius has left it us in writing, that when Tiberius went through Tuscany to Numantia, and found the country almost depopulated, there being hardly any free husbandmen or shepherds, but for the most part only barbarian, imported slaves, he then first conceived the course of policy which in the sequel proved so fatal to his family. Though it is also most certain that the people themselves chiefly excited his zeal and determination in the prosecution of it, by setting up writings upon the porches, walls, and monuments, calling upon him to reinstate the poor citizens in their former possessions.

However, he did not draw up his law without the advice and assistance of those citizens that were then most eminent for their virtue and authority; amongst whom were Crassus, the high-priest, Mucius Scævola, the lawyer, who at that time was consul, and Claudius Appius, his father-in-law. Never did any law appear more moderate and gentle, especially being enacted against such great oppression and avarice. For they who ought to have been severely punished for transgressing the former laws, and should at least have lost all their titles to such lands which they had unjustly usurped, were notwithstanding to receive a price for quitting their unlawful claims, and giving up their lands to those fit owners who stood in need of help. But though this reformation was managed

[1] Cf. No. 181.

with so much tenderness, that, all the former transactions being passed over, the people were only thankful to prevent abuses of the like nature for the future, yet, on the other hand, the moneyed men, and those of great estates, were exasperated, through their covetous feelings against the law itself, and against the lawgiver, through anger and party spirit. They therefore endeavored to seduce the people, declaring that Tiberius was designing a general redivision of lands, to overthrow the government, and put all things into confusion.

But they had no success. . . .

After this, they brought other accusations and writs against him [Caius] for exciting insurrection amongst the allies, and being engaged in the conspiracy that was discovered about Fregellæ. But having cleared himself of every suspicion, and proved his entire innocence, he now at once came forward to ask for the tribuneship; in which, though he was universally opposed by all persons of distinction, yet there came such infinite numbers of people from all parts of Italy to vote for Caius, that lodgings for them could not be supplied in the city; and the Field not being large enough to contain the assembly, there were numbers who climbed upon the roofs and the tilings of the houses to use their voices in his favor. However, the nobility so far forced the people to their pleasure and disappointed Caius's hope, that he was not returned the first, as was expected, but the fourth tribune. . . .

. . . He proposed two laws. The first was, that whoever was turned out of any public office by the people, should be thereby rendered incapable of bearing any office afterwards; the second, that if any magistrate condemn a Roman to be banished, without a legal trial, the people be authorized to take cognizance thereof.

One of these laws was manifestly levelled at Marcus Octavius, who, at the instigation of Tiberius, had been deprived of his tribuneship. The other touched Popilius, who, in his prætorship, had banished all Tiberius's friends; whereupon Popilius, being unwilling to stand the hazard of a trial, fled out of Italy. As for the former law, it was withdrawn by Caius himself, who said he yielded in the case of Octavius, at the request of his mother Cornelia. . . .

Of the laws which he now proposed, with the object of gratifying the people and abridging the power of the senate, the first was concerning the public lands, which were to be divided amongst the poor citizens ; another was concerning the common soldiers, that they should be clothed at the public charge, without any diminution of their pay, and that none should be obliged to serve in the army who was not full seventeen years old ; another gave the same right to all the Italians in general, of voting at elections, as was enjoyed by the citizens of Rome ; a fourth related to the price of corn, which was to be sold at a lower rate than formerly to the poor ; and a fifth regulated the courts of justice, greatly reducing the power of the senators. For hitherto, in all causes senators only sat as judges, and were therefore much dreaded by the Roman knights and the people. But Caius joined three hundred ordinary citizens of equestrian rank with the senators, who were likewise three hundred in number, and ordained that the judicial authority should be equally vested in the six hundred. While he was arguing for the ratification of this law, his behavior was observed to show in many respects unusual earnestness, and whereas other popular leaders had always hitherto, when speaking, turned their faces towards the senate-house, and the place called the comitium, he, on the contrary, was the first man that in his harangue to the people turned himself the other way, towards them, and continued after that time to do so. An insignificant movement and change of posture, yet it marked no small revolution in state affairs, the conversion, in a manner, of the whole government from an aristocracy to a democracy ; his action intimating that public speakers should address themselves to the people, not the senate.

When the commonalty ratified this law, and gave him power to select those of the knights whom he approved of, to be judges, he was invested with a sort of kingly power, and the senate itself submitted to receive his advice in matters of difficulty; nor did he advise anything that might derogate from the honor of that body. As, for example, his resolution about the corn which Fabius the proprætor sent from Spain, was very just and honorable; for he persuaded the senate to sell the corn, and return the money to the same provinces which had furnished them with it; and also that Fabius should be censured for rendering the Roman government odious and insupportable. This got him extraordinary respect and favor among the provinces. Besides all this, he proposed measures for the colonization of several cities, for making roads, and for building public granaries, of all which works he himself undertook the management and superintendence, and was never wanting to give necessary orders for the despatch of all these different and great undertakings, and that with such wonderful expedition and diligence, as if he had been but engaged upon one of them, insomuch that all persons, even those who hated or feared him, stood amazed to see what a capacity he had for effecting and completing all he undertook.

82. Roman Roads

Plutarch: *Life of C. Gracchus*, chapter 7

His most especial exertions were given to constructing the roads, which he was careful to make beautiful and pleasant, as well as convenient. They were drawn by his directions through the fields, exactly in a straight line, partly paved with hewn stone, and partly laid with solid masses of gravel. When he met with any valleys or deep watercourses crossing the line, he either caused them to be filled up with rubbish, or bridges to be built over them, so well levelled, that all being of an equal height on both sides, the work presented one uniform and beautiful prospect. Besides this, he caused the roads to be all divided into miles (each mile containing little less than eight furlongs), and erected pillars of

stone to signify the distance from one place to another. He likewise placed other stones at small distances from one another, on
both sides of the way, by the help of which travellers might get
easily on horseback without wanting a groom.

83. Gaius Gracchus and His Reforms

Appian: *Civil Wars*, Book I, Paragraphs 22–24

22. Thus Gaius Gracchus became tribune a second time. Having bought the plebeians, as it were, he began, by another like
political manœuvre, to court the equestrian order, who hold the
middle place between the senate and the plebeians. He transferred the courts of justice, which had become discredited by
reason of bribery, from the senators to the knights, reproaching
the former, especially with the recent examples of Aurelius Cotta,
Salinator, and, third in the list, Manius Aquilius (the one who subdued Asia), all notorious bribe-takers, who had been acquitted by
the judges, although ambassadors sent to complain against them
were still present, going around uttering hateful accusations against
them. The senate was extremely ashamed of these things and
yielded to the law, and the people ratified it. In this way were
the courts of justice transferred from the senate to the knights. It
is said that soon after the passage of this law Gracchus remarked
that he had broken the power of the senate once for all. This
saying of Gracchus has been even more confirmed by experience
in the course of events. This power of sitting in judgment on
all Romans and Italians, including the senators themselves, in all
matters as to property, civil rights, and banishment, exalted the
knights like rulers over them and put senators on the same level
with subjects. Moreover, as the knights voted in the election to
sustain the power of the tribunes, and obtained from them whatever they wanted in return, they became more and more formidable to the senators. So it shortly came about that the political
mastery was turned upside down, the power being in the hands

of the knights, and the honor only remaining with the senate. The knights went so far that they not only held power over the senators, but they openly flouted them beyond their right. They also became addicted to bribe-taking, and having once tasted these enormous gains, they indulged in them even more basely and immoderately than the senators had done. They suborned accusers against the rich and did away with prosecutions for bribe-taking altogether, partly by concert of action and partly by force and violence, so that the practice of this kind of investigation became entirely obsolete. Thus the judiciary law gave rise to another struggle of factions, which lasted a long time and was not less baneful than the former ones.

23. Gracchus made long roads throughout Italy and thus put a multitude of contractors and artisans under obligations to him and made them ready to do whatever he wished. He proposed the founding of numerous colonies.[1] He also called on the Latin allies to demand the full rights of Roman citizenship, since the senate could not with decency refuse this privilege to their blood relations. To the other allies, who were not allowed to vote in Roman elections, he sought to give the right of suffrage, in order to have their help in the enactment of laws which he had in contemplation. The senate was very much alarmed at this, and it ordered the consuls to give the following public notice, " Nobody who does not possess the right of suffrage shall stay in the city or approach within forty stades of it while voting is going on concerning these laws." The senate also persuaded Livius Drusus, another tribune, to interpose his veto against the laws proposed by Gracchus, but not to tell the people his reasons for doing so ; for a tribune was not required to give reasons for his veto. In order to conciliate the people, they gave Drusus the privilege of founding twelve colonies, and the plebeians were so much pleased with this that they began to scoff at the laws proposed by Gracchus.

---

1 The founding of colonies, which was originally a method of guarding the frontier, now became a method of providing for the poorer citizens.

24. Having lost the favor of the rabble, Gracchus sailed for Africa in company with Fulvius Flaccus, who, after his consulship, had been chosen tribune for the same reasons as Gracchus himself. A colony had been voted to Africa on account of its reputed fertility, and these men had been expressly chosen the founders of it in order to get them out of the way for a while, so that the senate might have a respite from demagogism. They marked out a town for the colony on the place where Carthage had formerly stood, disregarding the fact that Scipio, when he destroyed it, had devoted it with curses to sheep-pasturage forever. They assigned six thousand colonists to this place, instead of the smaller number fixed by law, in order further to curry favor with the people thereby. When they returned to Rome they invited the six thousand from the whole of Italy. The functionaries who were still in Africa laying out the city wrote home that wolves had pulled up and scattered the boundary marks made by Gracchus and Fulvius, and the soothsayers considered this an ill omen for the colony. So the senate summoned the comitia, in which it was proposed to repeal the law concerning this colony. . . .

Sources : The Gracchi

Appian: *Civil Wars*, I, 7–26; Cicero: *Concerning the Agrarian Law*, II, 31; Florus, III, 13–15; Livy: *Epitome*, LVIII–LXI; Plutarch: *Tiberius and Gaius Gracchus;* Sallust: *Jugurthine War;* Velleius Paterculus, II, 1–4, 6, 7.

VIII. (b) THE CIVIL WARS

I. MARIUS — SULLA (100–78 B.C.). — Abbott, ch. 6, par. 88–97; Allcroft: *The Making of the Monarchy*, ch. 1; Allen, ch. 13, 14; Beesly: *The Gracchi, Marius and Sulla*, ch. 4–15; Botsford, ch. 7, pp. 160–174; Duruy, Vol. II, ch. 39–47; Fowler, ch. 9; Freeman: *Historical Essays, Second Series: Lucius Cornelius Sulla;* How and Leigh, ch. 35–44; Ihne, Bk. VII, ch. 7–23; Leighton, ch. 32–39; Long: *Decline of the Roman Republic*, I, ch. 29; II, ch. 1–29; Masom: *Decline of the Oligarchy;* Merivale: *General History of Rome*, ch. 30–34; Merivale: *The Fall of the Roman Republic*, ch. 2–5; Mommsen, Bk. IV, ch. 4–10; V, ch. 1, 2; Morey, ch. 20; Myers, ch. 12;

p. 223–ch. 13; Pelham, Bk. IV, ch. 1–3; Robinson, ch. 18–21; Seignobos, ch. 14; Shuckburgh, ch. 36–40; Taylor, ch. 9, 10, 11; West, Pt. IV, par. 419–430; Wolfson, ch. 29.

II. CÆSAR AND POMPEY (78–44 B.C.). — Abbott, ch. 6, par. 98–117; Allcroft, ch. 2–9; Allen, ch. 15–17; Beesly, E. S.: *Catiline, Clodius, and Tiberius;* Boissier: *Cicero and his Friends;* Botsford, ch. 8; Church: *Roman Life in the Days of Cicero;* Dodge: *Cæsar;* Duruy, Vol. II, ch. 48; Vol. III, ch. 58; Forsyth: *Cicero;* Fowler: *Julius Cæsar;* Freeman, E. A.: *The Three Chief Periods of European History,* Lecture II; Froude: *Cæsar;* Greenidge, ch. 9; How and Leigh, ch. 40–54; Long, Vol. II, ch. 30–33; Vols. III–V; Mackail: *Latin Literature,* Bk. I, ch. 4–7; Mahaffy: *Greek World under Roman Sway,* ch. 4; Merivale: *History of the Romans under the Empire,* I, II, ch. 1–22; Merivale, *Roman Triumvirates,* ch. 1–8; Middleton: *Life and Letters of Cicero;* Mommsen, Bk. V, ch. 1–12; Morey, ch. 21; Myers, ch. 14; Pelham, Bk. IV, ch. 2, 3; Bk. V. ch. 1, 2; Robinson, ch. 22–28; Seeley: *Roman Imperialism,* Lecture I; Seignobos, ch. 15, 16, 17; Shuckburgh, ch. 41–45; Strachan-Davidson: *Cicero and the Fall of the Roman Republic;* Taylor, ch. 12–15; Trollope: *Cicero;* Van Santvoord: *The House of Cæsar;* West, Pt. IV, par. 431–451; Wolfson, ch. 30, 31.

663 A.U.C.   **84. Drusus**   B.C. 91

Velleius Paterculus, Book II, chapters 13–14

13. At the end of a few succeeding years, Marcus Livius Drusus entered on the office of tribune; a man of the noblest birth, the greatest eloquence, and the strictest purity of life, but who, in all his undertakings, was more distinguished by ability and good intention than by success. He formed a design of restoring to the senate its ancient dignity, and of transferring from the knights to that body the right of being judges; because when the knights, by the Sempronian laws, were invested with that authority, they had treated with cruel severity many of the most illustrious and most innocent citizens, and in particular had brought to trial for extortion Publius Rutilius, a man distinguished for virtue not only above his own, but above any age, and to the exceeding great grief of the public had condemned him to pay a penalty. But in those very efforts which he made in favor of the senate, he

found the senate itself opposed to him. For they did not perceive that whatever he brought forward in favor of the plebeians was intended to allure and attract the multitude, in order that being gratified in smaller matters they might consent to others of greater importance. Such, indeed, was the fate of Drusus, that the senate favored the injurious proceedings of his colleagues more than his own excellent designs, rejecting with scorn the honor offered by him, while they submitted patiently to the wrong done them by the others; looking, in short, with envy on his very exalted reputation, and with indulgence on the mean characters of his opponents.

14. When such well-intended plans were badly received, the purpose of Drusus was changed, and he resolved to extend the civic franchise to all Italy. As he was taking measures for this purpose, on coming home one day from the forum, surrounded by the immense disorderly crowd that constantly attended him, he was stabbed in the court-yard of his own house with a knife which was left sticking in his side, and within a few hours expired. While he was drawing almost his last breath, he uttered an expression, as he looked on the crowd standing round and lamenting over him, very consonant to his inward feelings. "My relations and friends," said he, "will the Commonwealth ever again have a citizen like me?" Thus ended the life of this illustrious man.

85. Caius Marius

Plutarch: *Life of Marius* (Extracts)

. . . Being naturally valiant and warlike, and more acquainted also with the discipline of the camp than of the city, he could not moderate his passion when in authority. He is said never to have either studied Greek, or to have made use of that language in any matter of consequence, thinking it ridiculous to bestow time in that learning, the teachers of which were little better than slaves. . . .

He was born of parents altogether obscure, indigent, who supported themselves by their daily labor. . . . He had spent a considerable part of his life before he saw and tasted the pleasures of the city, having passed previously in Cirrhæton, a village of the territory of Arpinum, a life compared with city delicacies rude and unrefined, yet temperate and conformable to the ancient Roman severity. . . .

. . . In the city he had neither riches nor eloquence to trust to, with which the leading men of the time obtained power with the people, but his vehement disposition, his indefatigable labors, and his plain way of living, of themselves gained him esteem and influence. . . .

Marius was now in his fifth consulship, and he sued for his sixth in such a manner as never any man before him had done, even for his first; he courted the people's favor and ingratiated himself with the multitude by every sort of complaisance, not only derogating from the state and dignity of his office, but also belying his own character, by attempting to seem popular and obliging, for which nature had never designed him. His passion for distinction did indeed, they say, make him exceedingly timorous in any political matters, or in confronting public assemblies, and that undaunted presence of mind he always showed in battle against the enemy forsook him when he was to address the people; he was easily upset by the most ordinary commendation or dispraise. . . .

. . . Being a man altogether ignorant of civil life and ordinary politics, he received all his advancement from war, and supposing his power and glory would by little and little decrease by his lying quietly out of action, he was eager by every means to excite some new commotion. . . .

When Marius again returned to Rome [from the war with Mithradates], he built a house close by the forum, either as he himself gave out, that he was not willing his clients should be tired with going far, or that he imagined distance was the reason why more

did not come. This, however, was not so ; the real reason was
that, being inferior to others in agreeableness of conversation and
the arts of political life, like a mere tool and implement of war,
he was thrown aside in time of peace. Amongst all those whose
brightness eclipsed his glory, he was most incensed against Sulla,
who had owed his rise to the hatred which the nobility bore
Marius, and had made his disagreement with him the one principle
of his political life. . . .

667 a.u.c.   **86. Revenge of Marius**   b.c. 87

Velleius Paterculus, Book II, chapters 22, 23

22. Soon after, Caius Marius made his entry into the city,
an entry fatal to his countrymen. Nothing could have surpassed
his victorious irruption in cruelty had not that of Sulla speedily
followed. Nor was the licentious barbarity of the sword inflicted
only on the middling ranks ; but men of the highest stations, and
most eminent characters, were destroyed under various kinds of
sufferings ; among these the consul Octavius, a man of the mildest
disposition, was slain by order of Cinna. Merula, who, on the
approach of Cinna, had resigned the consulship, having opened
his veins and sprinkled his blood on the altars, implored the same
gods, whom, as priest of Jupiter, he had often entreated to preserve the Commonwealth, to pour curses on Cinna and his party,
and then resigned a life, which had greatly served the State.
Marcus Antonius, a man as eminent in civil dignity as in eloquence,
was, by order of Marius and Cinna, stabbed by the swords of the
soldiers whom he long caused to hesitate by the power of his
eloquence. Quintus Catulus, celebrated for his other merits, as
well as for the fame acquired in the Cimbrian war, which was
common to him and Marius, when search was made for him by
executioners, shut himself up in a place lately plastered with
mortar, had fire brought in to raise a strong smell, and then, by
inhaling the noxious vapor, and holding in his breath, he found a

death agreeable to the wishes, though not to the intentions, of his enemies.   Everything was falling headlong into ruin, but no person was yet found who dared to make a donation of the property of a Roman citizen, or to ask for it.   Afterwards this additional evil was introduced, that avarice supplied motives for cruelty ; magnitude of guilt was estimated by magnitude of wealth ; whoever was rich, was criminal, and became a reward, as it were, for his own destruction ; nor was anything considered dishonorable that was gainful.

23. Cinna now entered on his second consulship, and Marius on his seventh, to the utter disgrace of the former six.   In the early part of it he fell sick and died, leaving a character for having been implacable in war toward his enemies, and in peace toward his countrymen, and utterly impatient of quiet. . . .

87. Lucius Cornelius Sulla and His Times

a. Plutarch : *Life of Sulla* (Extracts)

Lucius Cornelius Sulla was descended of a patrician or noble family. . . .   The time in which he lived was no longer an age of pure and upright manners, but had already declined, and yielded to the appetite for riches and luxury ; yet still, in the general opinion, they who deserted the hereditary poverty of their family were as much blamed as those who had run out a fair patrimonial estate. . . .

His general personal appearance may be known by his statues : only his blue eyes, of themselves extremely keen and glaring, were rendered all the more forbidding and terrible by the complexion of his face, in which white was mixed with rough blotches of fiery red.   Hence, it is said, he was surnamed Sulla. . . .

Nor is it out of place to make use of marks of character like these, in the case of one who was by nature so addicted to raillery that in his youthful obscurer years he would converse freely

with players and professed jesters, and join them in all their low
pleasures. And when supreme master of all, he was often wont
to muster together the most impudent players and stage-followers
of the town, and to drink and bandy jests with them without
regard to his age or the dignity of his place, and to the prejudice
of important affairs that required his attention. When he was
once at table, it was not in Sulla's nature to admit of anything
that was serious; and whereas at other times he was a man
of business, and austere of countenance, he underwent all of
a sudden, at his first entrance upon wine and good-fellowship,
a total revolution, and was gentle and tractable with common
singers and dancers, and ready to oblige any one that spoke
with him. . . .

. . . Sulla not only accepted with pleasure the credit of such
divine felicities and favors, but joining himself in extolling and
glorifying what was done [in the Social War], gave the honor
of all to Fortune, whether it were out of boastfulness, or a real
feeling of divine agency. . . . And in the character which he
gives of himself [in his *Memoirs*], that he was born for fortune
rather than war, he seems to give Fortune a higher place than
merit, and, in short, makes himself entirely the creature of a
superior power. . . .

In general he would seem to have been of a very irregular
character, full of inconsistencies with himself; much given to
rapine, to prodigality yet more; in promoting or disgracing whom
he pleased, alike unaccountable; cringing to those he stood in
need of, and domineering over others who stood in need of him,
so that it was hard to tell, whether his nature had more in it of
pride or of servility. As to his unequal distribution of punishments, as, for example, that upon slight grounds he would put to
the torture, and again would bear patiently with the greatest
wrongs; would readily forgive and be reconciled after the most
heinous acts of enmity, and yet would visit small and inconsiderable offences with death, and confiscation of goods; one might

judge that in himself he was really of a violent and revengeful nature, which however he could qualify, upon reflection, for his interest. . . .

. . . The commanders of these times, attaining to superiority by force, not worth, and having need of arms one against another, rather than against the public enemy, were constrained to temporize in authority, and in order to pay for the gratifications with which they purchased the labor of their soldiers, were driven before they knew it to sell the Commonwealth itself, and, to gain the mastery over men better than themselves, were content to become slaves to the vilest of wretches. These practices drove Marius into exile, and again brought him in against Sulla. These made Cinna the assassin of Octavius, and Fimbria of Flaccus. To which courses Sulla contributed not the least; for to corrupt and win over those who were under the command of others, he would be munificent and profuse towards those who were under his own; and so, while tempting the soldiers of other generals to treachery, and his own to dissolute living, he was naturally in want of a large treasury. . . .

At the point of transportation [at Dyrrhachium, after the war with Mithradates], Sulla being in alarm, lest at their first setting foot upon Italy the soldiers should disband and disperse one by one among the cities, they of their own accord first took an oath to stand firm by him, and not of their good-will to injure Italy; then seeing him in distress for money, they made, so to say, a voluntary offering, and contributed each man according to his ability. However, Sulla would not accept of their offering. . . .

. . . Sulla gathered together in the circus, these as well as other survivors of the party [of Marius], to the number of six thousand, and just as he commenced speaking to the senate, . . . proceeded to cut them down, by men appointed for that service. . . . This gave the most stupid of the Romans to understand that they had merely exchanged, not escaped, tyranny. For Marius, being of a naturally harsh temper, had not altered, but merely continued what he had been, in authority; whereas Sulla, using his fortune moderately and unambitiously at first, and giving good hopes of a true patriot, firm to the interests both of the nobility and commonalty, being, moreover, of a gay and cheerful temper from his youth, and so easily moved to pity as to shed tears readily, had, perhaps deservedly, cast a blemish upon offices of great authority, as if they deranged men's former habits and character, and gave rise to violence, pride, and inhumanity. . . .

Sulla being thus wholly bent upon slaughter, filled the city with executions without number or limit, many wholly uninterested persons falling a sacrifice to private enmity, through his permission and indulgence to his friends. . . .

There were other things, besides this bloodshed, which gave offence. For Sulla had declared himself dictator, an office which had then been laid aside for the space of one hundred and twenty years. There was, likewise, an act of grace passed on his behalf, granting indemnity for what was passed, and for the future intrusting him with the power of life and death, confiscation, division of lands, erecting and demolishing of cities, taking away of kingdoms, and bestowing them at pleasure.

. . . It is said that the Roman ladies contributed such vast heaps of spices [at his funeral] that besides what was carried on two hundred and ten litters, there was sufficient to form a large figure of Sulla himself, and another, representing a lictor, out of the costly frankincense and cinnamon. . . .

b. Sallust: *Jugurthine War*, chapter 95

. . . Sulla was of patrician descent, but of a family almost sunk in obscurity by the degeneracy of his forefathers. He was skilled, equally and profoundly, in Greek and Roman literature. He was a man of large mind, fond of pleasure, but fonder of glory. His leisure was spent in luxurious gratifications, but pleasure never kept him from his duties. . . . He was eloquent and subtle, and lived on the easiest terms with his friends. His depth of thought in disguising his intentions was incredible ; he was liberal of most things, but especially of money. And though he was the most fortunate of all men before his victory in the civil war, yet his fortune was never beyond his desert ; and many have experienced a doubt whether his success or his merit were the greater. As to his subsequent acts, I know not whether more of shame or of regret must be felt at the recital of them.

673 A.U.C.   ## 88. Sulla's Constitutional Changes   B.C. 81

Appian : *Civil Wars*, Book I, paragraph 100

Nevertheless, as the form of the republic remained, he allowed them to appoint consuls. . . .   But Sulla, like a reigning sovereign, was dictator over the consuls.   Twenty-four axes were borne in front of him, as was customary with dictators, the same number that were borne before the ancient kings, and he had a large body-guard also.   He repealed laws and enacted others. He forbade anybody to hold the office of prætor until after he had held that of quæstor, or to be consul before he had been prætor, and he prohibited any man from holding the same office a second time till after the lapse of ten years.   He reduced the tribunitian power to such an extent that it seemed to be destroyed.   He curtailed it by a law which provided that one holding the office of tribune should never afterward hold any other office ; for which reason all men of reputation or family, who formerly contended for this office, shunned it hereafter.   I am not able to say positively whether Sulla transferred this office from the people to the senate, where it is now lodged, or not. To the senate itself, which had been much thinned by the seditions and wars, he added about three hundred members from the best of the knights, taking the vote of the tribes for each one. To the plebeians he added more than ten thousand slaves of proscribed persons, choosing the youngest and strongest, to whom he gave freedom and Roman citizenship, and he called them

Cornelii after himself. In this way he made sure of having ten thousand men among the plebeians always ready to obey his commands. In order to provide the same kind of safeguard throughout Italy, he distributed to the twenty-three legions that had served under him a great deal of land among the communities, as I have already related, some of which was public property and some taken from the communities by way of fine.

89. Pompey

a. Plutarch : *Life of Pompey* (Extracts)

. . . Never had any Roman the people's good-will and devotion more zealously throughout all the changes of fortune, more early in its first springing up, or more steadily rising with his prosperity, or more constant in his adversity than Pompey had. . . . In Pompey there were many [causes] that helped to make him the object of their love; his temperance, his skill and exercise in war, his eloquence of speech, integrity of mind, and affability in conversation and address ; insomuch that no man ever asked a favor with less offence, or conferred one with a better grace. When he gave, it was without assumption ; when he received, it was with dignity and honor.

In his youth, his countenance pleaded for him, seeming to anticipate his eloquence, and win upon the affections of the people before he spoke. His beauty even in his bloom of youth had something in it at once of gentleness and dignity ; and when his prime of manhood came, the majesty and kingliness of his character at once became visible in it. His hair sat somewhat hollow or rising a little ; and this, with the languishing motion of his eyes, seemed to form a resemblance in his face, though perhaps more talked of than really apparent, to the statues of King Alexander. . . .

About that time Cæsar, returning from military service, started a course of policy which brought him great present favor, and

much increased his power for the future, and proved extremely
destructive both to Pompey and the Commonwealth.   For now
he stood candidate for his first consulship, and well observing the
enmity betwixt Pompey and Crassus, and finding that by joining
with one he should make the other his enemy, he endeavored by
all means to reconcile them, an object in itself honorable and
tending to the public good, but as he undertook it, a mischievous
and subtle intrigue.   For he well knew that opposite parties or
factions in a commonwealth, like passengers in a boat, serve to
trim and balance the unsteady motions of power there ; whereas
if they combine and come all over to one side, they cause a shock
which will be sure to overset the vessel and carry down everything.   And therefore Cato wisely told those who charged all the
calamities of Rome upon the disagreement betwixt Pompey and
Cæsar, that they were in error in charging all the crime upon the
last cause ; for it was not their discord and enmity, but their
unanimity and friendship, that gave the first and greatest blow to
the Commonwealth. . . .

For the city now at once began to roll and swell, so to say,
with the stir of the coming storm.   Things everywhere were in
a state of agitation, and everybody's discourse tended to division,
now that death had put an end to that relation which hitherto had
been a disguise rather than a restraint to the ambition of these
men.   Besides, not long after [the death of Julia] came messengers from Parthia with intelligence of the death of Crassus there,
by which another safeguard against civil war was removed, since
both Cæsar and Pompey kept their eyes on Crassus, and awe of
him held them together more or less within the bounds of fair-
dealing all his lifetime. . . .

b. Velleius Paterculus, Book II, chapter 29

. . . He was distinguished for temperance, was eminent for
integrity, and had a moderate share of eloquence.   He was excessively covetous of power, when conferred on him from regard to

his merit, but had no desire to acquire it by irregular means. In war, he was the most skilful of generals ; in peace, the most modest of citizens, except when he was jealous of having an equal. He was constant in his friendships, placable when offended, most cordial in reconciliation, most ready to receive an apology. He never, or very rarely, stretched his power to excess, and was almost exempt from vice, unless it be counted among the greatest vices, that, in a free state, the mistress of the world, though, in right, he saw every citizen his equal, he could not endure to behold any one on a level with him in dignity. . . .

90. Cicero

a. Plutarch: *Life of Cicero* (Extracts)

. . . His readiness and address in sarcasm, and generally in witty sayings, was thought to suit a pleader very well, and to be highly attractive, but his using it to excess offended many, and gave him the repute of ill-nature.

He was appointed quæstor at a time when there was a great scarcity of corn, and had Sicily for his province, where, though at first he displeased many, by compelling them to send in their provisions to Rome, yet after they had had experience of his care, justice, and clemency, they honored him more than ever they did any of their governors before. It happened, also, that some young Romans of good and noble families, charged with neglect of discipline and misconduct in military service, were brought before the prætor in Sicily. Cicero undertook their defence, which he conducted admirably, and got them acquitted. So returning to Rome with a great opinion of himself for these things, a ludicrous incident befell him, as he himself tells us. Meeting an eminent citizen in Campania, whom he accounted his friend, he asked him what the Romans said and thought of his actions, as if the whole city had been filled with the glory of what he had done. His friend asked him in reply, " Where is it you have been, Cicero?" This for the time utterly mortified and cast him down, to perceive that the report of his actions had sunk into the city of Rome as into an immense ocean, without any visible effect or result in reputation. And afterwards considering with himself that the glory he contended for was an infinite thing, and that there was no fixed end nor measure in its pursuit, he abated much of his ambitious thoughts. Nevertheless, he was always excessively pleased with his own praise, and continued to the very last to be passionately fond of glory, which often interfered with the prosecution of his wisest resolutions. . . .

For Cicero, it may be said, was the one man, above all others, who made the Romans feel how great a charm eloquence lends to what is good, and how invincible justice is, if it be well spoken ; and that it is necessary for him who would dexterously govern a commonwealth, in action always to prefer that which is honest before that which is popular, and in speaking to free the right and useful measure from everything that may occasion offence. . . .

At this time [in his consulship] his authority was very great in the city; but he created himself much envy, and offended very many, not by any evil action, but because he was always lauding and magnifying himself. For neither senate, nor assembly of the people, nor court of judicature could meet, in which he was not heard to talk of Catiline and Lentulus. Indeed, he also filled his books and writings with his own praises, to such an excess as to render a style, in itself most pleasant and delightful, nauseous and irksome to his hearers ; this ungrateful humor, like a disease, always cleaving to him. Nevertheless, though he was intemperately fond of his own glory, he was very free from envying others, and was, on the contrary, most liberally profuse in commending both the ancients and his contemporaries, as any one may see in his writings.

. . . As soon as it was publicly known that he had fled, Clodius proposed to the people a decree of exile, and by his own order interdicted him fire and water, prohibiting any within five hundred miles in Italy to receive him into their houses. Most people, out of respect for Cicero, paid no regard to this edict, offering him every attention, and escorting him on his way. . . . Although many visited him with respect, and the cities of Greece contended which should honor him most, he yet continued disheartened and disconsolate, like an unfortunate lover, often casting his looks back upon Italy; and, indeed, he was become so poor-spirited, so humiliated and dejected by his misfortunes, as none could have expected in a man who had devoted so much of his life to study and learning. And yet he often desired his friends not to call him orator, but philosopher, because he had made philosophy his business, and had only used rhetoric as an instrument for attaining his objects in public life. . . .

. . . Cicero's immeasurable boasting of himself in his orations argues him guilty of an uncontrollable appetite for distinction, his cry being evermore that arms should give place to the toga, and the soldier's laurel to the tongue. . . .

b. Quintilian: *Institutes*, Book XII, chapters 16, 17

16. Nor do I see that the feeling of an upright citizen was, in any respect, wanting to Cicero. As proofs of his integrity may be mentioned his consulship, in which he conducted himself with so much honor; his honorable administration of his province; his refusal to be one of the twenty commissioners;[1] and, during the civil wars, which fell with great severity on his times, his uprightness of mind, which was never swayed, either by hope or by fear, from adhering to the better party, or the supporters of the Commonwealth.

17. He is thought by some to have been deficient in courage, but he has given an excellent reply to this charge, when he says, that he was timid, not in encountering dangers, but in taking precautions against them, an assertion of which he proved the truth at his death, to which he submitted with the noblest fortitude.

[1] For dividing the lands of Campania, see Vell. Pat. II, 45.

91. Cato the Younger

a. Plutarch: *Life of Cato* (Extracts)

It is said of Cato, that even from his infancy, in his speech, his countenance, and all his childish pastimes, he discovered an inflexible temper, unmoved by any passion, and firm in everything. He was resolute in his purposes, much beyond the strength of his age, to go through with whatever he undertook. He was rough and ungentle toward those that flattered him, and still more unyielding to those that threatened him. It was difficult to excite him to laughter; his countenance seldom relaxed even into a smile; he was not quickly or easily provoked to anger, but if once incensed, he was no less difficult to pacify.

. . . Having gained the intimate acquaintance of Antipater, the Tyrian, the Stoic philosopher, he devoted himself to the study, above everything, of moral and political doctrine. And though possessed, as it were, by a kind of inspiration for the pursuit of every virtue, yet what most of all virtue and excellence fixed his affection, was that steady and inflexible justice, which is not to be wrought upon by favor or compassion. . . .

. . . Though it was now the time that he should become quæstor, he would not stand for the place till he had studied the laws relating to it, and by inquiry from persons of experience had attained a distinct understanding of the duty and authority belonging to it. With this knowledge, as soon as he came into the office, he made a great reformation among the clerks and under-officers of the treasury, people who had long practice and familiarity in all the public records and the laws, and, when new magistrates came in year by year, so ignorant and unskilful as to be in absolute need of others to teach them what to do, did not submit and give way, but kept the power in their own hands, and were in effect the treasurers themselves. Till Cato, applying himself roundly to the work, showed that he possessed not only the title and honor of a quæstor, but the knowledge and understanding and full authority of his office. So that he used the clerks and under-officers like servants, as they were, exposing their corrupt practices and instructing their ignorance. . . .

Cato's assiduity, also, and indefatigable diligence won very much upon the people. He always came first of any of his colleagues to the treasury, and went away the last. He never missed any assembly of the people, or sitting of the senate; being always anxious and on watch for those who lightly, or as a matter of interest, passed votes in favor of this or that person, for remitting debts or granting away customs that were owing to the State. . . .

. . . It was not in the hope of gaining honors or riches, nor out of mere impulse, nor by chance, that he engaged in politics, but he undertook the service of the State, as the proper business of an honest man, and therefore he thought himself obliged to be as constant to his public duty as the bee to the honeycomb. To this end, he took care to have his friends and correspondents everywhere, to send him reports of the edicts, decrees, judgments, and all the important proceedings that passed in any of the provinces. . . .

. . . The people were at that time extremely corrupted by the gifts of those who sought offices, and most made a constant trade of selling their voices. Cato was eager utterly to root this corruption out of the Commonwealth; he therefore [as prætor] persuaded the senate to make an order, that those who were chosen into any office, though nobody should accuse them, should be obliged to come into the court, and give account upon oath of their proceedings in their election. . . .

b. Velleius Paterculus, Book II, chapter 35

. . . He was great-grandson of Marcus Cato, the founder of the Porcian family, and was a man who closely resembled virtue itself, and, in every particular of his conduct, seemed more like the gods than mankind; who never acted rightly, that he might appear to do so, but because he could not act otherwise; who never thought anything reasonable, that was not likewise just; and who, exempt from every vice, kept his own fortune always in his own power. . . .

92. Julius Cæsar

a. Plutarch: *Life of Cæsar* (Extracts)

. . . In his pleadings at Rome, his eloquence soon obtained him great credit and favor, and he won no less upon the affections of the people by the affability of his manners and address, in which he showed a tact and consideration beyond what could have been expected at his age; and the open house he kept, the entertainments he gave, and the general splendor of his manner of life contributed little by little to create and increase his political influence. His enemies slighted the growth of it at first, presuming it would soon fail when his money was gone; whilst in the meantime it was growing up and flourishing among the common people. . . . Cicero was the first who had any suspicions of his designs upon the government, and . . . saw the designing temper of the man through his disguise of good-humor and affability, and said that, in general, in all he did and undertook, he detected the ambition for absolute power, "but when I see his hair so carefully arranged, and observe him adjusting it with one finger, I cannot imagine it should enter into such a man's thoughts to subvert the Roman State."

. . . He was so profuse in his expenses, that before he had any public employment he was in debt thirteen hundred talents, and many thought that by incurring such expense to be popular, he changed a solid good for what would prove but a short and uncertain return; but in truth he was purchasing what was of the greatest value at an inconsiderable rate. When he was made surveyor of the Appian Way, he disbursed, besides the public money, a great sum out of his private purse; and when he was ædile, he provided such a number of gladiators, that he entertained the people with three hundred and twenty single combats, and by his great liberality and magnificence in theatrical shows, in processions, and public feastings, he threw into the shade all the attempts that had been made before him, and gained so much upon the people, that every one was eager to find out new offices and new honors for him in return for his munificence.

There being two factions in the city, one that of Sulla, which was very powerful, the other that of Marius, which was then broken and in a very low condition, he undertook to revive the latter and to make it his own. . . .

FIG. 12. — GLADIATORS.   (From wall painting at Pompeii)
Baumeister, fig. 2351

The love of honor and passion for distinction were inspired into them [the soldiers] and cherished in them by Cæsar himself, who, by his unsparing distribution of money and honors, showed them that he did not heap up wealth from the wars for his own luxury, or the gratifying of his private pleasures, but that all he received was but a public fund laid by for the reward and encouragement of valor, and that he looked upon all he gave to deserving soldiers as so much increase to his own riches.   Added to this, also, there was no danger to which he did not willingly expose himself, no labor from which he pleaded exemption.   His contempt of danger was not so much wondered at by his soldiers, because they knew how much he coveted honor.   But his enduring so much hard-

FIG. 13.—GLADIATORS. (From the tomb of Scaurus)

Baumeister, fig. 2353

ship, which he did to all appearance beyond his natural strength, very much astonished them. For he was a spare man, had a soft and white skin, was distempered in the head, and subject to an epilepsy. . . . But he did not make the weakness of his constitution a pretext for his ease, but rather used war as the best physic against his indispositions; whilst by indefatigable journeys, coarse diet, frequent lodgings in the field, and continual laborious exercise, he struggled with his diseases, and fortified his body against all attacks. . . .

Cæsar had long ago resolved upon the overthrow of Pompey, as had Pompey, for that matter, upon his. For Crassus, the fear of whom had hitherto kept them in peace, having now been killed in Parthia, if the one of them wished to make himself the greatest man in Rome, he had only to overthrow the other; and if he again wished to prevent his own fall, he had nothing for it but to be beforehand with him whom he feared. . . . Making the Gallic wars his exercise-ground, Cæsar had at once improved the strength of his soldiery, and had heightened his own glory by his great actions, so that he was looked on as one who might challenge comparison with Pompey. Nor did he let go any of those advantages which were now given him both by Pompey himself and the times, and the ill-government of Rome, where all who were candidates for office publicly gave money, and without any shame bribed the people, who having received their pay, did not contend for their benefactors with bare suffrages, but with bows, swords, and slings. So that after having many times stained the place of election with the blood of men killed upon the spot, they left the city at last without a government at all, to be carried about like a ship without a pilot to steer her; while all who had any wisdom could only be thankful if a course of such wild and stormy disorder and madness might end no worse than in a monarchy. Some were so bold as to declare openly, that the government was incurable but by a monarchy, and that they ought to take that remedy from the hands of the gentlest physician, meaning Pompey, who, though in words he pretended to decline it, yet in reality made his utmost efforts to be declared dictator. Cato, perceiving his design, prevailed with the senate to make him sole consul, that with the offer of a more legal sort of monarchy he might be withheld from demanding the dictatorship. . . .

. . . After his triumphs [for Egypt, Pontus, and Africa], Cæsar distributed rewards to his soldiers, and treated the people with feasting and shows. He entertained the whole people together at one feast, where twenty-two thousand dining couches were laid out ; and he made a display of gladiators, and of battles by sea. . . . When these shows were over, an account was taken of the people, who from three hundred and twenty thousand were now reduced to one hundred and fifty thousand. So great a waste had the civil war made in Rome alone, not to mention what the other parts of Italy and the provinces suffered.

. . . Nevertheless his countrymen, conceding all this [the victory at Munda] to his fortune, and accepting the bit, in the hope that the government of a single person would give them time to breathe after so many civil wars and calamities, made him dictator for life. This was indeed a tyranny avowed, since his power now was not only absolute, but perpetual too. Cicero made the first proposals to the senate for conferring honors upon him, which might in some sort be said not to exceed the limits of ordinary human moderation. But others, striving which should deserve most, carried them so excessively high, that they made Cæsar odious to the most indifferent and moderate sort of men, by the pretension and extravagance of the titles which they decreed him. His enemies, too, are thought to have had some share in this, as well as his flatterers. It gave them an advantage against him, and would be their justification for any attempt they should make upon him ; for since the civil wars were ended, he had nothing else that he could be charged with. And they had good reason to decree a temple to Clemency, in token of their thanks for the mild use he made of his victory. For he not only pardoned many of those who fought against him, but, further, to some gave honors and offices ; as particularly to Brutus and Cassius, who both of them were præ-tors. Pompey's images that were thrown down, he set up again, upon which Cicero also said that by raising Pompey's statues he had fixed his own. When his friends advised him to have a guard, and several offered their service, he would not hear of it, but said it was better to suffer death once, than always to live in fear of it. He looked upon the affections of the people to be the best and surest guard, and entertained them again with public feasting and general distributions of corn ; and to gratify his army, he sent out colonies to several places, of which the most remarkable were Carthage and Corinth ; which, as before they had been ruined at the same time, so now were restored and re-peopled together.

Cæsar was born to do great things, and had a passion after honor, and the many noble exploits he had done did not now serve as an inducement to him to sit still and reap the fruit of his past labors, but were incentives and encouragements to go on, and raised in him ideas of still greater actions, and a desire of new glory, as if the present were all spent. It was, in fact, a sort of emulous struggle with himself, as it had been with another, how he might outdo his past actions by his future. In pursuit of these thoughts, he resolved to make war upon the Parthians, and when he had subdued them, to pass through Hyrcania ; thence to march along by the Caspian Sea to Mount Caucasus, and so on about Pontus, till he came into Scythia ; then to overrun all the countries bordering upon Germany, and Germany itself ; and so to return through Gaul into Italy, after completing the whole circle of his intended empire, and bounding it on every side by the ocean. . . .

But that which brought upon him the most apparent and mortal hatred, was his desire of being king ; which gave the common peo-ple the first occasion to quarrel with him, and proved the most specious pretence to those who had been his secret enemies all along. Those who would have procured him that title gave it out that it was foretold in the Sibyl's books that the Romans should conquer the Parthians when they fought against them under the conduct of a king, but not before. And one day, as Cæsar was coming down from Alba to Rome, some were so bold as to salute him by the name of king ; but he, finding the people disrelish it, seemed to resent it himself, and said his name was Cæsar, not king. . . .

He gave a fresh occasion of resentment by his affront to the tribunes. The *Lupercalia* were then celebrated. . . . Cæsar, dressed in a triumphal robe, seated himself in a golden chair at the rostra, to view this ceremony. Antony, as consul, was one of those who ran this course, and when he came into the forum, and the people made way for him, he went up and reached to Cæsar a diadem wreathed with laurel. Upon this there was a shout, but only a slight one, made by the few who were planted there for that purpose ; but when Cæsar refused it, there was universal applause. Upon the second offer, very few, and upon the second refusal, all again applauded. Cæsar, finding it would not take, rose up, and ordered the crown to be carried into the capitol. Cæsar's statues were afterwards found with royal diadems on their heads. Flavius and Marullus, two tribunes of the people, went presently and pulled them off, and having apprehended those who first saluted Cæsar as king, committed them to prison. The people followed them with acclamations, and called them by the name of Brutus, because Brutus was the first who ended the succession of kings, and transferred the power which before was lodged in one man into the hands of the senate and people. Cæsar so far resented this that he displaced Marullus and Flavius. . . .

b. Cicero: *Philippics*, II, chapter 45

. . . In that man were combined genius, method, memory, literature, prudence, deliberation, and industry. He had performed exploits in war which, though calamitous for the republic, were nevertheless mighty deeds. Having for many years aimed at being a king, he had with great labor, and much personal danger, accomplished what he intended. He had conciliated the ignorant multitude by presents, by monuments, by largesses of food, and by banquets ; he had bound his own party to him by rewards, his adversaries by the appearances of clemency. Why need I say much on such a subject? He had already brought a free city, partly by fear, partly by patience, into a habit of slavery.

705 A.U.C.   **93. Cicero on the Civil War**   B.C. 49

Cicero: *To Atticus*, VIII, 11(No. 341)

. . . Such a conception never occurred to our friend Gnæus [Pompey] in former times, and least of all in this controversy. Supremacy has been the object of both [Pompey and Cæsar] ; there has been no idea of securing the happiness and virtue of the citizens. Nor, indeed, did he abandon the city because he ' was unable to protect it, nor Italy because he was driven from it ; but his idea from the first was to stir up every land and sea, to rouse foreign princes, to bring barbarous tribes in arms into Italy, to collect the most formidable armies possible. For some time past a kind of royalty like Sulla's has been the object in view, and this is the eager desire of many who are with him. Do you suppose that some understanding between the two, some bargain has been impossible? To-day it is still possible. But the object of neither is our happiness : both want to be kings. . . .

94. M. Cato and C. Cæsar

Sallust: *Catiline*, 53 and 54

53. . . . Within my recollection, however, there arose two men of remarkable powers, though of very different character, Marcus Cato and Caius Cæsar, whom . . . it is not my intention to pass in silence, but to describe, to the best of my ability, the disposition and manners of each.

54. Their birth, age, and eloquence were nearly on an equality ; their greatness of mind similar, as was also their reputation,

though attained by different means. Cæsar grew eminent by generosity and munificence ; Cato by the integrity of his life. Cæsar was esteemed for his humanity and benevolence ; austereness had given dignity to Cato. Cæsar acquired renown by giving, relieving, and pardoning ; Cato by bestowing nothing. In Cæsar there was a refuge for the unfortunate ; in Cato, destruction for the bad. In Cæsar, his easiness of temper was admired ; in Cato, his firmness. Cæsar, in fine, had applied himself to a life of energy and activity ; intent upon the interests of his friends, he was neglectful of his own ; he refused nothing to others that was worthy of acceptance, while for himself he desired great power, the command of an army, and a new war in which his talents might be displayed. But Cato's ambition was that of temperance, discretion, and, above all, of austerity ; he did not contend in splendor with the rich, nor in faction with the seditious, but with the brave in fortitude, with the modest in simplicity, with the temperate in abstinence ; he was more desirous to be, than to appear, virtuous ; and thus, the less he courted popularity, the more it pursued him.

95. Apotheosis of Cæsar

Suetonius : *Life of Julius Cæsar*, chapter 88

He died in the fifty-sixth year of his age, and was ranked amongst the gods, not only by a formal decree, but in the belief of the vulgar. For during the first games which Augustus, his heir, consecrated to his memory, a comet blazed for seven days together, rising always about eleven o'clock ; and it was supposed to be the soul of Cæsar, now received into heaven ; for which reason, likewise, he is represented on his statue with a star on his brow. . . .

96. M. Antony

Plutarch : *Life of Antony* (Extracts)

He had a very good and noble appearance ; his beard was well grown, his forehead large, and his nose aquiline, giving him altogether a bold, masculine look, that reminded people of the faces of Hercules in paintings and sculptures. . . . What might seem to some very insupportable, his vaunting, his raillery, his drinking in public, sitting down by the men as they were taking their food, and eating, as he stood, off the common soldiers' tables, made him the delight and pleasure of the army. . . . And his generous ways, his open and lavish hand in gifts and favors, to his friends and fellow-soldiers, did a great deal for him in his first advance to power, and, after he had become great, long maintained his fortunes, when a thousand follies were hastening their over-throw. . . .

Antony was not long in getting the hearts of the soldiers, join-ing with them in their exercises, and for the most part living amongst them, and making them presents to the utmost of his abilities; but with all others he was unpopular enough. He was too lazy to pay attention to the complaints of persons who were injured; he listened impatiently to petitions; . . .

. . . For there was much simplicity in his character; he was slow to see his faults, but, when he did see them, was extremely repentant, and ready to ask pardon of those he had injured; prodi-gal in his acts of reparation, and severe in his punishments, but his generosity was much more extravagant than his severity; his raillery was sharp and insulting, but the edge of it was taken off by his readiness to submit to any kind of repartee; for he was as well contented to be rallied as he was pleased to rally others. And this freedom of speech was, indeed, the cause of many of his disasters. He never imagined that those who used so much liberty in their mirth would flatter or deceive him in business of consequence. . . .

Such being his temper, the last and crowning mischief that could befall him came in the love of Cleopatra, to awaken and kindle to fury passions that as yet lay dormant in his nature, and to stifle and finally corrupt any elements of goodness and a sound judgment that yet made resistance in him. . . .

97. Degeneracy of Roman Society (at the Death of J. Cæsar)

Appian: *Civil Wars*, Book II, paragraph 120

. . . They [the conspirators] hastened up to the Capitol with their gladiators. There they took counsel and decided to bribe the populace, hoping that if some would begin to praise the deed [the murder of Cæsar], others would join in from love of liberty and longing for the republic. They thought that the Roman people were still exactly the same as they had heard that they were at the time when the elder Brutus expelled the kings. They did not perceive that they were counting on two incompatible things, namely, that people could be lovers of liberty and bribe-takers at the same time. The latter class were much easier to find of the two, because the government had been corrupt for a long time. The plebeians were now mixed with foreign blood, freedmen had equal rights of citizenship with them, and slaves were dressed in the same fashion as their masters. Except in the case of the senatorial rank, the same costume was common to slaves and free citizens. Moreover, the distribution of corn to the poor, which took place in Rome only, drew thither the lazy, the beggars, the vagrants of all Italy. The multitude of discharged soldiers no longer returned one by one to their native places as formerly, . . . but were sent in groups to unjust allotments of lands and houses belonging to others. These were now encamped in temples and sacred enclosures under one standard, and one person appointed to lead them to their colony; and as they had already sold their own belongings preparatory to their departure, they were in readiness to be bought for any purpose.

Sources

I. MARIUS AND SULLA. — Appian: *Foreign Wars*, XII, par. 10–66; Appian: *Civil Wars*, I, par. 27–106; Eutropius, IV, 26–V, 9; Florus, III, 16–21; Justin, XXXVIII, 4 ff.; Livy, *Epitome*, LVIII–XC; Plutarch: *Marius, Sulla, Lucullus, Sertorius;* Sallust: *Jugurthine War;* Tacitus: *Annals*, XI, 22; XII, 60.

II. POMPEY — CÆSAR — CICERO — ANTONY. — Appian: *Foreign Wars*, XII, par. 67–121; Appian: *Civil Wars*, I, par. 107–121; II, III; Cæsar: *Commentaries on the Gallic and Civil Wars;* (Hirtius?) *Commentaries on the Alexandrine, African, and Spanish Wars;* Cicero: *Correspondence;* Cicero: *Orations*, especially *For the Manilian Law, Against Verres, Against Catiline, For Sestius, Against Vatinius, For Milo, On the Consular Provinces,* and the *Philippics;* Dio Cassius (German translation), XXXVI–LI; Eutropius, VI (entire); Florus, III, 22, 23; IV, 1, 2; Livy: *Epitome,* XC–CXXXIV; Lucan: *Pharsalia;* Plutarch: *Sertorius, Lucullus, Crassus, Pompey, Cæsar, Cicero, Cato (the Younger), Antony, Brutus;* Sallust: *Catiline;* Sallust: *Histories* (fragments); Suetonius: *J. Cæsar, Augustus;* Velleius Paterculus, II, 29–89.

IX. THE EARLY EMPIRE

Abbott, ch. 12, 13, 14; Allcroft: *The Making of the Monarchy*, ch. 12, 13; Allcroft and Haydon: *Early Principate (Tutorial)*; Allen, ch. 18–20; Beesly: *Catiline, Clodius, and Tiberius;* Botsford, ch. 9, 10; Bury: *The Student's Roman Empire (27 B.C. to 180 A.D.)*; Capes: *Early Empire (Epochs)*; Duruy, Vol. III, ch. 64–Vol. IV, ch. 78; Firth, J. B.: *Augustus Cæsar;* Freeman: *Historical Essays, II: The Flavian Emperors;* Gardthausen: *Augustus u. seine Zeit*, 2 vols.; Gibbon, Vol. I, ch. 1; Leighton, ch. 31–36; Mahaffy: *Greek World under Roman Sway*, ch. 1–12; Mau: *Pompeii, its Life and Art;* Merivale: *History of the Romans*, Vols. IV–VI; Morey, ch. 23, 24, 25; Myers, ch. 15, 16 (to p. 354); Pelham, Bk. V, ch. 1–4; Robinson, ch. 29, 30; Seignobos, ch. 20, 21; Taylor, ch. 17–19; West, Pt. IV, ch. 2; Wolfson, ch. 32, 33.

98. Policy of Augustus

Tacitus: *Annals*, Book I, chapter 2

When after the destruction of Brutus and Cassius there was no longer any army of the Commonwealth, when Pompeius was crushed in Sicily, and when, with Lepidus pushed aside and Antonius slain, even the Julian faction had only Cæsar left to lead it, then, dropping the title of triumvir, and giving out that he was a consul, and was satisfied with a tribune's authority for the protection of the people, Augustus won over the soldiers with gifts, the populace with cheap corn, and all men with the sweets of repose, and so grew greater by degrees, while he concentrated in himself the functions of the senate, the magistrates, and the laws.   He was wholly unopposed, for the boldest spirits had fallen

143

in battle, or in the proscription, while the remaining nobles, the readier they were to be slaves, were raised the higher by wealth and promotion, so that, aggrandized by revolution, they preferred the safety of the present to the dangerous past. Nor did the provinces dislike that condition of affairs, for they distrusted the government of the senate and the people because of the rivalries between the leading men and the rapacity of the officials, while the protection of the laws was unavailing, as they were continually deranged by violence, intrigue, and finally by corruption.

99. Official Version of the Principate

Monumentum Ancyranum, chapters 1, 6, 7, 34

1. In my twentieth year, acting upon my own judgment and at my own expense, I raised an army by means of which I restored to liberty the Commonwealth which had been oppressed by the tyranny of a faction. On this account the senate by laudatory decrees admitted me to its order, in the consulship of Gaius Pansa and Aulus Hirtius, and at the same time gave me consular rank in the expression of opinion, and gave me the *imperium*. It also voted that I as proprætor, together with the consuls, should see to it that the Commonwealth suffered no harm. In the same year, moreover, when both consuls had perished in war, the people made me consul and triumvir for organizing the Commonwealth.

6. During the consulship of . . ., by the consent of the senate and the Roman people, I was voted the sole charge of the laws and of morals, with the fullest power; but I accepted the proffer of no office which was contrary to the customs of the country. The measures of which the senate at that time wished me to take charge, I accomplished in virtue of my possession of the tribunitian power. In this office I five times associated with myself a colleague, with the consent of the senate.

7. For ten years in succession I was one of the triumvirs for organizing the Commonwealth. . . .

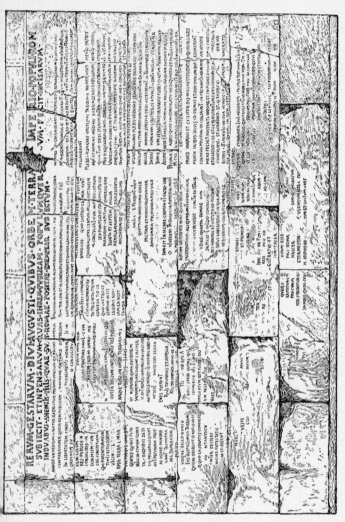

FIG. 14.—MONUMENTUM ANCYRANUM

Duruy, Vol. IV, p. 165

34. In my sixth and seventh consulships, when I had put an end to the civil wars, after having obtained complete control of affairs by universal consent, I transferred the Commonwealth from my own dominion to the authority of the senate and Roman people. In return for this favor on my part, I received by decree of the senate the title Augustus, . . . After that time I excelled all others in dignity, but of power I held no more than those also held who were my colleagues in any magistracy.

100. The Principate

Cassius Dio, Book LIII, chapters 17–18

The word " monarchy " was so odious to the Romans that they never called their Emperors dictators or kings or anything of that sort. Yet, as the ultimate power in the State lies with them, they do in effect reign. The various constitutional offices (except the censorship) do indeed subsist to this day ; but the Emperor for the time being manages and directs everything exactly as he chooses. That they may seem, however, to possess these powers in accordance with law and not by force, the Emperors assume the several offices, which, when there was a free democracy, carried with them the highest powers, with the one exception of the dictatorship. Thus for instance they frequently take the consulship ; on quitting the *pomœrium* they are always styled proconsuls ; instead of king or dictator they take the name of *Imperator*, and not merely those who have won victories, but all alike, as a symbol of irresponsible power. Dictators or kings indeed they do not style themselves, since those offices have been once for all abolished, but all their actual powers they have secured by this appellation of *Imperator*.

The powers bestowed by these various offices are these. As *Imperatores* they can levy troops, collect money, declare war, make peace, exercise at all times and in all places alike such complete authority over the army, whether of citizens or auxiliaries, that even

within the *pomœrium* they can put to death both knights and senators; and, in short, can do all that the consuls and other magistrates possessed of full *imperium* would be able to do.

Again, as censors they examine into our lives and morals, hold
the census, and enter or strike off names from the rolls of the
knights and senate, entirely at their own pleasure.

Once more, being invested with all priesthoods, especially that
of the *Pontifex Maximus*, and in the majority of cases being able
to confer them on others, they have complete control over everything connected with religion.

Lastly, the tribunitian power, exercised in old times by the men
of the greatest influence, gives them the means of absolutely putting a stop to any proceedings of which they do not approve, and
renders their persons inviolable, so that the least violence offered
to them, however trivial, whether by word or deed, makes the guilty
party liable to death without trial, as being under a curse. The
actual office of tribune they consider themselves debarred by the
sacred laws from taking, because they are always patricians, but
its powers they assume to the highest degree to which they ever
extended. And accordingly it is by it that they reckon the years
of their reign, as though they were colleagues of the annually elected
tribunes.

These titles they have taken from the usages of the democracy
in order that they may pose as having assumed nothing that was
not bestowed by the people. Yet they had been already rendered
unnecessary by one sweeping concession putting them above the
laws. In virtue of this, which was never given outright to any
Roman in old times, they might have done all they have ever done,
or anything else. The result is that they have invested themselves
with the complete powers of the State, with everything in short that
kings ever had, except the offensive name.

The appellations of Cæsar and Augustus add nothing to their
powers. The former is merely a symbol of a pretended descent,
the latter of an exalted position. The title *pater patriæ*, however,

does perhaps give them a certain authority over us all, such as formerly fathers had over their children. Not that this was the original idea of it. It was at first a mere title of honor, which yet conveyed the suggestion that, while they loved their subjects, their subjects were bound to reverence them.

101. Attempts to Restrain Luxury   A.D. 16

Tacitus: *Annals*, Book II, chapter 33

On the next day of the senate's meeting much was said against the luxury of the country by Quintus Haterius, an ex-consul, and by Octavius Fronto, an ex-prætor. It was decided that vessels of solid gold should not be made for the serving of food, and that men should not disgrace themselves with silken clothing from the East. Fronto went further, and insisted on restrictions being put on plate, furniture, and household establishments.

102. Expulsion of Egyptian and Jewish Worship   A.D. 19

Tacitus: *Annals*, Book II, chapter 85

There was a debate too about expelling the Egyptian and Jewish worship, and a resolution of the senate was passed that four thousand of the freedmen class who were infected with those superstitions and were of military age should be transported to the island of Sardinia, to quell the brigandage of the place, a cheap sacrifice should they die from the pestilential climate. The rest were to quit Italy, unless before a certain day they repudiated their impious rites.

103. Improper Use of the Emperor's Statues   A.D. 21

Tacitus: *Annals*, Book III, chapter 36

Next was exposed an abuse, hitherto the subject of many a whispered complaint. The vilest wretches used a growing freedom in exciting insult and obloquy against respectable citizens, and escaped punishment by clasping some statue of the Emperor.

The very freedman or slave was often an actual terror to his patron or master whom he would menace by word and gesture.

104. Character of Tiberius.

Tacitus: *Annals*, Book VI, chapter 51

It was a bright time in his life and reputation, while under Augustus he was a private citizen or held high offices; a time of reserve and crafty assumption of virtue, as long as Germanicus and Drusus were alive. Again, while his mother lived, he was a compound of good and evil; he was infamous for his cruelty, though he veiled his debaucheries, while he loved or feared Sejanus. Finally, he plunged into every wickedness and disgrace, when fear and shame being cast off he simply indulged his own inclinations.

105. Gross Sycophancy of the Time

Tacitus: *Annals*, Book III, chapter 65

So corrupted indeed and debased was that age by sycophancy that not only the foremost citizens who were forced to save their grandeur by servility, but every ex-consul, most of the ex-prætors, and a host of inferior senators would rise in eager rivalry to propose shameful and preposterous motions. Tradition says that Tiberius as often as he left the Senate-house used to exclaim in Greek, "How ready these men are to be slaves." Clearly, even he, with his dislike of public freedom, was disgusted at the abject abasement of his creatures.

106. Elections Transferred to Senate   A.D. 14

Tacitus: *Annals*, Book I, chapter 15

It was then for the first time that the elections were transferred from the Campus Martius to the senate. For up to that day, though the most important rested with the Emperor's choice, some were settled by the partialities of the tribes. Nor did the people complain of having the right taken from them, except in mere idle

talk ; and the senate, being now released from the necessity of
bribery and of degrading solicitations, gladly upheld the change,
Tiberius confining himself to the recommendation of only four
candidates who were to be nominated without rejection or
canvass.

107. Revival of the Law of Treason   A.D. 15
Tacitus: *Annals*, Book I, chapter 72

The title of " father of his country," which the people had so
often thrust on him, Tiberius refused, nor would he allow obedience to be sworn to his enactments, though the senate voted it ;
for he said repeatedly that all human things were uncertain, and
that the more he had obtained, the more precarious was his position. But he did not thereby create a belief in his patriotism, for
he had revived the law of treason, the name of which indeed was
known in ancient times, though other matters came under its jurisdiction, such as the betrayal of an army, or seditious stirring up
of the people, or, in short, any corrupt act by which a man had
impaired " the majesty of the people of Rome." Deeds only
were liable to accusation ; words went unpunished. It was
Augustus who first, under color of this law, applied legal inquiry
to libellous writings, provoked, as he had been, by the licentious
freedom with which Cassius Severus had defamed men and women
of distinction in his insulting satires. Soon afterwards, Tiberius,
when consulted by Pompeius Macer, the prætor, as to whether
prosecutions for treason should be revived, replied that the laws
must be enforced. He, too, had been exasperated by the publication of verses of uncertain authorship, which pointed at his cruelty,
his arrogance, and his dissensions with his mother.

108. The Tribunitian Power   A.D. 22
Tacitus: *Annals*, Book III, chapter 56

Tiberius, having gained credit for forbearance by the check
he had given to the growing terror of the informers, wrote a letter

to the senate, requesting the tribunitian power for Drusus. This was a phrase which Augustus devised as a designation of supremacy, so that without assuming the name of king or dictator he might have some title to mark his elevation above all other authority. He then chose Marcus Agrippa to be his associate in this power, and on Agrippa's death, Tiberius Nero, that there might be no uncertainty as to the succession. In this manner he thought to check the perverse ambition of others, while he had confidence in Nero's moderation and in his own greatness.

109. Treatment of Drusus by Tiberius

Tacitus: *Annals*, Book VI, chapter 24

And, what seemed most horrible of all, he [Tiberius] ordered a daily journal of all that he [Drusus] said and did to be read in public. That there had been spies by his side for so many years, to note his looks, his sighs, and even his whispered thoughts, and that his grandfather could have heard, read, and published all, was scarce credible. But letters of Attius, a centurion, and Didymus, a freedman, openly exhibited the names of slave after slave who had respectively struck or scared Drusus as he was quitting his chamber. The centurion had actually added, as something highly meritorious, his own language in all its brutality, and some utterances of the dying man in which, at first feigning loss of reason, he imprecated in seeming madness fearful things on Tiberius, and then, when hope of life was gone, denounced him with a studied and elaborate curse. "As he had slain a daughter-in-law, a brother's son, and son's sons, and filled his whole house with bloodshed, so might he pay the full penalty due to the name and race of his ancestors as well as to future generations."

110. The Profession of "Informer" (under Tiberius)

Tacitus: *Annals*, Book I, chapter 74

Crispinus then entered on a line of life afterwards rendered notorious by the miseries of the age and men's shamelessness.

Needy, obscure, and restless, he wormed himself by stealthy informations into the confidence of a vindictive prince, and soon imperilled all the most distinguished citizens; and having thus gained influence with one, hatred from all besides, he left an example in following which beggars became wealthy, the insignificant, formidable, and brought ruin first on others, finally on themselves.

And this was the most dreadful feature of the age, that leading members of the senate, some openly, some secretly, employed themselves in the very lowest work of the informer. One could not distinguish between aliens and kinsfolk, between friends and strangers, or say what was quite recent, or what half-forgotten from lapse of time. People were incriminated for some casual remark in the forum or at the dinner-table, for every one was impatient to be the first to mark his victim, some to screen themselves, most from being, as it were, infected with the contagion of the malady.

111. Reign of Terror (under Tiberius)

Tacitus: *Annals*, Book VI, chapter 19

Executions were now a stimulus to his fury, and he [Tiberius] ordered the death of all who were lying in prison under accusation of complicity with Sejanus. There lay, singly or in heaps, the unnumbered dead, of every age and sex, the illustrious with the obscure. Kinsfolk and friends were not allowed to be near them, to weep over them, or even to gaze on them too long. Spies were set round them, who noted the sorrow of each mourner and followed the rotting corpses, till they were dragged to the Tiber, where, floating or driven on the bank, no one dared to burn or to touch them. The force of terror had utterly extinguished the sense of human fellowship, and, with the growth of cruelty, pity was thrust aside.

112. Character of Gaius

A.D. 37–41

Tacitus: *Annals*, Book VI, chapter 20

He was a man who masked a savage temper under an artful guise of self-restraint, and neither his mother's doom nor the banishment of his brothers extorted from him a single utterance. Whatever the humor of the day with Tiberius, he would assume the like, and his language differed as little. Hence the fame of a clever remark from the orator Passienus, that "there never was a better slave nor a worse master."

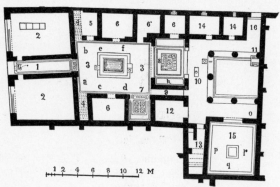

FIG. 15.—PLAN OF THE HOUSE OF THE TRAGIC POET

Mau's *Pompeii*, fig. 152

1. Fauces
2, 2. Shops
3. Atrium
4, 4. Stairways to upper floor
5. Porter's room
6, 6. Sleeping rooms
6'. Storeroom
7. Ala
8. Tablinum
9. Andron
10. Peristyle
11. House shrines
12, 14. Sleeping rooms
13. Kitchen
15. Dining room
16. Posticum

113. Charges against Seneca

A.D. 62

Tacitus: *Annals*, Book XIV, chapter 52

The death of Burrus was a blow to Seneca's power, for virtue had not the same strength when one of its champions, so to say, was removed, and Nero too began to lean on worse advisers. They assailed Seneca with various charges, representing that he continued to increase a wealth which was already so vast as to be beyond the scale of a subject, and was drawing to himself the attachment of the citizens, while in the picturesqueness of his gardens and the magnificence of his country-houses he almost surpassed the Emperor. They further alleged against him that he claimed for himself alone the honors of eloquence, and composed poetry more assiduously, as soon as a passion for it had seized on Nero. " Openly inimical to the prince's amusements, he disparaged his ability in driving horses, and ridiculed his voice whenever he sang. When was there to be an end of nothing being publicly admired but what Seneca was thought to have originated? Surely Nero's boyhood was over, and he was all but in the prime of youthful manhood. He ought to shake off a tutor, furnished as he was with sufficiently noble instructors in his own ancestors."

114. Petronius

Tacitus: *Annals*, Book XVI, chapters 18 and 19

18. With regard to Caius Petronius, I ought to dwell a little on his antecedents. His days he passed in sleep, his nights in the business and pleasure of life. Indolence had raised him to fame, as energy raises others, and he was reckoned not a debauchee and spendthrift, like most of those who squander their substance, but a man of refined luxury. And indeed his talk and his doings, the freer they were and the more show of carelessness they exhibited, were the better liked, for their look of a natural simplicity. Yet as proconsul of Bithynia and soon afterwards as consul, he showed himself a man of vigor and equal to business. Then falling back into vice or affecting vice, he was chosen by Nero to be one of his few intimate associates, as a critic in matters of taste, while the Emperor thought nothing charming or elegant in luxury unless Petronius had expressed to him his approval of it. Hence jealousy on the part of Tigellinus, who looked on him as a rival

and even his superior in the science of pleasure. And so he worked on the prince's cruelty, which dominated every other passion, charging Petronius with having been the friend of Scævinus, bribing a slave to become informer, robbing him of the means of defence, and hurrying into prison the greater part of his domestics.

19. It happened at the time that the Emperor was on his way to Campania, and that Petronius, after going as far as Cumæ, was there detained. He bore no longer the suspense of fear or of hope. Yet he did not fling away life with precipitate haste, but having made an incision in his veins and then, according to his humor, bound them up, he again opened them, while he conversed with his friends, not in a serious strain or on topics that might win for him the glory of courage. And he listened to them as they repeated, not thoughts on the immortality of the soul or on the theories of philosophers, but light poetry and playful verses. To some of his slaves he gave liberal presents, a flogging to others. He dined, indulged himself in sleep, that death, though forced on him, might have a natural appearance. Even in his will he did not, as did many in their last moments, flatter Nero or Tigellinus or any other of the men in power. On the contrary, he described fully the prince's shameful excesses, with the names of his male and female companions and their novelties in debauchery, and sent the account under seal to Nero. Then he broke his signet ring, that it might not be subsequently available for imperilling others.

115. Feelings at the Death of Nero   A.D. 68

Tacitus: *History*, Book I, chapter 4

. . . Welcome as the death of Nero had been in the first burst of joy, yet it had not only roused various emotions in Rome, among the senators, the people, or the soldiery of the capital, it had also excited all the legions and their generals ; for now had been divulged that secret of the empire, that Emperors could be made elsewhere than at Rome. The senators enjoyed the first exercise of freedom with the less restraint, because the Emperor was new to power, and absent from the capital. The leading men of the equestrian order sympathized most closely with the joy of the senators. The respectable portion of the people, which was connected with the great families, as well as the dependants and freedmen of condemned and banished persons, were high in hope. The degraded populace, frequenters of the arena and the theatre, the most worthless of the slaves, and those who having wasted their property were supported by the infamous excesses of Nero, caught eagerly in their dejection at every rumor.

116. Character of Previous Histories

Tacitus: *Annals*, Book I, chapter 1

. . . Fine intellects were not wanting to describe the times of Augustus, till growing sycophancy scared them away. The histories of Tiberius, Caius, Claudius, and Nero, while they were in power, were falsified through terror, and after their death were written under the irritation of a recent hatred.

117. Character of the Times

Tacitus: *History*, Book I, chapters 2 and 3

2. I am entering on the history of a period rich in disasters, frightful in its wars, torn by civil strife, and even in peace full of horrors. Four Emperors perished by the sword. There were three civil wars; there were more with foreign enemies; there were often wars that had both characters at once. There was success in the East, and disaster in the West. There were disturbances in Illyricum; Gaul wavered in its allegiance; Britain was thoroughly subdued and immediately abandoned; the tribes of the Suevi and the Sarmatæ rose in concert against us; the Dacians

had the glory of inflicting as well as suffering defeat; the armies of Parthia were all but set in motion by the cheat of a counterfeit Nero. Now, too, Italy was prostrated by disasters either entirely novel, or that recurred only after a long succession of ages; cities in Campania's richest plains were swallowed up and overwhelmed; Rome was wasted by conflagrations, its oldest temples consumed, and the Capitol itself fired by the hands of citizens. Sacred rites were profaned; there was profligacy in the highest ranks; the sea was crowded with exiles, and its rocks polluted with bloody deeds. In the capital there were yet worse horrors. Nobility, wealth, the refusal or the acceptance of office, were grounds for accusation, and virtue insured destruction. The rewards of the informers were no less odious than their crimes; for while some seized on consulships and priestly offices, as their share of the spoil, others on procuratorships, and posts of more confidential authority, they robbed and ruined in every direction amid universal hatred and terror. Slaves were bribed to turn against their masters, and freedmen to betray their patrons; and those who had not an enemy were destroyed by friends.

3. Yet the age was not so barren in noble qualities, as not also to exhibit examples of virtue. Mothers accompanied the flight of their sons; wives followed their husbands into exile; there were brave kinsmen and faithful sons-in-law; there were slaves whose fidelity defied even torture; there were illustrious men driven to the last necessity, and enduring it with fortitude; there were closing scenes that equalled the famous deaths of antiquity. Besides the manifold vicissitudes of human affairs, there were prodigies in heaven and earth, the warning voices of the thunder, and other intimations of the future, auspicious or gloomy, doubtful or not to be mistaken. Never surely did more terrible calamities of the Roman people, nor evidence more conclusive, prove that the gods take no thought for our happiness, but only for our punishment.

118. Peace in Rome for One Hundred Years

Tacitus: *History*, Book I, chapter 89

Indeed from the time that the Divine Augustus consolidated the power of the Cæsars, the wars of the Roman people had been in remote places, and had caused anxiety or brought honor to but one man. Under Tiberius and Caius, men dreaded for the Commonwealth only the miseries of peace. The rising of Scribonianus against Claudius was crushed as soon as heard of. Nero was driven from power by evil tidings and rumors rather than by the sword.

119. Part of Galba's Advice to Piso   A.D. 69

Tacitus: *History*, Book I, chapter 16

"The most practical and the shortest method of distinguishing between good and bad measures is to think what you yourself would or would not like under another Emperor. It is not here, as it is among nations despotically ruled, that there is a distinct governing family, while all the rest are slaves. You have to reign over men who cannot bear either absolute slavery or absolute freedom."

120. Sufferings of Italy   A.D. 69

Tacitus: *History*, Book II, chapter 56

Italy, however, was prostrated under sufferings heavier and more terrible than the evils of war. The soldiers of Vitellius, dispersed through the municipal towns and colonies, were robbing and plundering and polluting every place with violence and lust. Everything, lawful or unlawful, they were ready to seize or to sell, sparing nothing, sacred or profane. Some persons under the soldiers' guard murdered their private enemies. The soldiers themselves, who knew the country well, marked out rich estates and wealthy owners for plunder, or for death in case of resistance; their commanders were in their power and dared not check them.

121. Violence in Rome A.D. 69

Tacitus: *History*, Book IV, chapter 1

When Vitellius was dead, the war had indeed come to an end, but peace had yet to begin. Sword in hand, throughout the capital, the conquerors hunted down the conquered with merciless hatred. The streets were choked with carnage, the squares and temples reeked with blood, for men were massacred everywhere as chance threw them in the way. Soon, as their license increased, they began to search for and drag forth hidden foes. Whenever they saw a man tall and young they cut him down, making no distinction between soldiers and civilians. But the ferocity, which in the first impulse of hatred could be gratified only by blood, soon passed into the greed of gain. They let nothing be kept secret, nothing be closed; Vitellianists, they pretended, might be thus concealed. Here was the first step to breaking open private houses; here, if resistance were made, a pretext for slaughter. The most needy of the populace and the most worthless of the slaves did not fail to come forward and betray their wealthy masters; others were denounced by friends. Everywhere were lamentations, and wailings, and all the miseries of a captured city, till the license of the Vitellianist and Othonianist soldiery, once so odious, was remembered with regret. The leaders of the party, so energetic in kindling civil strife, were incapable of checking the abuse of victory.

122. Domitian's Reign A.D. 81–96

Tacitus: *Agricola*, chapters 2 and 3, 44 and 45

2. Certainly we showed a magnificent example of patience; as a former age had witnessed the extreme of liberty, so we witnessed the extreme of servitude, when the informer robbed us of the interchange of speech and hearing. We should have lost memory as well as voice, had it been as easy to forget as to keep silence.

3. Now at last our spirit is returning. And yet, though at the dawn of a most happy age Nerva Cæsar blended things once irreconcilable, sovereignty and freedom, though Nerva Trajan is now daily augmenting the prosperity of the time, and though the public safety has not only our hopes and good wishes, but has also the certain pledge of their fulfilment, still, from the necessary condition of human frailty the remedy works less quickly than the disease. As our bodies grow but slowly, perish in a moment, so it is easier to crush than to revive genius and its pursuits. Besides, the charm of indolence steals over us, and the idleness which at first we loathed we afterwards love. What if during those fifteen years, a large portion of human life, many were cut off by ordinary casualties, and the ablest fell victims to the Emperor's rage, if a few of us survive, I may almost say, not only others but our own selves, survive, though there have been taken from the midst of life those many years which brought the young in dumb silence to old age, and the old almost to the very verge and end of existence! Yet we shall not regret that we have told, though in language unskilful and unadorned, the story of past servitude, and borne our testimony to present happiness.

44. As his daughter and his wife survived him, it may be thought that he was even fortunate — fortunate, in that while his honors had suffered no eclipse, while his fame was at its height, while his kindred and his friends still prospered, he escaped from the evil to come. For, though to survive until the dawn of this most happy age and to see a Trajan on the throne was what 'he would speculate upon in previsions and wishes confined to my ears, yet he had this mighty compensation for his premature death, that he was spared those later years during which Domitian, leaving now no interval or breathing space of time, but, as it were, with one continuous blow, drained the life-blood of the Commonwealth. . . .

45. With Domitian it was the chief part of our miseries to

see and to be seen, to know that our sighs were being recorded,
to have, ever ready to note the pallid looks of so many faces, that

FIG. 16. — VIEW OF THE HOUSE OF THE TRAGIC POET. (After a photograph)

savage countenance reddened with the hue with which he defied
shame. . . .

Other Sources

Augustus: *Deeds* (*Monumentum Ancyranum*); *Translations and Reprints,* Univ. of Pa., Vol. V, No. 1; Dio Cassius (German translation), LI–LXVII; Eutropius, VII, 7–23; Florus, IV, 12; Josephus: *Antiquities of the Jews,* XVIII, 6–XX, 11; Josephus: *Jewish War,* II–VII; Livy: *Epitome,* CXXXIV–CXL; Plutarch: *Galba, Otho;* Suetonius: *Lives of the Twelve Cæsars;* Strabo: *Geography* (*passim*); Tacitus: *Annals; Histories,* I–V; *Agricola;* Velleius Paterculus, II, 88–131.

X. CHRISTIANITY AND STOICISM

I. CHRISTIANITY. — Adams, G. B.: *Civilization during the Middle Ages*, ch. 3; Allard : *Histoire des Persécutions*, 5 vols.; Allard : *Le Christianisme et l'Empire Romain;* Allen, pp. 300–306, *et passim;* Botsford, pp. 230–231, 262–265, 281–285; Bury, pp. 287, 288, 302–304, 445–448, 577–581; Capes : *The Age of the Antonines*, ch. 6; Carr : *The Church and the Roman Empire;* Duruy, Vol. V, ch. 87; Vol. VI, ch. 90, 91, 96, 100; Farrar : *Early Days of Christianity;* Fisher, G. P. : *Beginnings of Christianity;* Fisher, G. P.: *History of the Christian Church;* Friedländer: *Darstellungen aus der Sittengeschichte Roms*, Vol. III, ch. 4; Gibbon : *Decline and Fall of the Roman Empire* (ed. Bury), Vol. II, ch. 15, 16; Hardy : *Christianity and the Roman Government;* Hatch : *Organization of the Early Christian Churches;* Lanciani: *Pagan and Christian Rome;* Leighton, pp. 475–477, 490; Lightfoot: *Saint Clement of Rome;* Mason : *Persecution of Diocletian;* Milman : *History of Christianity*, Bks. I, II; Mommsen: In the *Historische Zeitschrift*, Vol. LXIV, 1890, pp. 389–424; Mommsen: *Provinces of the Roman Empire* (cf. Index); Morey (cf. Index); Munro and Bramhall: *Translations and Reprints*, Univ. of Pa., Vol. IV, No. 1 : *The Early Christian Persecutions;* Myers (cf. Index); Pelham, pp. 540, 557 ; Ramsay : *The Church in the Roman Empire before 170 A.D.;* Robinson, pp. 391, 399, 409; Renan : *Les Origines du Christianisme*, 6 vols.; Renan : *The Influence of Rome upon Christianity;* Seignobos, ch. 24, *et passim;* Stanley : *History of the Eastern Church*, Lectures 2–6; Uhlhorn, G.: *Conflict of Christianity with Heathenism;* West, par. 505–510; Wolfson, ch. 35, 36, pp. 457–463.

II. STOICISM. — Benn : *The Greek Philosophers*, Vol. II, ch. 1; Capes : *Stoicism;* Epictetus : *Discourses* and *Encheiridion;* Wallace : *Epicureanism*, ch. 1; Zeller : *Stoics, Epicureans, and Skeptics*, Pt. II, ch. 3–14.

123. Early Christians (under Claudius)   A.D. 41–54

Suetonius: *Life of Claudius*, chapter 25

. . . He banished from Rome all the Jews who were continually making disturbances at the instigation of one Chrestus.

124. Persecutions under Nero   A.D. 64

Tacitus: *Annals*, Book XV, chapter 44

. . . But all human efforts, all the lavish gifts of the Emperor, and the propitiations of the gods did not banish the sinister belief that the conflagration was the result of an order. Consequently, to get rid of the report, Nero fastened the guilt and inflicted the most exquisite tortures on a class hated for their abominations, called Christians by the populace. Christus, from whom the name had its origin, suffered the extreme penalty during the reign of Tiberius at the hands of one of our procurators, Pontius Pilatus, and a most mischievous superstition, thus checked for the moment, again broke out not only in Judæa, the first source of the evil, but even in Rome, where all things hideous and shameful from every part of the world find their centre and become popular. Accordingly, an arrest was first made of all who pleaded guilty; then, upon their information, an immense multitude was convicted, not so much of the crime of firing the city, as of hatred against mankind. Mockery of every sort was added to their deaths. Covered with the skins of beasts, they were torn by dogs and perished, or were nailed to crosses, or were doomed to the flames and burnt, to serve as a nightly illumination, when daylight had expired. Nero offered his gardens for the spectacle, and was exhibiting a show in the circus, while he mingled with the people in the dress of a charioteer or stood aloft on a car. Hence, even for criminals who deserved extreme and exemplary punishment, there arose a feeling of compassion; for it was not, as it seemed, for the public good, but to glut one man's cruelty, that they were being destroyed.

125. Attitude of Trajan A.D. 112

PLINY'S LETTER TO THE EMPEROR TRAJAN

Pliny: Book X, Letter 96

It is my custom, my Lord, to refer to you all things concerning which I am in doubt. For who can better guide my indecision or enlighten my ignorance?

I have never taken part in the trials of Christians : hence I do not know for what crime nor to what extent it is customary to punish or investigate. I have been in no little doubt as to whether any discrimination is made for age, or whether the treatment of the weakest does not differ from that of the stronger ; whether pardon is granted in case of repentance, or whether he who has ever been a Christian gains nothing by having ceased to be one ; whether the *name* itself without the proof of crimes, or the crimes, inseparably connected with the *name*, are punished. Meanwhile, I have followed this procedure in the case of those who have been brought before me as Christians. I asked them whether they were Christians a second and a third time and with threats of punishment ; I questioned those who confessed ; I ordered those who were obstinate to be executed. For I did not doubt that, whatever it was that they confessed, their stubbornness and inflexible obstinacy ought certainly to be punished. There were others of similar madness, whom, because they were Roman citizens, I have noted for sending to the City. Soon, the crime spreading, as is usual when attention is called to it, more cases arose. An anonymous accusation containing many names was presented. Those who denied that they were or had been Christians, ought, I thought, to be dismissed since they repeated after me a prayer to the gods and made supplication with incense and wine to your image, which I had ordered to be brought for the purpose together with the statues of the gods, and since besides they cursed Christ, not one of which things, they say, those who are really Christians can be compelled to do. Others, accused by the informer, said that they were Christians and afterwards denied it ; in fact they had been, but had ceased to be, some many years ago, some even twenty years before. All both worshipped your image and the statues of the gods, and cursed Christ. They continued to maintain that this was the amount of their fault or error, that on a fixed day they were accustomed to come together before daylight and to sing by turns a hymn to Christ as a god, and that they bound themselves by oath, not for some crime, but that they would not commit robbery, theft, or adultery, that they would not betray a trust nor deny a deposit when called upon. After this it was their custom to disperse and to come to-gether again to partake of food, of an ordinary and harmless kind, however ; even this they had ceased to do after the publication of my edict in which according to your command I had forbidden associations. Hence I believed it the more necessary to examine two female slaves, who were called deaconesses, in order to find out what was true, and to do it by torture. I found nothing but a vicious, extravagant superstition. Consequently I have post-poned the examination and make haste to consult you. For it seemed to me that the subject would justify consultation, especially on account of the number of those in peril. For many of all ages, of every rank, and even of both sexes are and will be called into danger. The infection of this superstition has not only spread to the cities but even to the villages and country districts. It seems possible to stay it and bring about a reform. It is plain enough that the temples, which had been almost deserted, have begun to be frequented again, that the sacred rites, which had been neglected for a long time, have begun to be restored, and that fodder for victims, for which till now there was scarcely a purchaser, is sold. From which one may readily judge what a number of men can be reclaimed if repentance is permitted.

TRAJAN'S REPLY

Pliny: Book X, Letter 97

You have followed the correct procedure, my Secundus, in conducting the cases of those who were accused before you as Christians, for no general rule can be laid down as a set form. They
ought not to be sought out; if they are brought before you and
convicted, they ought to be punished, provided that he who
denies that he is a Christian, and proves this by making supplication to our gods, however much he may have been under suspicion
in the past, shall secure pardon on repentance. In the case of no
crime should attention be paid to anonymous charges, for they
afford a bad precedent and are not worthy of our age.

126. Rescript of M. Aurelius to the Legate at Lyons A.D. 177

Eusebius: *Church History*, Book V, chapter 1, paragraph 47

For Cæsar commanded that they [the Christians] should be
put to death, but that any who might deny should be set free.

127. Effect of Persecutions

Tertullian: *Apology*, chapter 50

Nor does your cruelty, however exquisite, avail you; it is rather
a temptation to us. The oftener we are mown down by you, the
more in number we grow; *the blood of Christians is seed*. Many
of your writers exhort to the courageous bearing of pain and
death, as Cicero in the *Tusculans*, as Seneca in his *Chances*, as
Diogenes, Pyrrhus, Callinicus; and yet their words do not find
so many disciples as Christians do, teachers not by words, but by
their deeds. That very obstinacy you rail against is the precep-
tress. For who that contemplates it, is not excited to inquire
what is at the bottom of it? who, after inquiry, does not embrace
our doctrines? and when he has embraced them, desires not to
suffer that he may become partaker of the fulness of God's grace,

that he may obtain from God complete forgiveness, by giving in exchange his blood ? For that secures the remission of all offences.

128. Crimes of Christians

a. *Octavius* of Minucius Felix, chapter 10

" I purposely pass over many things, for those that I have mentioned are already too many ; and that all these, or the greater part of them, are true, the obscurity of their vile religion declares. For why do they endeavor with such pains to conceal and to cloak whatever they worship, since honorable things always rejoice in publicity, while crimes are kept secret ? Why have they no altars, no temples, no acknowledged images ? Why do they never speak openly, never congregate freely, unless for the reason that what they adore and conceal is either worthy of punishment, or something to be ashamed of ? " . . .

b. Tertullian: *Apology* (Extracts)

10. "You do not worship the gods," you say ; "and you do not offer sacrifice for the Emperors." Well, we do not offer sacrifice for others, for the same reason that we do not for ourselves, namely, that your gods are not at all the objects of our worship. So we are accused of sacrilege and treason. . . .

32. There is also another and a greater necessity for our offering prayer in behalf of the Emperors, nay, for the complete stability of the Empire, and for Roman interests in general. For we know that a mighty shock is impending over the whole earth — in fact, the very end of all things threatening dreadful woes is only retarded by the continued existence of the Roman Empire. We have no desire, then, to be overtaken by these dire events ; and in praying that their coming may be delayed, we are lending our aid to Rome's duration. . . .

33. But why dwell longer on the reverence and sacred respect of Christians to the Emperor, whom we cannot but look up

FIG. 17. — INTERIOR OF A HOUSE, LOOKING FROM THE ATRIUM TOWARD THE REAR. (After a photograph)

to as called by our Lord to his office ? so that on valid grounds I might say Cæsar is more ours than yours, for our God has appointed him.   Therefore, as having this property in him, I do more than you for his welfare, not merely because I ask it of Him who can give it, nor because I ask it as one who deserves to get it, but also because, in keeping the majesty of Cæsar within due limits, and putting it under the Most High, and making it less than divine, I commend him the more to the favor of the Deity, to whom alone I make him inferior.   But I place him in subjection to one I regard as more glorious than himself.   Never will I call the Emperor God. . . .

35. This is the reason, then, why Christians are counted public enemies : that they pay no vain, nor false, nor foolish honors to the Emperor ; that, as men believing in the true religion, they prefer to celebrate their festal days with a good conscience, instead of with the common wantonness. . . .

38. Ought not Christians, therefore, to receive not merely a somewhat milder treatment, but to have a place among the societies tolerated by law, seeing they are not chargeable with any such crimes as are commonly dreaded from societies of the illicit class?   For, unless I mistake the matter, the prevention of such associations is based on a prudential regard to public order, that the State may not be divided into parties, which would naturally lead to disturbance in the electoral assemblies, the councils, the *curiæ*, the special conventions, even in the public shows, by the collision of rival parties, especially when now, in pursuit of gain, men have begun to consider their violence an article to be bought and sold.   But as those in whom all ardor in the pursuit of glory and honor is dead, we have no pressing inducement to take part in your public meetings ; nor is there aught more entirely foreign to us than affairs of state.   We acknowledge one all-embracing commonwealth — the world.   We renounce all your spectacles, as strongly as we renounce the matters originating them, which we know were conceived of superstition, when we

give up the very things which are the basis of their representations. Among us nothing is ever said, or seen, or heard, which has anything in common with the madness of the circus, the immodesty of the theatre, the atrocities of the arena, the useless exercises of the wrestling ground. . . .

40. On the contrary, they deserve the name of faction who conspire to bring odium on good men and virtuous, who cry out against innocent blood, offering as justification of their enmity the baseless plea, that they think the Christians the cause of every public disaster, of every affliction with which the people are visited. If the Tiber rises as high as the city walls, if the Nile does not send its waters up over the fields, if the heavens give no rain, if there is an earthquake, if there is famine or pestilence, straightway the cry is, " Away with the Christians to the lions ! "

42. But we are called to account as harm-doers on another ground, and are accused of being useless in the affairs of life. How in all the world can that be the case with people who are living among you, eating the same food, wearing the same attire, having the same habits, under the same necessities of existence ? . . . So we sojourn with you in the world, abjuring neither forum, nor shambles, nor bath, nor booth, nor workshop, nor inn, nor weekly market, nor any other places of commerce. We sail with you, and fight with you, and till the ground with you ; and in like manner we unite with you in your traffickings — even in the various arts we make public property of our works for your benefit. How it is we seem useless in your ordinary business, living with you and by you as we do, I am not able to understand. But if I do not frequent your religious ceremonies, I am still on the sacred day a man.

129. Numbers of the Christians

Tertullian : *Apology*, chapter 37

We are men of yesterday ; yet we have filled all your places of resort — cities, lodging-houses, forts, towns, markets, even the camp, tribes, town-councils, palace, senate, forum ; we have left' you nothing but your temples.   For what war should not we have been fit and ready, though with unequal forces, who are so willing to be slaughtered, if according to our teaching it were not better to be killed than to kill? We could have fought against you even without arms, yet without rebellion, simply by the civil discord of an unfriendly separation.   For if such a force of men as we had broken off from you to some far corner of the world, your Empire would undoubtedly have been put to shame by the loss of so many citizens of whatever sort, or rather, actual bankruptcy would have been your punishment.

130. Christian Worship

Tertullian : *Apology*, chapter 39

We are made a body by common religious feeling, unity of discipline, and the bond of hope.   We come together in a meeting and assembly, that we may as it were form a troop, and so in prayer to God beset Him with our supplications.   This violence is well-pleasing to God.   We pray also for Emperors, for their ministers and for them that are in power, for the welfare of the world, for peace therein, for the delay of the end.   We meet together for the reading of the divine writings, if the character of the times compels us in any way to forewarning or reminder.   However that may be, with the holy words we nourish our faith, lift up our hope, confirm our confidence, and no less make strong our discipline by impressing the precepts.   At these meetings we have also exhortations, rebukes, and a divine censorship.   For judgment also is executed with much gravity, as before men who are sure that they are in the sight of God ; and it is a notable foretaste of judgment to come if a man has so sinned as to be banished from the communion of our prayer and meeting and all holy intercourse.   Our presidents are the approved elders, obtaining that honor not for a price, but by attested character ; for indeed the things of God are not sold for a price. Even if there is a sort of common fund, it is not made up of money paid in fees, as for a worship by contract. Each of us puts in a trifle on the monthly day, or when he pleases ; but only if he pleases, and only if he is able, for no man is obliged, but contributes of his own free will. These are as it were deposits of piety ; for it is not paid out thence for feasts and drinkings and thankless eating-houses, but for feeding and burying the needy, for boys and girls deprived of means and parents, for old folk now confined to the house ; also for them that are shipwrecked, for any who are in the mines, and for any who in the islands or in the prison, if only it be for the cause of God's people, become the nurslings of their own confession.

131. Inconveniences

Tertullian : *To His Wife*, Book II, chapters 3–6

. . . Without doubt a wife cannot satisfy the Lord according to discipline, when she has at her side a servant of the devil, an agent of *his* lord to hinder the works and duties of believers ; so that if there is a meeting to attend, her husband the first thing in the morning makes her an appointment for the baths ; if there are fasts to be observed, her husband that same day gives a dinner ; if she has to go out [on charitable errands], never is household business more in the way. For who would let his wife go round from street to street to other men's houses, and indeed to all the poorer cottages, for the sake of visiting the brethren? Who will willingly allow her to be taken from his side for nocturnal meetings, if her duty be so? Who in short will bear without anxiety her absence all night for the ceremonial of Easter? Who will let her go without suspicion of his own to that Lord's Supper which they defame? Who will suffer her to creep into a prison to kiss a martyr's bonds? or indeed to meet one of the brethren for the kiss? to offer water for the feet of the saints? to seize [for them] from her food or from her cup, to long for them, to keep them in mind? If a brother come on a journey, what welcome is there for him in an alien house? If there is a case for liberality, the granary and the larder are shut up. . . . The handmaid of God dwells with alien labors, and amongst them she will be persecuted with the odor of incense at all the festivals of demons, all the ceremonials of kings, the beginning of the year, the beginning of the month. She will come forth too from a laurelled gateway hung with lanterns as from some new abode of public lusts. She will dine with her husband in clubs, often in taverns, and sometimes she, who was used to minister to saints will minister to the unjust; and will she not recognize in this a sentence that carries her damnation, as she attends on those whom she is to judge hereafter?

132. Edicts of Diocletian against the Christians A.D. 303

Eusebius: *Church History*, Book VIII, chapters 2 and 6

2. This was the nineteenth year of the reign of Diocletian, in Dystrus (which the Romans call March), when the feast of the Saviour's passion was near at hand, and royal edicts were published everywhere, commanding that the churches should be razed to the ground, the Scriptures destroyed by fire, those who held positions of honor degraded, and the household servants, if they persisted in the Christian profession, be deprived of their liberty.

And such was the first decree against us. But issuing other decrees not long after, the Emperor commanded that all the rulers of the churches in every place should be first put in prison and afterwards compelled by every device to offer sacrifice.

6. Then as the first decrees were followed by others commanding that those in prison should be set free, if they would offer sacrifice, but that those who refused should be tormented with countless tortures; who could again at that time count the multitude of martyrs throughout each province, and especially throughout Africa and among the race of the Moors, in Thebais and throughout Egypt, from which having already gone into other cities and provinces, they became illustrious in their martyrdoms!

133. Constantine's Cross A.D. 312

Eusebius: *Life of Constantine*, Book I, chapters 28 and 29

. . . And while he was thus praying with fervent entreaty, a most marvellous sign appeared to him from heaven, the account of which it might have been hard to believe had it been related by any other person. But since the victorious Emperor himself long afterwards declared it to the writer of this history, when he was honored with his acquaintance and society, and confirmed his statement by an oath, who could hesitate to accredit the relation, especially since the testimony of after-time has established its truth? He said that about noon, when the day was already beginning to decline, he saw with his own eyes the trophy of a cross of light in the heavens, above the sun, and bearing the inscription, CONQUER BY THIS. At this sight he himself was struck with amazement, and his whole army also, which followed him on this expedition, and witnessed the miracle.

He said, moreover, that he doubted within himself what the import of this apparition could be. And while he continued to ponder and reason on its meaning, night suddenly came on; then in his sleep the Christ God appeared to him with the same sign which he had seen in the heavens, and commanded him to make a likeness of that sign which he had seen in the heavens, and to use it as a safeguard in all engagements with his enemies.

134. Edict of Toleration by Galerius A.D. 311

Lactantius: *On the Death of the Persecutors*, chapters 34 and 35

34. Among other arrangements which we are always accustomed to make for the prosperity and welfare of the Republic, we had desired formerly to bring all things into harmony with the ancient laws and public order of the Romans, and to provide that even the Christians who had left the religion of their fathers should come back to reason; since, indeed, the Christians themselves, for some reason, had followed such a caprice and had fallen into

such a folly that they would not obey the institutes of antiquity, which perchance their own ancestors had first established; but at their own will and pleasure, they would thus make laws unto themselves which they should observe, and would collect various peoples in divers places in congregations.   Finally, when our law had been promulgated to the effect that they should conform to the institutes of antiquity, many were subdued by the fear of danger, many even suffered death.   And yet since most of them persevered in their determination, and we saw that they neither paid the reverence and awe due to the gods nor worshipped the God of the Christians, in view of our most mild clemency and the constant habit by which we are accustomed to grant indulgence to all, we thought that we ought to grant our most prompt indulgence also to these, so that they may again be Christians and may hold their conventicles, provided they do nothing contrary to good order.   But we shall tell the magistrates in another letter what they ought to do.

Wherefore, for this our indulgence, they ought to pray to their God for our safety, for that of the Republic, and for their own, that the Republic may continue uninjured on every side, and that they may be able to live securely in their homes.

35. This edict is published at Nicomedia on the day before the Kalends of May, in our eighth consulship and the second of Maximinus.

135. Stoic Philosophy

a. MEDITATIONS OF MARCUS AURELIUS

Book III, Ch. 7. Never value anything as profitable to thyself which shall compel thee to break thy promise, to lose thy self-respect, to hate any man, to suspect, to curse, to act the hypocrite, to desire anything which needs walls and curtains; for he who has preferred to everything else his own intelligence, and the dæmon [within him] and the worship of its excellence, acts no tragic part, does not groan, will not need either solitude or much company; and, what is chief of all, he will live without either pursuing or flying from [life]; but whether for a longer or a shorter time he shall have the soul inclosed in the body, he cares not at all; for even if he must depart immediately, he will go as readily as if he were going to do anything else which can be done with decency and order, taking care of this only all through life, that his thoughts turn not away from anything which belongs to an intelligent animal and a member of a civil community.

Book V, Ch. 21. Reverence that which is best in the universe; and this is that which makes use of all things and directs all things. And in like manner also reverence that which is best in thyself; and this is of the same kind as that. For in thyself also, that which makes use of everything else, is this, and thy life is directed by this.

Ch. 24. Think of the universal substance, of which thou hast a very small portion; and of universal time, of which a short and indivisible interval has been assigned to thee; and of that which is fixed by destiny, and how small a part of it thou art.

Book VI, Ch. 2. Let it make no difference to thee whether thou art cold or warm, if thou art doing thy duty; and whether thou art drowsy or satisfied with sleep; and whether ill-spoken of or praised; and whether dying or doing something else. For it is one of the acts of life, this act by which we die: it is sufficient then in this act also to do well what we have in hand.

Ch. 21. If any man is able to convince me and show me that I do not think or act right, I will gladly change; for I seek the truth by which no man was ever injured. But he is injured who abides in his error and ignorance.

Ch. 22. [I do my duty: other things trouble me not . . .

b. THE ENCHEIRIDION OF EPICTETUS

Ch. 15. Remember that in life you ought to behave as at a banquet. Suppose that something is carried round and is opposite to you. Stretch out your hand and take a portion with decency. Sup-

pose that it passes by you.   Do not detain it.   Suppose that it is
not yet come to you.   Do not send your desire forward to it, but
wait till it is opposite to you.   Do so with respect to children, so
with respect to a wife, so with respect to magisterial offices, so with
respect to wealth, and you will be some time a worthy partner at
the banquets of the gods.   But if you take none of the things which
are set before you, and even despise them, then you will be not
only a fellow-banqueter with the gods, but also a partner with them
in power.   For by acting thus Diogenes and Heracleitus and
those like them were deservedly divine and were so called.

XI. ROMAN LIFE AND SOCIETY

(*a*) SLAVERY.   (*b*) EDUCATION.   (*c*) MANNERS, CUSTOMS, AMUSE-
MENTS, ETC.

a. Slavery

Allen, pp. 150, 158 ff.; Becker: *Gallus*, pp. 199–225; Beesly: *The Grac-
chi*, 10–14; Botsford, pp. 341–344, *et passim;* Bury (cf. Index); Church:
Roman Life in the Days of Cicero; Duruy, Vol. II, ch. 38, pp. 383–396; Fried-
länder: *Sittengeschichte Roms*, 3 vols., *passim;* Guhl and Koner: *Life of the
Greeks and Romans*, pp. 764–772; How and Leigh, pp. 316 ff., *et passim;*
Inge: *Society in Rome under the Cæsars*, ch. 6; Leighton, pp. 179 ff., 193,
194; Marquardt: *Privat-Leben der Römer*, ch. 4; Merivale: *Fall of the
Roman Republic*, ch. 1; Mommsen (see Index); Morey, pp. 140, 154, 156;
Myers, pp. 523–525; 14, 15, 445 ff.; Pelham (cf. Index); Pellison: *Roman
Life in Pliny's Time*, ch. 4; Preston and Dodge: *The Private Life of the
Romans*, pp. 66–76; Robinson, pp. 18, 453 ff.; Seignobos, ch. 12, pp. 163–
166; Shuckburgh, ch. 21, pp. 283 ff., 403, 404; Wallon, H.: *Histoire de
l'Esclavage dans l'Antiquité*, 2 vols.; West, par. 405 and 406; Wolfson (see
Index).

136. Slaves, Freemen, and Freedmen

Justinian : *Institutes*, Titles III, IV, V

Title III : Of the Law of Persons.   In the law of persons,
then, the first division is into freemen and slaves. Freedom,
from which men are called free, is a man's natural power of doing
what he pleases, so far as he is not prevented by force or law ;
slavery is an institution of the law of nations, against nature sub-
jecting one man to the dominion of another. The name " slave "
is derived from the practice of generals to order the preservation
and sale of captives, instead of killing them ; hence they are also

called *mancipia*, because they are taken from the enemy by the strong hand.   Slaves are either born so, their mothers being slaves themselves ; or they become so, and this either by the law of nations, that is to say by capture in war, or by the civil law, as when a freeman, over twenty years of age, collusively allows himself to be sold in order that he may share the purchase money. The condition of all slaves is one and the same : in the conditions of free men there are many distinctions ; to begin with, they are either free born, or made free.

Title IV: Of Men Free Born.   A free-born man is one free from his birth, being the offspring of parents united in wedlock, whether both be free born or both made free, or one made free and the other free born.   He is also free born if his mother be free, even though his father be a slave.

Title V: Of Freedmen.   Those are freedmen, or made free, who have been manumitted from legal slavery.   Manumission is the giving of freedom ; for while a man is in slavery he is subject to the power known as *manus;* and from that power he is set free by manumission.   All this originated in the law of nations ; for by natural law all men were born free, — slavery, and by consequence manumission, being unknown.   But afterwards slavery came in by the law of nations, and was followed by the boon of manumission. . . .

137. Duties of the Proprietor

Cato : *On Agriculture*, chapter 2

When the proprietor (*pater familias*) comes to his domain (*villa*), after paying his respects to the patron-god (*lar familiaris*), he ought, if possible, to inspect his estate on that same day ; at the latest, on the day after.   When he has examined the state of his lands, how they have been cultivated, what work has been done, what remains unfinished, then let him call the manager (*vilicus*) and demand of him an account of what has been accomplished, what remains to be done, whether the work has been completed in good time, and whether it is possible to finish what remains [to be done], how much wine, grain, and other products are on hand. Having secured this information, he ought to compare the work done with the number of [work] days. If the work done does not seem sufficient, the manager says that he has done his best, but that the slaves have been sick, the weather unfavorable, that some slaves have fled, or that work on the public roads had to be done. When he shall have alleged all these excuses and many more, call back the manager to an accounting of his services and of the work done. When the weather was unfavorable, see what work might have been done during the rainy season, *e.g.*, jars washed and lined with pitch, the villa cleaned, grain transported, the dung carried out of doors, a dung-pit made, the seed cleaned, old ropes repaired and new ones made, the hoods and clothes of the slaves mended. On holidays, old ditches could have been repaired, the public roads paved, bramble-bushes cut down, the garden dug, the meadow cleared, twigs woven, thorns weeded out, corn ground, everything made neat and clean. When the slaves are sick, they must be put on diet. Then orders shall be given to finish the rest of the work. An account shall be made of the silver on hand, of the grain in the granaries, of the fodder, wine, and oil; the sales and expenditures shall be recorded, also what remains to be sold, what is still owing. If there is a deficit for the current year, the neces-

FIG. 18.—ALTAR OF THE LARES COMPITALES

Schreiber, plate 18, fig. 4

saries shall be bought; if a surplus, this shall be disposed of. . . .
If they command good prices, the surplus of oil, wine, and grain
shall be sold.   It is necessary to sell the old oxen, blemished
cattle [unfit for ploughing], and sheep, wool, skins, old wagons,
old iron, old and sick slaves, and whatever else is useless.   The
proprietor ought to be eager to sell and not to buy.

138. The Duties of a Manager (Vilicus)

Cato: *On Agriculture*, chapter 5

His conduct shall always be well regulated.   He shall observe
the holidays.   He shall respect the property of others and shall
diligently watch over his own.   He shall settle the disputes of
slaves of the household; if any one commits a wrong, the punishment shall be proportioned to the offence.   He shall see to it that
the slaves are well-kept, that they suffer neither hunger nor thirst.
. . .   He shall be grateful for favors shown him, that others also
may be encouraged to do good.   He shall not be an idler; he
shall always be sober and shall not go out to dinner.   He shall
keep the slaves busy at work and shall see to it that his master's
orders are carried out.   He shall not deem himself wiser than his
master.   His master's friends shall be his friends.   He shall listen
to those whom he has been commanded to obey.   He shall perform no sacred rite, except to the Lares at the hearth or at the
cross-roads (*Lares Compitales*).   He shall lend to no one without
his master's order, and he shall render an account of whatever
he lends.   He shall lend to no one seed, provisions, meal, wine,
or oil.   In lending or borrowing the necessaries, he shall confine
his relations to two or three neighboring farms.   He shall frequently give an account to his master.   He shall not retain a day-
laborer, hired servant, or cultivator longer than one day.   He
shall buy nothing without his master's knowledge, neither shall he
conceal anything from him.   He shall not have a parasite.   He
shall consult no soothsayer, no augur, no fortune-teller, nor

Chaldæan. He shall not be sparing with the sowing; that is poor economy. He shall personally superintend all the work on the farm and shall himself often lend a hand, without, however, tiring himself out. In this way, he will come to know the dispositions of the slaves under his authority, and they will be all the more eager to work. He himself will be less disposed to idle, will get along better, and will sleep more soundly. He shall be the first to rise and the last to go to bed. Before retiring, he shall see to it that the "villa" is carefully closed, that every one is in his own lodging, that the cattle are provided with fodder; that the oxen are well taken care of. He shall sometimes humor the plough-men that they may the more willingly care for their oxen. He shall see to it also that the ploughs and ploughshares are in good condition.

139. The Duties of a Vilica

Cato: *On Agriculture*, chapter 143

If the master give her to you in marriage, be content with her. Make her respect you. Let her not be too extravagant. She shall employ women of the neighborhood and others as little as possible, and not receive them in her house. She shall not go out anywhere for dinner, nor be an idler. She shall perform no sacred rite, nor bid any one to perform it for her, without the command of her master or mistress. Know that the master performs the sacred rites for the whole household. She shall be neat. . . . On the kalends, ides, nones, on every holiday, she shall place a wreath on the hearth, and on these same days she shall pray to the patron god (*lar familiaris*) for plenty. She shall see to the cooking for you and the household. She shall have many chickens and eggs, dried-pears, sorb-apples, figs, raisins, sorb-apples in must, preserved pears and grapes and sparrow-apples and grapes with grapestones, preserved in jars buried in the earth, fresh nuts of Præneste. . . . She shall know how to make good flour and fine meal.

140. Treatment of Slaves

a. Cato: *On Agriculture*, chapters 56, 57, 58, 104

56. *Provisions* for the household of slaves. When they work, they shall receive three *modii* [about three pecks] of wheat during the winter, four and one-half *modii* during the summer. The manager, the overseer, and the shepherd shall receive three *modii,* the slaves in fetters four pounds of bread during the winter, and five pounds from the commencement of the vintage-season to the time when the figs are ripe ; after that, four pounds again.

57. *Wine* for the slaves. When the vintage is over, they shall drink after-wine for three months ; during the fourth month a *hemina* [about one-half pint] a day ; *i.e.,* two and one-half *congii* [one *congius* equals about one gallon] for the month. During the fifth, sixth, seventh, and eighth months, one *sextarius* [about one pint] a day ; *i.e.,* five *congii* per month. During the ninth, tenth, eleventh, and twelfth months, three *heminæ* a day ; *i.e.,* an *amphora* [about twenty-seven quarts] per month ; this to be increased to a *congius* per man on the Saturnalia and *Compitalia.* . . .

58. *Relish* for slaves. Save as many fallen olives as possible ; next, ripe olives which will yield but little oil, and, be sparing with them that they may last longer. When the olives shall have been consumed, give them some pickle and vinegar. Distribute to each man one *sextarius* of oil each month. A *modius* of salt per man is enough for the year.

Clothing. A tunic three and one-half feet long and a cloak every other year. As often as you give them a tunic or cloak, first take back the old one ; patched garments can be made of them. Give them every year a good pair of shoes.

104. *Wine* for the winter. Put in a cask ten parts of must [wine not fermented] and two parts of very pungent vinegar ; add two parts of boiled wine and fifty of fresh water. With a stick mix all this three times a day for five consecutive days. Add one forty-eighth of brine several days old. Place a lid on the

cask, and let the mixture ferment for ten days. This wine shall be consumed up to the solstice. If any remains after that date, it will make excellent sour vinegar.

713 A.U.C.

b. Appian: *Civil Wars*, Book V, paragraph 35   B.C. 41

. . . There [at Perusia] he [Lucius] took an account of the remaining provisions, and forbade the giving of any to the slaves, and prohibited them from escaping, lest the enemy should gain better knowledge of his desperate situation. The slaves wandered about in crowds, threw themselves upon the ground in the city, and between the city and their forts, and ate grass or green leaves wherever they could find them. Those who died Lucius buried in long trenches, lest, if he burned them, the enemy should discover what was taking place, and, if they were unburied, disease should result from the poisonous exhalations.

141. The Slave Trade

Strabo: *Geography* XIV, 5, page 668

. . . The exportation of slaves [from Cilicia] was the chief cause of inducing them [the Cilicians] to commit criminal acts; for this traffic was attended with very great profit, and the slaves were easily taken. Delos was at no great distance, a large and rich mart, capable of receiving and transporting, when sold the same day, ten thousand slaves; so that hence arose a proverbial saying: —

"Merchant, come into port, discharge your freight; everything is sold."

The Romans, having acquired wealth after the destruction of Carthage and Corinth, employed great numbers of domestic slaves, and were the cause of this traffic. The pirates, observing the facility with which slaves could be procured, issued forth in numbers from all quarters, committing robbery and dealing in slaves. . . .

142. Slaves' Vengeance

Pliny: *Letters*, Book III, 14

The atrocious treatment that Largius Macedo, a man of prætorian rank, lately received at the hands of his slaves is so extremely tragical that it deserves a place rather in public history than in a private letter ; though it must, at the same time, be acknowledged there was a haughtiness and severity in his behavior towards them which showed that he little remembered, indeed, almost entirely forgot, the fact that his own father had once been in that station of life. He was bathing at his Formian Villa, when he found himself suddenly surrounded by his slaves ; one seized him by the throat, another struck him on the mouth, whilst others trampled upon his breast, stomach, and even other parts which I need not mention. When they thought the breath must be quite out of his body, they threw him down upon the heated pavement of the bath, to try whether he were still alive, where he lay outstretched and motionless, either really insensible or only feigning to be so, upon which they concluded him to be actually dead. In this condition they brought him out, pretending that he had got suffocated by the heat of the bath. Some of his more trusty servants received him, and his mistresses came about him shrieking and lamenting. The noise of their cries and the fresh air together brought him a little to himself ; he opened his eyes, moved his body, and showed them (as he now safely might) that he was not quite dead. The murderers immediately made their escape ; but most of them have been caught again, and they are after the rest. He was, with great difficulty, kept alive for a few days, and then expired, having, however, the satisfaction of finding himself as amply revenged in his lifetime as he would have been after his death. Thus you see to what affronts, indignities, and dangers we are exposed. Lenity and kind treatment are no safeguard ; for it is malice and not reflection that arms such ruffians against their masters. . . .

143. Protection of Slaves (under Claudius)

Suetonius : *Life of Claudius*, chapter 25

. . . He confiscated the estates of all freedmen who presumed to take upon themselves equestrian rank. Such of them as were ungrateful to their patrons, and were complained of by them, he reduced to their former condition of slavery ; and declared to their advocates that he would always give judgment against the freedmen in any suit at law which the masters might happen to have with them. Some persons having exposed their sick slaves, in a languishing condition, on the island of Æsculapius, because of the tediousness of their cure, he declared all who were so exposed perfectly free ; never more to return, if they should recover, to their former servitude ; and that if any one chose to kill at once, rather than expose, a slave, he should be liable for murder. . . .

144. Position of Freedmen   A.D. 56

Tacitus : *Annals*, Book XIII, chapters 26 and 27

26. During the same time there was a discussion in the senate on the misconduct of the freedmen class, and a strong demand was made that, as a check on the undeserving, patrons should have the right of revoking freedom. There were several who supported this. But the consuls did not venture to put the motion without the Emperor's knowledge, though they recorded the senate's general opinion, to see whether he would sanction the arrangement. . . .

27. It was argued in reply that, though the guilt of a few ought to be the ruin of the men themselves, there should be no diminution of the rights of the entire class. " For it was," they contended, " a widely diffused body ; from it the city tribes, the various public functionaries, the establishments of the magistrates and priests were for the most part supplied, as well as the cohorts of the city-guard ; very many, too, of the knights, and several of the senators, derived their origin from no other source. If freed-

men were to be a separate class, the paucity of the free-born would be conspicuously apparent. Not without good reason had our ancestors, in distinguishing the position of the different orders, thrown freedom open to all. Again, two kinds of enfranchisement had been instituted, so as to leave room for retracting the boon, or for a fresh act of grace. Those whom the patron had not emancipated with the freedom-giving rod, were still held, as it were, by the bonds of slavery. Every master should carefully consider the merits of each case, and be slow to grant what once given could not be taken away.

This view prevailed, and the Emperor replied to the senate that, whenever freedmen were accused by their patrons, they were to investigate each case separately, and not to annul any right to their common injury. . . .

145. Punishment of Slaves   A.D. 61

Tacitus: *Annals*, Book XIV, chapters 42, 44, 45

42. Soon afterwards one of his own slaves murdered the city-prefect, Pedanius Secundus, either because he had been refused his freedom, for which he had made a bargain, or in the jealousy of a love in which he could not brook his master's rivalry. Ancient custom required that the whole slave-establishment which had dwelt under the same roof should be dragged to execution, when a sudden gathering of the populace, which was for saving so many innocent lives, brought matters to actual insurrection. Even in the senate there was a strong feeling on the part of those who shrank from extreme rigor, though the majority were opposed to any innovation. Of these, Caius Cassius, in giving his vote, argued to the following effect : —

44. . . . "Our ancestors always suspected the temper of their slaves, even when they were born on the same estates, or in the same houses with themselves, and thus inherited from their birth an affection for their masters. But now that we have in our

households nations with different customs from our own, with a foreign worship or none at all, it is only by terror you can hold in such a motley rabble. But, it will be said, the innocent will perish. Well, even in a beaten army when every tenth man is felled by the club, the lot falls also on the brave. There is some injustice in every great precedent, which, though injurious to individuals, has its compensation in the public advantage."

45. No one indeed dared singly to oppose the opinion of Cassius, but clamorous voices rose in reply from all who pitied the number, age, or sex, as well as the undoubted innocence of the great majority. Still, the party which voted for their execution prevailed. But the sentence could not be obeyed in the face of a dense and threatening mob, with stones and firebrands. Then the Emperor reprimanded the people by edict, and lined with a force of soldiers the entire route by which the condemned had to be dragged to execution. Cingonius Varro had proposed that even all the freedmen under the same roof should be transported from Italy. This the Emperor forbade, as he did not wish an ancient custom, which mercy had not relaxed, to be strained with cruel rigor.

146. Vices of Slaves

Pliny: *Natural History*, Book XXXIII, chapter 6

. . . How happy the times, how truly innocent, in which no seal was ever put to anything! At the present day, on the contrary, our very food even and our drink have to be preserved from theft through the agency of the ring: a result owing to those legions of slaves, those throngs of foreigners which are introduced into our houses, multitudes so numerous that we require the services of a nomenclator even to tell us the names of our own servants. Very different was it in the times of our forefathers when each person possessed a single servant only, one of his master's own lineage, called *Marcipor* or *Lucipor*,[1] from his

---

[1] Meaning "*Marci puer*" or "*Luci puer*,"—"Marcus's boy" or "Lucius's boy."

master's name, as the case might be, and taking all his meals with him in common ; when, too, there was no occasion for taking precautions at home by keeping a watch upon the domestics. But at the present day we not only procure dainties which are sure to be pilfered, but hands to pilfer them as well; and so far is it from being sufficient to have the very keys sealed, that the signet-ring is often taken from off the owner's finger while he is overpowered with sleep or lying on his death-bed. . . .

147. Immense Wealth in Slaves

Pliny: *Natural History*, Book XXXIII, chapter 47

. . . M. Crassus . . . used to say that no man was rich who could not maintain a legion upon his yearly income. He possessed in land two hundred millions of sesterces, being the richest Roman citizen next to Sulla. . . . And yet, although he was the first to become memorable for his opulence . . . we have known of many manumitted slaves, since his time, much more wealthy than he ever was ; three, for example, all at the same time, in the reign of the Emperor Claudius : Pallas, Callistus, and Narcissus. . . . Let us turn to C. Cæcilius Claudius Isidorus, who, in the consulship of C. Asinius Gallus and C. Marcius Censorinus (A.U.C. 746), upon the sixth day before the Kalends of February declared by his will, that though he had suffered great losses through the civil wars, he was still able to leave behind him four thousand one hundred and sixteen slaves, three thousand six hundred pairs of oxen, and two hundred and fifty-seven thousand heads of other kind of cattle, besides, in ready money, sixty millions of sesterces. Upon his funeral, also, he ordered eleven hundred thousand sesterces to be expended. . . .

148. Influence and Rise of Slaves

Pliny: *Natural History*, Book XXXV, chapter 58

. . . Other instances Rome has beheld of persons rising to high positions from the slave market ; Chrysogonus, for example, the freedman of Sulla; . . . and many others as well, whom it would be superfluous to enumerate, and who have enriched themselves at the cost of Roman blood, and the license that results from proscription.

Such is the mark that is set upon those droves of slaves which we see on sale, such the opprobrium thrown upon them by a capricious fortune! And yet some of these very men have we beheld in the enjoyment of such power and influence that the senate itself has decreed them — at the command of Agrippina, wife of the Emperor Claudius — the decorations even of the prætorship; all but honored with the fasces and their laurels, in fact, and sent back in state to the very place from which they originally came, with their feet whitened with the slave dealer's chalk!

149. Restraint of Masters

Seneca: *On Benefits*, paragraph 22

. . . Now an official has been appointed to hear complaints of the wrongs done by masters to their slaves, whose duty it is to restrain cruelty and lust, or avarice in providing them with the necessaries of life. . . .

150. Sale of a Slave   A.D. 129

Oxyrhynchus Papyri, Volume I, number 95

The thirteenth year of the Emperor Cæsar Trajanus Hadrianus Augustus, *Payni* 29, at Oxyrhynchus in the Thebaid. Agathodæmon, also called Dionysius, son of Dionysius, his mother being Hermione, of Oxyrhynchus, agrees with Gaius Julius Germanus, son of Gaius Julius Domitianus (the agreement being executed in the street), that he hereby assents to the autograph contract, made on *Tybi* 25 of the present thirteenth year, for the sale to Julius Germanus of a slave named Dioscorous, about twenty-five years old, with no distinguishing marks, which slave was his by purchase, having previously belonged to Heraclides, also called

Theon, son of Machon, son of Sosicosmius, also called Althæeus.
This slave Julius Germanus then took from him just as she was, free
from blemish except epilepsy and marks of punishment, at the
price of twelve hundred drachmæ of silver, which sum Agathodæmon, also called Dionysius, thereupon received from Julius
Germanus in full, together with the autograph contract.   In consequence of this contract Julius Germanus paid the tax upon the
sale of the said slave Dioscorous on *Phamenoth* 3 of the same year,
in accordance with the receipt issued to him.   Agathodæmon, also
called Dionysius, is the guarantor of the said slave Dioscorous in
all respects, as the autograph contract states.   If the terms of it
should be broken, or it in any other way be rendered invalid,
Julius Germanus has the right to demand. . . .

151. Legal Provisions Concerning Slaves

Gaius, Book I, chapters 52 and 53

52. Slaves are in the power of their proprietors, a power recognized by Gentile law, for all nations present the spectacle of masters invested with power of life and death over slaves ; and by the
Roman law the owner is entitled to everything acquired by the
slave.

53. But in the present day neither citizens of Rome, nor any
other persons under the empire of the people of Rome, are permitted to indulge in excessive or causeless harshness towards their
slaves.   By a constitution of the Emperor Pius Antoninus, a man
who kills a slave of whom he is owner, is as liable to punishment
as a man who kills a slave of whom he is not owner ; and inordinate cruelty on the part of owners is checked by another constitution whereby the same Emperor, in answer to inquiries from
presidents of provinces concerning slaves who take refuge at temples of the gods, or statues of the Emperor, commanded that on
proof of intolerable cruelty a proprietor should be compelled to
sell his slaves.

b. Education

Becker, pp. 28–38, 322–340; Botsford, pp. 93, 235, 335, *et seq.;* Bury, pp. 598–600; Capes: *Antonines,* ch. 8, pp. 165–170; Dill: *Roman Society in the Last Century of the Western Empire,* Bk. V, ch. 1; Friedländer, Vol. III, ch. 2, 3; How and Leigh, pp. 320 ff.; Inge, ch. 7; Kingsley: *Alexandria and her Schools* (in *Historical Lectures*); Leighton, ch. 56, pp. 399–404; Marquardt: *Das Privatleben der Römer,* ch. 3; Mommsen, Bk. IV, ch. 12; Monroe: *Greek and Roman Education;* Morey, p. 260; Myers, pp. 409, 512 ff.; Pellison, ch. 1; Preston and Dodge, ch. 3, pp. 57–66; Robinson, pp. 459–462; Seignobos, pp. 153 ff.; Thomas: *Roman Life under the Cæsars,* ch. 9; West, par. 483, 484; Wolfson, pp. 340, 341.

152. Old Roman Education and Education in Imperial Times

Tacitus: *Dialogue concerning Oratory,*[1] chapters 28 and 29

28. . . . The infant, as soon as born, was not consigned to the mean dwelling of a hireling nurse, but was reared and cherished in the bosom of its mother, whose highest praise it was to take care of her household affairs and attend to her children. It was customary, likewise, for each family to choose some elderly female relation of approved conduct, to whose charge the children were committed. In her presence not one indecent word was uttered; nothing was done against propriety and good manners. The hours of study and serious employment were settled by her direction; and not only so, but even the diversions of the children were conducted with modest reserve and sanctity of manners. Thus it was that Cornelia, the mother of the Gracchi, superintended the education of her illustrious issue. It was thus that Aurelia trained up Julius Cæsar; and thus Atia formed the mind of Augustus. The consequence of this regular discipline was that the young mind, whole and sound, and unwarped by irregular passions, received the elements of the liberal arts with hearty avidity. Whatever was the peculiar bias, whether to the military art, the study of the laws, or the profession of eloquence, that engrossed the whole attention, that was imbibed thoroughly and totally.

[1] The scene of the dialogue is laid in the sixth year of Vespasian, 75 A.D.

29. In the present age what is our practice? The infant is committed to a Greek chambermaid, and a slave or two, chosen for the purpose, generally the worst of the whole household train, and unfit for any office of trust. From the idle tales and gross absurdities of these people, the tender and uninstructed mind is suffered to receive its earliest impressions. Throughout the house not one servant cares what he says or does in the presence of his young master; and, indeed, how should it be otherwise? since the parents themselves are so far from training their young families to virtue and modesty, that they set them the first examples of luxury and licentiousness. Thus our youth gradually acquire a confirmed habit of impudence, and a total disregard of that reverence they owe both to themselves and to others. To say truth, it seems as if a fondness for horses, actors, and gladiators, the peculiar and distinguishing folly of this our city, was impressed upon them even in the womb; and when once a passion of this contemptible sort has seized and engaged the mind, what opening is there left for the noble arts? Who talks of anything else in our houses? If we enter the schools, what other subjects of conversation do we hear among the boys? The pre-

FIG. 19.—YOUTH READING AT BOOKCASE.
WRITING MATERIALS

Seignobos, History of Rome, p. 165

ceptors themselves choose no other topic more frequently to
entertain their hearers ; for it is not by establishing a strict discipline, nor by giving proofs of their genius, that this order of men
gain pupils, but by fawning and flattery. Not to mention how
ill instructed our youth are in the very elements of literature,
sufficient pains are by no means taken in making them acquainted
with the best authors, or in giving them a proper notion of history,
together with a knowledge of men and things. The whole that
seems to be considered in their education is, to find out a person
for them called a rhetorician. . . .

153. Early Roman Education

Suetonius: *Lives of Eminent Rhetoricians*, chapter 1

Rhetoric, also, as well as grammar, was not introduced amongst
us till a late period, and with still more difficulty, inasmuch as we
find that, at times, the practice of it was even prohibited. . . .

"After some interval, the censors[1] Cnæus Domitius Ænobarbus
and Lucius Licinius Crassus issued the following edict upon the
same subject : ' It is reported to us that certain persons have instituted a new kind of discipline ; that our youth resort to their
schools ; that they have assumed the title of Latin rhetoricians ;
and that young men waste their time there for whole days together. Our ancestors have ordained what instruction it is fitting
their children should receive, and what schools they should attend.
These novelties, contrary to the customs and instructions of our
ancestors, we neither approve, nor do they appear to us good.
Wherefore it appears to be our duty that we should notify our
judgment both to those who keep such schools, and those who are
in the practice of frequenting them, that they meet our disappro-
bation.' "

However, by slow degrees, rhetoric manifested itself to be a
useful and honorable study, and many persons devoted themselves

[1] 92 B.C.

to it both as a means of defence and of acquiring reputation. . . .
In consequence, public favor was so much attracted to the study
of rhetoric, that a vast number of professors and learned men
devoted themselves to it; and it flourished to such a degree that
some of them raised themselves by it to the rank of senators
and to the highest offices.

154. Horace's Education

Horace: *Satires*, Book I, 6, lines 65–80

And yet, if the faults and defects of my nature are moderate
ones, and with their exception my life is upright (just as if one
were to censure blemishes found here and there on a handsome
body), if no one can truly lay to my charge avarice, meanness,
or frequenting vicious haunts, if (that I may praise myself) my
life is pure and innocent, and my friends love me, I owe it all
to my father; he, though not rich, for his farm was a poor one,
would not send me to the school of Flavius, to which the first
youths of the town, the sons of the centurions, the great men there,
used to go, with their bags and slates on their left arm, taking the
teacher's fee on the Ides of eight months in the year; but he had
the spirit to carry me, when a boy, to Rome, there to learn the
liberal arts which any knight or senator would have his own
sons taught.   Had any one seen my dress, and the attendant
servants, so far as would be observed in a populous city, he
would have thought that such expense was defrayed from an old
hereditary estate.   He himself was ever present, a guardian incor-
ruptible, at all my studies.

155. The Cost of an Education

Juvenal, Satire VII

The baths will cost six hundred sestertia, and the colonnade still
more, in which the great man rides whenever it rains.   Is he to

wait, forsooth, for fair weather? or bespatter his horses with fresh mud? Nay, far better here! for here the mule's hoof shines unsullied. On the other side must rise a spacious dining room, supported on stately columns of Numidian marble, and catch the cool sun. However much the house may have cost, he will have besides an *artiste* who can arrange his table scientifically; another, who can season made-dishes. Yet amid all this lavish expenditure, two poor sestertia will be deemed an ample remuneration for Quintilian. Nothing will cost a father less than his son's education. . . .

156. Letter of a Schoolboy   2d or 3d century A.D.

Oxyrhynchus Papyri, Volume I, number 119

Theon to his father Theon, greeting. It was a fine thing of you not to take me with you to the city! If you won't take me with you to Alexandria, I won't write you a letter nor speak to you nor say good-bye to you; and if you go to Alexandria, I won't take your hand nor ever greet you again. That is what will happen if you won't take me. Mother said to Archelaus, "It quite upsets him to be left behind." It was good of you to send me presents . . . on the twelfth, the day you sailed. Send me a lyre, I implore you. If you don't, I won't eat, I won't drink; there now!

c. Roman Life: Amusements

Becker, scenes 1–12; Botsford, pp. 345–348; Bury, ch. 30, 31; Friedländer, Vol. II, ch. 1–3; Vol. III, ch. 1; Gibbon, Vol. 1, ch. 2, 31; Gilman, A.: *The Story of Rome*, ch. 18, pp. 271–291; Guhl and Koner, pp. 553–564; How and Leigh, pp. 318–321; Ihne, Vol. I. ch. 18; Vol. IV, ch. 12, 14, 15; Inge, ch. 8, 9; Lecky, W. E. H.: *History of European Morals from Augustus to Charlemagne*, Vol. I, ch. 2; Leighton, ch. 56; Marquardt, ch. 7; Merivale: *Empire*, Vol. IV, ch. 41; Mommsen, Bk. II, ch. 8, 9; Bk. III, ch. 13, 14; Bk. IV, ch. 12, 13; Bk. V, ch. 12; Morey, ch. 25, pp. 252–258; Myers, ch. 25; Pellison, ch. 2–10; Preston and Dodge, ch. 2, 4, 6; Ramsay and Lanciani, ch. 14; Robinson, ch. 34; Seignobos, ch. 19, 23; Shuckburgh, *passim;* Thomas, ch. 4; West. par. 476–500; Wolfson, ch. 34

157. Patria Potestas

Justinian: *Institutes*, Title 9

Our children whom we have begotten in lawful wedlock are in our power. Wedlock or matrimony is the union of male and female, involving the habitual intercourse of daily life. The power which we have over our children is peculiar to Roman citizens and is found in no other nation. The offspring then of you and your wife is in your power, and so too is that of your son and his wife, that is to say, your grandson and granddaughter, and so on. But the offspring of your daughter is not in your power, but in that of its own father.

158. Agreement of Marriage   A.D. 36

Oxyrhynchus Papyri, Volume II, number 267

"Tryphon, son of Dionysius, a Persian of the Epigone, to Saræus, daughter of Apion, under the wardship of Onnophis, son of Antipater, greeting. I acknowledge the receipt from you at the Serapeum at Oxyrhynchus through the bank of Sarapion, son of Kleandrus, of 40 silver drachmæ of the Imperial and Ptolemaic coinage, and for the value of one pair of gold earrings, 20 drachmæ of silver, and for a milk-white robe, 12 drachmæ of silver, making a total sum of 72 drachmæ of silver, to which nothing at all has been added, in consideration of which I have consented (to our marriage). And I will repay to you the 72 drachmæ of silver on the 30th of *Phaophi* in the coming second year of Gaius Cæsar Germanicus Novus Augustus Imperator, without any delay. If I do not repay in accordance with the above terms I will forfeit to you the said sum with the addition of half its amount, for which you are to have the right of execution upon me and upon all my property, as in accordance with a legal decision. If we separate from each other, you shall be empowered to have the pair of earrings at their present value. . . . This receipt is valid wherever and by whomsoever it is produced."

159. Invitation to a Wedding Feast 3d century A.D.

Oxyrhynchus Papyri, Volume I, number 111

Herais requests your company at dinner in celebration of the marriage of her children at her house to-morrow, the fifth, at nine o'clock.

160. A Roman Funeral

Polybius, Book VI, chapters 53 and 54

53. Whenever one of their illustrious men dies, in the course of his funeral, the body with all its paraphernalia is carried into the forum to the *Rostra*, as a raised platform there is called, and sometimes is propped upright upon it so as to be conspicuous, or, more rarely, is laid upon it. Then, with all the people standing round, his son, if he has left one of full age and he is there, or, failing him, one of his relations, mounts the *Rostra* and delivers a speech concerning the virtues of the deceased, and the successful exploits performed by him in his lifetime. . . . After the burial and all the usual ceremonies have been performed, they place the likeness of the deceased in the most conspicuous spot in his house, surmounted by a wooden canopy or shrine. This likeness consists of a mask made to represent the deceased with extraordinary fidelity both in shape and color. These likenesses they display at public sacrifices adorned with much care. And when any illustrious member of the family dies, they carry these masks to the funeral, putting them on men whom they thought as like the originals as possible in height and other personal peculiarities. And these substitutes assume clothes according to the rank of the person represented ; if he was a consul or prætor, a toga with purple stripes ; if a censor, whole purple ; if he had also celebrated a triumph or performed any exploit of that kind, a toga embroidered with gold. These representatives also ride in chariots, while the fasces and axes, and all the other customary insignia of the particular offices, lead the way, according to the dignity of the rank

in the state enjoyed by the deceased in his lifetime; and on arriving at the *Rostra* they all take their seats on ivory chairs in their order.   There could not easily be a more inspiring spectacle than this for a young man of noble ambitions and virtuous aspirations. . . .

54. Besides, the speaker over the body about to be buried, after having finished the panegyric of this particular person, starts upon the others whose representatives are present, beginning with the most ancient, and recounts the successes and achievements of each. By this means the glorious memory of brave men is continually renewed; the fame of those who have performed any noble deed is never allowed to die; and the renown of those who have done good service to their country becomes a matter of common knowledge to the multitude, and part of the heritage of posterity. But the chief benefit of the ceremony is that it inspires young men to shrink from no exertion for the general welfare, in the hope of obtaining the glory which awaits the brave. . . .

FIG. 20. — A BAKER'S MONUMENT, ROME
Schreiber, plate 67, fig. 5

161. The Funeral Eulogy of a Roman Lady 9 or 10 B.C.

Corpus Inscriptionum Latinarum, Volume VI, number 1527 (Abridged)

Before the day fixed for our marriage, you were suddenly left an orphan, by the murder of your parents in the solitude of the country. . . .

Through your efforts chiefly, their death did not remain unavenged. For I had departed for Macedonia and C. Cluvius, your sister's husband, into the province of Africa.

So active were you in the performance of this pious duty, in searching out and insistently demanding the punishment [of the guilty] that, had we ourselves been present, we could not have done more. You share the credit for this with that pious woman, your sister.

While you were busy with these matters, to shield your honor, immediately after the punishment of the assassins, you retired from your father's house to the home of your mother's sister, where you awaited my return. . . .

In our day, marriages of such long duration, not dissolved by divorce, but terminated by death alone, are indeed rare. For our union was prolonged in unclouded happiness for forty-one years. Would that it had been my lot to put an end to this our good fortune and that I as the older — which was more just — had yielded to fate.

Why recall your inestimable qualities, your modesty, deference, affability, your amiable disposition, your faithful attendance to the household duties, your enlightened religion, your unassuming elegance, the modest simplicity and refinement of your manners? Need I speak of your attachment to your kindred, your affection for your family, — when you respected my mother as you did your own parents and cared for her tomb as you did for that of your own mother and father, — you who share countless other virtues with Roman ladies most jealous of their fair name? These qualities which I claim for you are your own, equalled or excelled by but few; for the experience of men teaches us how rare they are.

With common prudence we have preserved all the patrimony which you received from your parents. Intrusting it all to me, you were not troubled with the care of increasing it; thus did we share the task of administering it, that I undertook to protect your fortune, and you to guard mine. On this point, I pass by many things in silence, for fear of attributing to myself a portion of your own deserts. Suffice it for me to indicate your sentiments.

You gave proof of your generosity not only towards several of your kin, but especially in your filial devotion. . . . You brought up in your own home, in the enjoyment of mutual benefits, some young girls of your kinship. And that these might attain to a station in life worthy of our family, you provided them with dowries. C. Cluvius and myself, by common accord, executed your intentions, and, approving of your generosity, in order that your patrimony might suffer no diminution, offered our own family possessions instead and gave up our personal property to provide the dowries, settled upon by you. This I relate, not to sing my own praises, but to show the unanimity of our counsels, that we held ourselves in honor bound to execute those obligations, incurred by you out of the fulness of your heart.

I owe you no less a debt than Cæsar Augustus himself, for this my return from exile to my native land. For unless you had prepared the way for my safety, even Cæsar's promises of assistance had been of no avail. So I owe no less a debt to your loyal devotion than to the clemency of Cæsar.

Why shall I now conjure up the memory of our domestic counsels and plans stored away in the hidden recesses of the heart? — That, aroused by the sudden arrival of messages from you to a realization of the present and imminent perils, I was saved by your counsel? That you suffered me not to be recklessly carried away by a foolish rashness, or that, when bent on more temperate plans, you provided for me a safe retreat, having as sharers in your plans for my safety, when an exile, — fraught with danger as they were for you all, — your sister and her husband, C. Cluvius. But I should not finish, were I to attempt to touch on all these matters. Suffice it for me, and for your memory, that the retreat provided by you insured my safety.

I should confess, however, that on this occasion I suffered one of the bitterest experiences of my life, in the fate that befell you, much against my will. When the favor and permission of Cæsar Augustus, then absent [from Rome], had restored me to my country, still a useful citizen perhaps, M. Lepidus, his colleague, then present in the city, interposed objections. Then prostrating yourself at his feet, he not only did not raise you up, — but, dragged along and abused as though a common slave, your body all covered with bruises, yet with unflinching steadfastness of purpose, you recalled to him Cæsar's edict [of pardon] and the letter of felicitation on my return, that accompanied it. Braving his taunts and suffering the most brutal treatment, you denounced these cruelties publicly so that he [Lepidus] was branded as the author of all my perils and misfortunes. And his punishment was not long delayed.

Could such courage remain without effect? Your unexampled patience furnished the occasion for Cæsar's clemency, and, by guarding my life, he branded the infamous and savage cruelty [of the tyrant Lepidus]. . . .

When all the world was again at peace and the Republic reëstablished, peaceful and happy days followed. We longed for children, which an envious fate denied us. Had Fortune smiled on us in this, what had been lacking to complete our happiness? But an adverse destiny put an end to our hopes. . . . Disconsolate to see me without children . . . you wished to put an end to my chagrin by proposing to me a divorce, offering to yield the place to another spouse more fertile, with the only intention of searching for and providing for me a spouse worthy of our mutual affection, whose children you assured me you would have treated as your own. . . . Nothing would have been changed, only you would have rendered to me henceforth the services of a devoted sister or mother-in-law.

I will admit that I was so irritated and shocked by such a proposition that I had difficulty in restraining my anger and remaining master of myself. You spoke of divorce before the decree of fate had forced us to separate, and I could not comprehend how you could conceive of any reason why you, still living, should not be my wife, you who during my exile had always remained most faithful and loyal. . . .

Would that our time of life had permitted our union to have endured until I, the older, had passed away — which was more just — and that you might perform for me the last sad rites and that I might have departed, leaving you behind, with a daughter to replace me at your side.

By fate's decree your course was run before mine. You left me the grief, the heart-ache, the longing for you, the sad fate to live alone. . . .

The conclusion of this discourse will be that you have deserved all, and that I remain with the chagrin of not being able to give you all. Your wishes have always been my supreme law; and whatever it will be permitted me to accord them still, in this I shall not fail.

May the gods, the Manes, assure and protect your repose !

162. Cato's Opinion of Farmers

Cato: *On Agriculture*, Introduction

. . . When our fathers pronounced the eulogy of a worthy man, they praised him as a worthy farmer and a worthy landlord ; only one who was thus commended was thought to have received the highest praise. The merchant I deem energetic and diligent in the pursuit of gain ; but his calling is too much exposed to perils and mischances. On the other hand, farmers furnish the bravest men and the ablest soldiers ; no calling is so honorable, safe, and

Copyright, 1892, by Houghton, Mifflin & Co.

FIG. 21. — COLUMBARIUM

Lanciani, Ruins and Excavations of Ancient Rome, p. 332

inoffensive as theirs, and those who occupy themselves with it are least liable to evil thoughts.[1]

163. Servile and Liberal Occupations

Cicero: *Offices*, Book I, chapter 42

Now with regard to what arts and means of acquiring wealth are to be regarded as worthy and what disreputable, we have been taught as follows.   In the first place, those sources of emolument are condemned that incur the public hatred ; such as those of tax-gatherers and usurers. We are likewise to account as ungenteel and mean the gains of all hired workmen, whose source of profit is not their art but their labor ; for their very wages are the consideration of their servitude. We are likewise to despise all who retail from merchants goods for prompt sale ; for they never can succeed unless they lie most abominably.   Now nothing is more disgraceful than insincerity.   All mechanical laborers are by their profession mean.   For a workshop can contain nothing befitting a gentleman.   Least of all are those trades to be approved that serve the purposes of sensuality, such as (to speak after Terence) fishmongers, butchers, cooks, pastry-cooks, and fishermen ; to whom we shall add, if you please, perfumers, dancers, and the whole tribe of gamesters.

But those professions that involve a higher degree of intelligence or a greater amount of utility, such as medicine, architecture, the teaching the liberal arts, are honorable in those to whose rank in life they are suited.   As to merchandising, if on a small scale it is mean ; but if it is extensive and rich, bringing numerous commodities from all parts of the world, and giving bread to numbers without fraud, it is not so despicable.   But if a merchant, satiated, or rather satisfied with his profits, as he sometimes used to leave the open sea and make the harbor, shall from the harbor step into an estate and lands, such a man seems most justly deserving of

1 Quoted in Pellison: *Roman Life in Pliny's Time*, p. 112.

praise. For of all gainful professions, nothing is better, nothing more pleasing, nothing more delightful, nothing better becomes a well-bred man than agriculture.

600 ? A.U.C. **164. No Permanent Theatres** B.C. 154?

Livy: *Epitome*, XLVIII

A theatre which the censors had contracted for, being built, Cornelius Nasica moves, and carries the question, that it be pulled down, as being not only useless, but injurious to the morals of the people ; the people, therefore, continue to behold the public shows standing. . . .

165. Games and Sports of Augustus

Suetonius: *Life of Augustus*, chapter 83

As soon as the civil wars were ended, he [Augustus] gave up riding and other military exercises in the Campus Martius, and took to playing at ball, or foot-ball ; but soon afterwards used no other exercise than that of going abroad in his litter, or walking. Towards the end of his walks, he would run leaping, wrapped up in a short cloak or cape. For amusement he would sometimes angle, or play with dice, pebbles, or nuts, with little boys, collected from various countries, and particularly Moors and Syrians, for their beauty or amusing talk. . . .

166. Magnificence of Public Spectacles Given by Augustus

Suetonius : *Life of Augustus*, chapter 43

In the number, variety, and magnificence of his public spectacles, he surpassed all former example. . . . The performances took place sometimes in the different streets of the city, and upon several stages, by players in all languages. The same he did not only in the forum and amphitheatre, but in the circus likewise, and

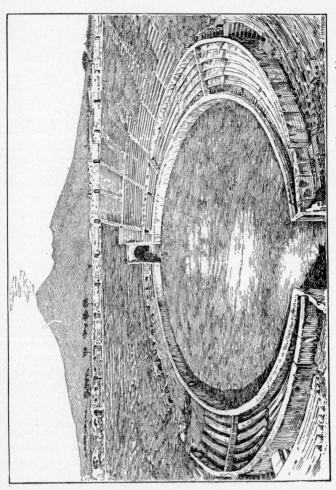

FIG. 22. — INTERIOR OF THE AMPHITHEATRE AT POMPEII.   (After a photograph)

in the *Septa*, and sometimes he exhibited only the hunting of wild beasts. He entertained the people with wrestlers in the Campus Martius, where wooden seats were erected for the purpose; and also with a naval fight, for which he excavated the ground near the Tiber, where there is now the grove of the Cæsars. . . . Sometimes he engaged Roman knights to act upon the stage, or to fight as gladiators; but only before the practice was prohibited by a decree of the senate. Thenceforth, the only exhibition he made of that kind was that of a young man named Lucius, of a good family, who was not quite two feet in height, and weighed only seventeen pounds, but had a stentorian voice. . . . He used, likewise, at times when there were no public entertainments, if anything was brought to Rome which was uncommon, and might gratify curiosity, to expose it to public view, in any place whatever; as he did a rhinoceros in the *Septa*, a tiger upon a stage, and a snake fifty cubits long, in the *Comitium*. . . .

167. Amusements (under the Empire)

Juvenal : *Satires*, X, lines 81 ff.

For that sovereign people that once gave away military command, consulships, legions, and everything, now bridles its desires, and limits its anxious longings to two things only — bread, and the games of the circus ! (*panem et circenses*).

168. Games in the Provinces   A.D. 57

Tacitus : *Annals*, Book XIII, chapter 31

. . . The Emperor [Nero], by an edict, forbade any magistrate or procurator in the government of a province to exhibit a show of gladiators, or of wild beasts, or indeed any other public entertainment ; for hitherto our subjects had been as much oppressed by such bribery as by actual extortion, while governors sought to screen by corruption the guilty deeds of arbitrary caprice.

169. Nero's Amusements

Tacitus : *Annals*, Book XIV, chapter 14

He had long had a fancy for driving a four-horse chariot, and a no less degrading taste for singing to the harp, in a theatrical fashion, when he was at dinner. This, he would remind people, was a royal custom, and had been the practice of ancient chiefs ; it was celebrated, too, in the praises of poets, and was meant to show honor to the gods. Songs indeed, he said, were sacred to Apollo, and it was in the dress of a singer that that great and prophetic deity was seen in Roman temples as well as in Greek cities. He could no longer be restrained, when Seneca and Burrus thought it best to concede one point that he might not persist in both. A space was enclosed in the Vatican valley, where he might manage his horses, without the spectacle being public. Soon he actually invited all the people of Rome, who extolled him in their praises, like a mob which craves for amusements and rejoices when a prince draws them the same way. However, the public exposure of his shame acted on him as an incentive, instead of sickening him, as men expected. Imagining that he mitigated the scandal by disgracing many others, he brought on the stage descendants of noble families, who sold themselves because they were paupers. As they have ended their days, I think it due to their ancestors not to hand down their names. And indeed the infamy is his who gave them wealth to reward their degradation rather than to deter them from degrading themselves. He prevailed, too, on some well-known Roman knights, by immense presents, to offer their services in the amphitheatre ; only pay from one who is able to command, carries with it the force of compulsion.

170. Feelings about Nero's Performances

Tacitus: *Annals*, Book XVI, chapter 5

All, however, who were present from remote towns, and still retained the Italy of strict morals and primitive ways ; all, too, who had come on embassies or on private business from distant provinces, where they had been unused to such wantonness, were unable to endure the spectacle or sustain the degrading fatigue, which wearied their unpractised hands, while they disturbed those who knew their part, and were often struck by soldiers, stationed in the seats, to see that not a moment of time passed with less vigorous applause or in the silence of indifference. It was a known fact that several knights, in struggling through the narrow approaches and the pressure of the crowd, were trampled to death, and that others while keeping their seats day and night were seized with some fatal malady. For it was a still worse danger to be absent from the show, as many openly, and many more secretly, made it their business to scrutinize names and faces and to note the delight or the disgust of the company. Hence came cruel severities, immediately exercised on the humble, and resentments, concealed for the moment, but subsequently paid off, towards men of distinction. There was a story that Vespasian was insulted by Phœbus, a freedman, for closing his eyes in a doze, and that having with difficulty been screened by the intercessions of the well-disposed, he escaped imminent destruction through his grander destiny.

171. Gladiatorial Shows at Pompeii A.D. 59

Tacitus: *Annals*, Book XIV, chapter 17

About the same time a trifling beginning led to frightful bloodshed between the inhabitants of Nuceria and Pompeii, at a gladiatorial show exhibited by Livineius Regulus, who had been, as I have related, expelled from the senate. With the unruly spirit of townsfolk, they began with abusive language of each other ; then they took up stones and at last weapons, the advantage resting with the populace of Pompeii, where the show was being exhibited. And so there were brought to Rome a number of the people of Nuceria, with their bodies mutilated by wounds, and many lamented the deaths of children or of parents. The Emperor intrusted the trial of the case to the senate, and the senate to the consuls, and then again the matter being referred back to the senators, the inhabitants of Pompeii were forbidden to have any such public gatherings for ten years, and all associations they had formed in defiance of the laws were dissolved. Livineius and the others who had excited the disturbance were punished with exile.

FIG. 23. — THE AMPHITHEATRE AT POMPEII.   (After a photograph)

172. Amusements under Domitian   A.D. 81–96

Suetonius: *Life of Domitian*, chapter 4

He frequently entertained the people with most magnificent and costly shows, both in the amphitheatre, and in the circus; where, besides the usual races with chariots drawn by two or four horses abreast, he exhibited the representation of an engagement between both horse and foot, and a sea-fight in the amphitheatre. The people were also entertained with the chase of wild beasts and the combat of gladiators, even in the night-time, by torch-light. Nor did men only fight in these spectacles, but women also. He constantly attended at the games given by the quæstors, which had been disused for some time, but were revived by him; and upon these occasions always gave the people the liberty of demanding two pair of gladiators out of his own school, who appeared last in court uniforms. Whenever he attended the shows of gladiators, there stood at his feet a little boy dressed in scarlet, with a prodigiously small head, with whom he used to talk very much, and sometimes seriously. . . . He likewise celebrated the secular games. . . . In these, upon the day of the Circensian sports, in order to have a hundred races performed, he reduced each course from seven rounds to five. He likewise instituted, in honor of Jupiter Capitolinus, a solemn contest in music to be performed every five years; besides horse-racing and gymnastic exercises, with more prizes than are at present allowed. There was also a public performance in elocution, both Greek and Latin; and besides the musicians who sung to the harp, there were others who played concerted pieces or solos, without vocal accompaniment. Young girls also ran races in the Stadium, at which he presided in his sandals, dressed in a purple robe, made after the Grecian fashion, and wearing upon his head a golden crown bearing the effigies of Jupiter, Juno, and Minerva. . . . He thrice bestowed upon the people a largess of three hundred sesterces for each man ; and, at a public show of gladiators, a very plentiful feast. At the festival of the Seven Hills he distributed large hampers of provisions to the senatorial and equestrian orders, and small baskets to the common people, and encouraged them to eat by setting them the example. The day after, he scattered among the people a variety of cakes and other delicacies to be scrambled for ; and on the greater part of them falling amidst the seats of the crowd, he ordered five hundred tickets to be thrown into each range of benches belonging to the senatorial and equestrian orders.

173. Gladiatorial Shows at Bononia

Martial: *Epigrams*, Book III, 59 [1]

A paltry cobbler, O elegant Bononia, has exhibited to thee a show of gladiators ; a dyer has done the same to Mutina. Now where will the innkeeper exhibit?

[1] Cf. Bk. III, 3.

174. Public Games in the Provincial Towns

Pliny: *Letters*, Book IV, 22

I lately attended our excellent Emperor [Trajan] as one of his assessors, in a case where he himself presided. A certain person left by his will a fund for the establishment of the gymnastic games at Vienne.[1] These my worthy friend Trebonius Rufinus, when he exercised the office of duumvir, had ordered the total abolition of; and it was now alleged against him that he had no legal authority for their suppression. . . . It was determined that these games should be suppressed, for they had greatly depraved the morals of the people of Vienne, just as ours have those of the world at large. . . .

175. Factions at the Circus

Juvenal: *Satires*, XI, lines 180 ff.

. . . If I may say so without offence to the immense and over-grown crowd, the circus to-day encloses the whole of Rome; and a din reaches my ears, from which I infer the success of the green faction. For should it not win, you would see this city in mourning and amazement, as when the consuls were conquered in the dust of Cannæ. Let young men be spectators of these, in whom shouting and bold betting, and sitting by a trim damsel, is becoming.

176. Liberality of a Citizen of Ostia   2d cent. A.D.

Ephemeris Epigraphica, Volume II, pages 320–322

Lucilius Gamala, having received from the municipal treasury a fund for the games, has refused it and has preferred to pay the whole cost himself. He has paved, at his own expense, the street near the Forum, which connects the two triumphal arches. He has invited all the inhabitants to a great banquet in one hundred

[1] Near Lyons.

and seventeen dining rooms. He has offered two repasts to all his fellow-citizens. He has repaired or reconstructed at his own expense the temple of Vulcan, the temple of Venus, the temple of Fortune, the temple of Ceres, the temple of Hope, the temple of Castor and Pollux, and the temple of the Tiber. He has elevated a marble tribunal in the Forum. He has caused the public weights of the market and the measures of the wine-hall to be made. He has reconstructed the baths of Antoninus Pius, destroyed by a fire, and has repaired the portico. He has rebuilt the workshop for shipbuilding, which was constructed by L. Coilus and has since fallen almost into ruins.

As the city had pledged itself to furnish to the State a certain sum of money for a naval war, and as, on account of its inability to make the payment, it placed on sale the communal property, Gamala gave to it three millions of sesterces.

177. Letter Concerning a Mouse-catcher Late 1st cent. A.D.

Oxyrhynchus Papyri, Volume II, number 299

" Horus to his esteemed Apion, greeting. Regarding Lampon the mouse-catcher I paid him for you as earnest money eight drachmæ in order that he may catch the mice while they are with young. Please send me the money. I have also lent Dionysius, the chief man of Nemeræ, eight drachmæ, and he has not repaid them, to which I call your attention. Good-by. *Payni* 24."

178. Declaration by an Egg-seller A.D. 327

Oxyrhynchus Papyri, Volume I, number 83

" To Flavius Thennyras, logistes of the Oxyrhynchite nome, from Aurelius Nilus, son of Didymus, of the illustrious and most illustrious city of Oxyrhynchus, an egg-seller by trade. I hereby agree on the august, divine oath by our lords the Emperor and the Cæsars to offer my eggs in the market-place publicly, for sale and for the supply of the said city, every day without intermission, and I acknowledge that it shall be unlawful for me in the future to sell secretly or in my house. If I am detected so doing [I shall be liable to the penalty for breaking the oath]."

Additional References to Sources

Torturing of Slaves: Juvenal, XIV, 16, *et seq.;* Sources of Slaves: Cicero: *For Cluentius,* 7; Suetonius: *Life of Tiberius,* 8; *Life of Augustus,* 32; Cicero's Treatment of Slaves: *To his Brother Quintus,* I, 16, 6; Endowments and Scholarships: Pliny: *Letter to Tacitus,* IV, 13; A Plea for a Vacation: Martial, X, 62; Early Roman Education: Plautus: *Bacchides,* ll. 420, *et seq.;* Old Roman Simplicity: Livy, *Epitome,* XLVIII; Roman Society under the Empire: Juvenal, I, ll. 101, *et seq.* (Clients); III, 35, *et seq.;* Importunacy of People for Gladiatorial Shows: Suetonius: *Tiberius,* 37; Chariot-racing (under Theodoric): Cassiodorus, III, 51; Factions at the Circus: Suetonius: *Vitellius,* 7; Gladiatorial Games at Verona: Pliny: *Letter to Maximus,* VI, 34; Guilds of Coppersmiths (338 A.D.): *Oxyrhynchus Papyri,* I, 85.

XII. PROVINCES AND PROVINCIAL ADMINISTRATION

Abbott, pp. 88–91 (cf. Index) ; Allcroft and Masom, pp. 281–286; Arnold: *Roman System of Provincial Administration;* Boissier: *Roman Africa;* Botsford, pp. 129–133, 205–210, *et passim;* Church: *Roman Life in the Days of Cicero,* ch. 13; Duruy, Vol. II, ch. 34, 44; Vol. III, ch. 62, 63; How and Leigh, pp. 310–313, *et passim;* Ihne, Vol. IV, ch. 9, 10, 11; Leighton, pp. 128 ff., *et passim;* Mommsen, Bk. III, ch. 11 ; Bk. IV, ch. 1, 7 ; Mommsen: *Provinces of the Roman Empire;* Morey, pp. 146–148, 264, 271, *et passim;* Myers, pp. 154, 279, 280, 313, 314, 319, 320; Pelham, pp. 173–188, 327–329; Pelham: *Imperial Domains;* Robinson (see Index); Seeley, J. R.: *Roman Imperialism,* ch. 3; Seignobos, ch. 12, pp. 173–176, *et passim;* Shuckburgh, pp. 648, *et seq.,* 654–656; Taylor, pp. 200–211; West, par. 401–404, *et passim;* Wolfson (consult Index).

179. Roman Theory of Conquest

Polybius: Book XXXVI, chapter 4

. . . "Those who thus surrender themselves to the Roman authority surrender all territory and the cities in it, together with all men and women in all such territory or cities, likewise rivers, harbors, temples, and tombs, so that the Romans should become actual lords of all these, and those who surrender should remain lords of nothing whatever."

180. The Roman Public Domain

Appian: *Civil Wars,* Book I, paragraph 7

The Romans, as they subdued the Italian nations successively in war, seized a part of their lands and built towns there, or established their own colonies in those already existing, and used them in place of garrisons. Of the land acquired by war they assigned the cultivated part forthwith to settlers, or leased or sold it. Since they had no leisure as yet to allot the part which then lay desolated by war (this was generally the greater part), they made proclamation that in the meantime those who were willing to work it might do so for a share of the yearly crops — a tenth of the grain and a fifth of the fruit. From those who kept flocks was required a share of the animals, both oxen and small cattle. They did these things in order to multiply the Italian race, which they considered the most laborious of peoples, so that they might have plenty of allies at home. But the very opposite thing happened; for the rich, getting possession of the greater part of the undistributed lands, and being emboldened by the lapse of time to believe that they would never be dispossessed, and adding to their holdings the small farms of their poor neighbors, partly by purchase and partly by force, came to cultivate vast tracts instead of single estates, using for this purpose slaves as laborers and herdsmen, lest free laborers should be drawn from agriculture into the army. The ownership of slaves itself brought them great gain from the multitude of their progeny, who increased because they were exempt from military service. Thus the powerful ones became enormously rich and the race of slaves multiplied throughout the country, while the Italian people dwindled in numbers and strength, being oppressed by penury, taxes, and military service. If they had any respite from these evils they passed their time in idleness, because the land was held by the rich, who employed slaves instead of freemen as cultivators.

181. The Provinces, the Estates of the Roman People

Cicero: *Against Verres*, III, chapter 3

And since our tributary nations and our provinces are, as it were, farms belonging to the Roman people; just as one is most pleased with those farms which are nearest to one, so too the suburban character of this province [Sicily] is very acceptable to the Roman people. And as to the inhabitants themselves, O judges, such is their patience, their virtue, and their frugality, that they appear to come very nearly up to the old-fashioned manners of our country, and not to those which now prevail. . . . Moreover, they are so fond of our nation that they are the only people where neither a publican nor a money-changer is unpopular. . . .

688 A.U.C. **182. Publicani and the Public Revenue** B.C. 66

Cicero: *For the Manilian Law*, chapter 7

And even this must not be neglected by you, which I had proposed to myself as the last thing to be mentioned, when I was to speak of the kind of war, for it concerns the property of many Roman citizens ; whom you, as becomes your wisdom, O Romans, must regard with the most careful solicitude. The publicans, most honorable and accomplished men, have taken all their resources and all their wealth into that province, and their property and fortunes ought, by themselves, to be an object of your especial care. In truth, if we have always considered the revenues as the sinews of the Republic, certainly we shall be right if we call that order of men which collects them, the prop and support of all the other orders. In the next place, clever and industrious men, of all the other orders of the State, are some of them actually trading themselves in Asia, and you ought to show a regard for their interests in their absence ; and others of them have large sums invested in that province [Asia]. It will, therefore, become your humanity to protect a large number of those citizens from misfortune ; it will become your wisdom to perceive that the misfortune of many citizens cannot be separated from the misfortune of the Republic. . . .

183. Maladministration of Provinces

Cicero: *Against Verres*, I, chapters 1 and 5

1. For an opinion has now become established, pernicious to us and pernicious to the public, which has been the common talk of every one, not only of Rome, but among foreign nations also, — that in the courts of law as they exist at present no wealthy man, however guilty he may be, can possibly be convicted. Now, at this time of peril to your order, and to your tribunals, when men are ready to attempt by harangues and by the proposal of new laws, to increase the existing unpopularity of the senate, Caius Verres is brought to trial as a criminal, a man condemned in the opinion of every one by his life and actions, but acquitted by the enormousness of his wealth, according to his own hope and boast.

5. No legal decision for three years was given on any other ground but his will; no property was so secure to any man, even if it had descended to him from his father and grandfather, but he was deprived of it at his command; enormous sums of money were exacted from the property of the cultivators of the soil by a new and nefarious system. The most faithful of the allies were classed in the number of enemies. Roman citizens were tortured and put to death like slaves; the greatest criminals were acquitted in the courts of justice through bribery; the most upright and honorable men, being prosecuted while absent, were condemned and banished without being heard in their own defence; the most fortified harbors, the greatest and strongest cities, were laid open to pirates and robbers; the sailors and soldiers of the Sicilians, our own allies and friends, died of hunger; the best built fleets on the most important stations were lost and destroyed, to the great disgrace of the Roman people. This same man while prætor plundered and stripped those most ancient monuments, some erected by wealthy monarchs and intended by them as ornaments for their cities; some, too, the work of our own generals, which they either gave or restored as conquerors to the different states

in Sicily. And he did this not only to public statues and ornaments, but he also plundered all the temples consecrated in the
deepest religious feelings of the people. He did not leave, in
short, one god to the Sicilians which appeared to him to be made
in a tolerably workmanlike manner, and with any of the skill of
the ancients.

184. Provinces under Augustus

Suetonius: *Life of Augustus*, paragraph 47

The more important provinces, which could not with ease or
safety be intrusted to the government of annual magistrates, he
reserved for his own administration; the rest he distributed by lot
amongst the proconsuls; but sometimes he made exchanges, and
frequently visited most of both kinds in person. . . . There is
not, I believe, a province, except Africa and Sardinia, which he
did not visit. . . .

185. Postal-service in the Empire

Suetonius: *Life of Augustus*, paragraph 47

. . . In order to obtain the earliest intelligence of what was
passing in the provinces, he [Augustus] established posts, consisting at first of young men stationed at moderate distances along
the military roads, and afterwards of regular couriers with fast
vehicles, which appeared to him the most commodious, because
the persons who were bearers of despatches, written on the spot,
might then be questioned about the business, as occasion occurred.

186. Organization of the Empire A.D. 14

Tacitus: *Annals*, Book I, chapter 11

. . . They (the senators) raised their hands to the gods, to the
statue of Augustus, and to the knees of Tiberius, when he ordered
a document to be produced and read. This contained a description of the resources of the State, of the number of citizens and
allies under arms, of the fleets, subject-kingdoms, provinces, taxes,

direct and indirect, necessary expenses, customary bounties. All
these details Augustus had written with his own hand, and had
added a counsel, that the Empire should be confined to its present
limits, either from fear or out of jealousy.

187. Census of the Roman People

Monumentum Ancyranum, paragraph 8

. . . In my sixth consulship,[1] with Marcus Agrippa as colleague,
I made a census of the people. I performed the lustration after
forty-one years. In this lustration the number of Roman citizens
was four million and sixty-three thousand. Again assuming the
consular power in the consulship of Gaius Censorinus and Gaius
Asinius,[2] I alone performed the lustration. At this census the
number of Roman citizens was four million, two hundred and
thirty thousand. A third time, assuming the consular power in
the consulship of Sextus Pompeius and Sextus Appuleius,[3] with
Tiberius Cæsar as colleague, I performed the lustration. At this
lustration the number of Roman citizens was four million, nine
hundred and thirty-seven thousand. . . .

188. "Client Princes"

Monumentum Ancyranum, paragraph 27

. . . Of greater Armenia, when its king Artaxes was killed, I
could have made a province, but I preferred, after the example of
our fathers, to deliver that kingdom to Tigranes. . . .

189. Government of Egypt   A.D. 14

a. Tacitus: *History*, Book I, chapter 2

Ever since the time of the divine Augustus, Roman knights have
ruled Egypt as kings, and the forces by which it has to be kept in
subjection. It has been thought expedient thus to keep under
home control a province so difficult of access, so productive of

---

[1] 735–736 A.U.C., or 19–18 B.C.   [2] 746 A.U.C., or 8 B.C.   [3] 767 A.U.C., or 14 A.D.

corn, ever distracted, excitable, and restless through the superstition and licentiousness of its inhabitants, knowing nothing of laws, and unused to civil rule. . . .

A.D. 19

b. Tacitus: *Annals*, Book II, chapter 59

. . . Germanicus set out for Egypt to study its antiquities. His ostensible motive, however, was solicitude for the province. He reduced the price of corn by opening the granaries, and adopted many practices pleasing to the multitude. He would go about without soldiers, with sandalled feet, and apparelled after the Greek fashion in imitation of Publius Scipio. . . . Tiberius having gently expressed his disapproval of his dress and manners, pronounced a very sharp censure on his visit to Alexandria without the Emperor's leave, contrary to the regulations of Augustus. That prince, among other secrets of the imperial policy, had forbidden senators and Roman knights of the higher rank to enter Egypt except by permission, and he had specially reserved the country, from a fear that any one who held a province containing the key of the land and of the sea, with ever so small a force against the mightiest army, might distress Italy by famine.

190. Importance of the Provinces

Tacitus: *Annals*, Book III, chapter 54

No one represents to the senate that Italy requires supplies from abroad, and that the very existence of the people of Rome is daily at the mercy of uncertain waves and storms. And unless masters, slaves, and estates have the resources of the provinces as their mainstay, our shrubberies, forsooth, and our country houses will have to support us. . . .

191. Tiberius's Administration of the Empire   A.D. 23

Tacitus: *Annals*, Book IV, chapter 6

It is, however, I think, a convenient opportunity for me to review the hitherto prevailing methods of administration in the other departments of the State, inasmuch as that year brought with it the beginning of a change for the worse in Tiberius's policy. In the first place, public business and the most important private matters were managed by the senate; the leading men were allowed freedom of discussion, and when they stooped to flattery, the Emperor himself checked them. He bestowed honors with regard to noble ancestry, military renown, or brilliant accomplishments as a civilian, letting it be clearly seen that there were no better men to choose. The consul and the prætor retained their prestige; inferior magistrates exercised their authority; the laws, too, with the single exception of cases of treason, were properly enforced.

As to the duties on corn, the indirect taxes and other branches of the public revenue, they were in the hands of companies of Roman knights. The Emperor intrusted his own property to men of the most tried integrity, or to persons known only by their general reputation, and once appointed they were retained without any limitation, so that most of them grew old in the same employments. The city populace indeed suffered much from high prices, but this was no fault of the Emperor, who actually endeavored to counteract barren soils and stormy seas with every resource of wealth and foresight. And he was also careful not to distress the provinces by new burdens, and to see that in bearing the old they were safe from any rapacity or oppression on the part of governors. Corporal punishments and confiscations of property were unknown.

192. Divisions in the Provinces

Strabo, Book XIII, chapter 4, paragraph 12

The places situated next to these [the Catacecaumene-Mysia?] towards the south, and extending to Mount Taurus, are so intermixed, that parts of Phrygia, Lydia, Caria, and Mysia running into one another are difficult to be distinguished. The Romans have contributed not a little to produce this confusion, by not dividing the people according to tribes, but, following another principle, have arranged them according to jurisdictions, in which they have appointed days for holding courts and administering justice. . . .

193. Provincial Organization A.D. 47

Tacitus: *Annals*, Book XI, chapter 19

. . . The Frisians . . . gave hostages and settled down on territories marked out by Corbulo, who, at the same time, gave them a senate, magistrates, and a constitution. That they might not throw off their obedience, he built a fort among them. . . .

194. Extortion by a Tax-collector A.D. 50

a. *Oxyrhynchus Papyri*, Volume II, number 284

" To Tiberius Claudius Pasion, strategus, from Alexandrus, son of Apollonius, a weaver of Oxyrhynchus, living in the quarter of the square of Thoëris. Apollophanes, ex-collector of taxes, in the eighth year of Tiberius Claudius Cæsar Augustus Germanicus Imperator extorted from me among other people sixteen drachmæ of silver. I therefore beg you to proceed against him as you may think fit."

A.D. 50

b. *Oxyrhynchus Papyri*, Volume II, number 285

" To Tiberius Claudius Pasion, strategus, from Sarapion, son of Theon, a weaver of the city of Oxyrhynchus, living in Gymnasium square quarter. Apollophanes, ex-collector of the trade tax upon weavers, in the first year of Tiberius Claudius Cæsar Augustus Germanicus Imperator, using great violence, seized from me a linen tunic which I was wearing, worth eight drachmæ. He also extorted from me four more drachmæ, and two drachmæ each month during the six months from the month *Neos Sebastos* in the ninth year of Tiberius Claudius Cæsar Augustus Germanicus Imperator to *Pharmuthi;* total, 24 drachmæ. I therefore beg you to proceed against him as you may think fit."

195. Public Revenues and Taxation   A.D. 58

Tacitus: *Annals*, Book XIII, chapters 50 and 51

50. That same year repeated demands on the part of the people, who denounced the excessive greed of the revenue collectors, made Nero doubt whether he should not order the repeal of all indirect taxes, and so confer a most splendid boon on the human race. But this sudden impulse was checked by the senators, who, having first heartily praised the grandeur of his conception, pointed out " that the dissolution of the Empire must ensue if the revenues which supported the State were to be diminished ; for as soon as the customs were swept away, there would follow a demand for the abolition of the direct taxes. . . . Certainly some restraint, they admitted, must be put on the cupidity of the revenue collectors, that they might not by new oppressions bring into odium what for so many years had been endured without a complaint."

51. Accordingly the Emperor issued an edict that the regulations about every branch of public revenue, which had hitherto been kept secret, should be published ; that claims which had been dropped should not be revived after a year ; that the prætor at Rome, the proprætor or proconsul in the provinces, should give judicial precedence to all cases against the collectors ; that the soldiers should retain their immunities except when they traded for profit, with other very equitable arrangements, which for a short time were maintained and were subsequently disregarded. However, the repeal of the two per cent and two-and-a-half per cent taxes remains in force, as well as that of others bearing names invented by the collectors to cover their illegal exactions. In our transmarine provinces the conveyance of corn was rendered less costly, and it was decided that merchant ships should not be assessed with their owner's property, and that no tax should be paid on them.

196. Legate *versus* Proconsul A.D. 70

Tacitus: *History*, Book IV, chapter 48

. . . The legion and the auxiliaries stationed in Africa to guard the frontiers of the Empire were under the proconsul's authority during the reigns of the divine Augustus and Tiberius. But in the course of time Caligula, prompted by his restless temper and by his fear of Marcus Silanus, who then held Africa, took away the legion from the proconsul, and handed it over to a legate whom he sent for that purpose. The patronage was equally divided between the two officers. A source of disagreement was thus studiously sought in the continual clashing of their authority, and it was further developed by an unprincipled rivalry. The power of the legates grew through their lengthened tenure of office, and, perhaps, because an inferior feels greater interest in such a competition. All the more distinguished of the proconsuls cared more for security than for power.

197. Cæsar's Account of Britain

Gallic Wars, Book V, chapters 12 and 14

12. The inland parts of Britain are inhabited by those whom fame reports to be natives of the soil. The sea-coast is peopled with Belgians, drawn thither by the love of war and plunder. These last, passing over from different parts, and settling in the country, still retain the names of the several states whence they are descended. The island is well-peopled, full of houses, built after the manner of the Gauls, and abounds in cattle. They use brass money and iron rings of a certain weight. The provinces remote from the sea produce tin, and those on the coast iron ; but the latter in no great quantity. Their brass is all imported. All kinds of wood grow here the same as in Gaul, except the fir and beech tree. They think it unlawful to feed on hares, pullets, or

geese ; yet they breed them up for their diversion and pleasure.
The climate is more temperate than in Gaul, and the cold less
intense. . . .

14. The inhabitants of Kent, which lies wholly on the sea-coast,
are the most civilized of all the Britons, and differ but little in their
manner from the Gauls. The greater part of those within the
country never sow their lands, but live on flesh and milk, and go
clad in skins. All the Britons in general paint themselves with
woad, which gives a bluish cast to the skin, and makes them look
dreadful in battle. They are long-haired, and shave all the rest
of the body except the head and upper lip.

198. Tacitus's Account of Britain

Agricola, chapters 13 and 21

13. The Britons themselves bear cheerfully the conscription,
the taxes, and the other burdens imposed on them by the Empire, if there be no oppression. Of this they are impatient ; they
are reduced to subjection, not as yet to slavery. To proceed, the
deified Julius, the very first Roman who entered Britain with an
army, though by a successful engagement he struck terror into the
inhabitants and gained possession of the coast, must be regarded as
having indicated rather than transmitted the acquisition to future
generations. Then the civil wars, and the arms of our leaders,
were turned against their country, and even when there was peace,
there was a long neglect of Britain. This Augustus spoke of as
policy, Tiberius as an inherited rule. That Caius Cæsar meditated
an invasion of Britain is perfectly clear ; but his purposes, rapidly
formed, were easily changed, and his vast attempts on Germany
had failed. Claudius was the first to renew the attempt, and conveyed over into the island some legions and auxiliaries, choosing
Vespasian to share with him the campaign, whose approaching
elevation had this beginning. Several tribes were subdued and
kings made prisoners, and destiny learned to know its favorite.

21. The succeeding winter was employed in the most salutary measures. In order, by a taste of pleasures, to reclaim the natives from that rude and unsettled state which prompted them to war, and reconcile them to quiet and tranquillity, he incited them, by private instigations and public encouragements, to erect temples, courts of justice, and dwelling-houses. He bestowed commendations upon those who were prompt in complying with his intentions, and reprimanded such as were dilatory ; thus promoting a spirit of emulation which had all the force of necessity. He was also attentive to provide a liberal education for the sons of their chieftains, preferring the natural genius of the Britons to the attainments of the Gauls ; and his attempts were attended with such success, that they who lately disdained to make use of the Roman language, were now ambitious of becoming eloquent. Hence the Roman habit began to be held in honor, and the toga was frequently worn. At length they gradually deviated into a taste for those luxuries which stimulate to vice ; porticoes, and baths, and the elegances of the table ; and this, from their inexperience, they termed politeness, whilst, in reality, it constituted a part of their slavery.

199. Management of the Imperial Revenue

Pliny to Trajan, Book X, Letter 62

The debts which were owing to the public are, by the prudence, Sir, of your counsels, and the care of my administration, either actually paid in or now being collected ; but I am afraid the money must lie unemployed. For as on one side there are few or no opportunities of purchasing land, so, on the other, one cannot meet with any person who is willing to borrow of the public (especially at twelve per cent interest) when they can raise money upon the same terms from private sources. You will consider, then, Sir, whether it may not be advisable, in order to invite responsible persons to take this money, to lower the interest ; or if that scheme should not succeed, to place it in the hands of the *decurii*, upon

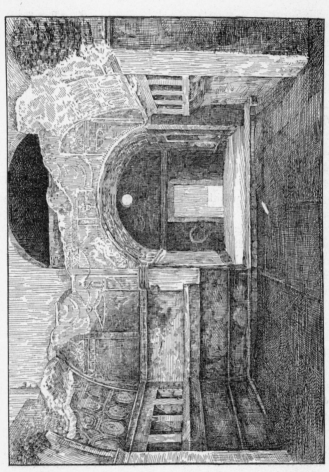

FIG. 24. — APODYTERIUM OF THE STABIAN BATHS, WITH THE ANTE-ROOM LEADING FROM THE PALÆSTRA

Mau's Pompeii, plate v

their giving sufficient security to the public. And though they should not be willing to receive it, yet as the rate of interest will be diminished, the hardship will be so much the less.

Trajan to Pliny, Book X, Letter 63

I agree with you, my dear Pliny, that there seems to be no other method of facilitating the placing out of the public money than by lowering the interest, the measure of which you will determine according to the number of the borrowers. But to compel persons to receive it who are not disposed to do so, when possibly they themselves may have no opportunity of employing it, is, by no means, consistent with the justice of my government.

200. Removal of a Temple

Pliny to Trajan, Book X, Letter 58

The Nicomedians, Sir, before my arrival in this province, had begun to build a new forum adjoining their former, in a corner of which stands an ancient temple dedicated to the *mother of the gods*.[1] This fabric must either be repaired or removed, and for this reason chiefly, because it is a much lower building than that very lofty one which is now in process of erection. Upon inquiry whether this temple had been consecrated, I was informed that their ceremonies of dedication differ from ours. You will be pleased therefore, Sir, to consider whether a temple which has not been consecrated according to our rites may be removed, consistently with the reverence due to religion; for, if there should be no objection from that quarter, the removal in every other respect would be extremely convenient.

Trajan to Pliny, Book X, Letter 59

You may without scruple, my dearest Secundus, if the situation requires it, remove the temple of the *mother of the gods*, from the

[1] Cybele.

place where it now stands, to any other spot more convenient. You need be under no difficulty with respect to the act of dedication; for the ground of a foreign city is not capable of receiving that kind of consecration which is sanctified by our laws.

201. Privileges of a City

Pliny to Trajan, Book X, Letter 56

Upon intimating, Sir, my intention to the city of Apamea of examining into the state of their public dues, their revenue, and expenses, they told me they were all extremely willing I should inspect their accounts, but that no proconsul had ever yet looked them over, as they had a privilege (and that of a very ancient date) of administering the affairs of their corporation in the manner they thought proper. I required them to draw up a memorial of what they then asserted, which I transmit to you precisely as I received it, though I am sensible it contains several things foreign to the question. I beg you will deign to instruct me as to how I am to act in this affair, for I should be extremely sorry either to exceed or fall short of the duties of my commission.

Trajan to Pliny, Book X, Letter 57

The memorial of the Apameans annexed to your letter has saved me the necessity of considering the reasons they suggest why the former proconsuls forebore to inspect their accounts, since they are willing to submit them to your examination. Their honest compliance deserves to be rewarded; and they may be assured the inquiry you are to make in pursuance of my orders shall be with a full reserve of their privileges.

202. Societies Discountenanced by Trajan

a. *Trajan to Pliny*, Book X, Letter 43

You are of the opinion it would be proper to establish a company of firemen in Nicomedia, agreeably to what has been practised in other cities. But it is to be remembered that societies of this sort have greatly disturbed the peace of the province in general, and of those cities in particular. Whatever name we may give them, and for whatever purposes they may be founded, they will not fail to form themselves into factious assemblies, however short their meetings may be. It will therefore be safer to provide such machines as are of service in extinguishing fires, enjoining the owners of houses to assist in preventing the mischief from spreading, and, if it should be necessary, to call in the aid of the populace.

b. *Pliny to Trajan*, Book X, Letter 93

The free and confederate city of the Amiseni enjoys, by your indulgence, the privilege of its own laws. A memorial being presented to me there, concerning a charitable institution, I have subjoined it to this letter that you may consider, Sir, whether, and how far, this society ought to be licensed or prohibited.

c. *Trajan to Pliny*, Book X, Letter 94

If the petition of the Amiseni which you have transmitted to me, concerning the establishment of a charitable society, be agreeable to their own laws, which by the articles of alliance it is stipulated they shall enjoy, I shall not oppose it, especially if these contributions are employed, not for the purchase of riot and faction, but for the support of the indigent. In other cities, however, which are subject to our laws, I would have all assemblies of this nature prohibited.

203. Senators in the Provinces

a. *Pliny to Trajan*, Book X, Letter 113

The Pompeian law, Sir, which is observed in Pontus and Bithynia, does not direct that any money for their admission shall be paid in by those who are elected into the senate by the censors. It has, however, been usual for such members as have been admitted into those assemblies, in pursuance of the privilege which you were pleased to grant to some particular cities, of receiving above their legal number, to pay one [1] or two [2] thousand denarii on their election. Subsequent to this, the proconsul Anicius Maximus ordained (though indeed his edict related to some few cities only) that those who were elected by the censors should also pay into the treasury a certain sum, which varied in different places. It remains, therefore, for your consideration whether it would not be proper to settle a certain fixed sum for each member who is elected into the councils to pay upon his entrance ; for it well becomes you, whose every word and action deserves to be immortalized, to establish laws that shall endure forever.

b. *Trajan to Pliny*, Book X, Letter 114

I can give no general directions applicable to all the cities of Bithynia, in relation to those who are elected members of their respective councils, whether they shall pay an honorary fee upon admission or not. I think that the safest method which can be pursued is to follow the particular laws of each city ; and I also think that the censors ought to make the sum less for those who are chosen into the senate contrary to their inclinations than for the rest.

c. *Trajan to Pliny*, Book X, Letter 116

You might well be doubtful, my dear Secundus, what reply to give to the censors, who consulted you concerning their right to elect into the senate foreign citizens, though of the same province. The authority of the law on one side, and long custom prevailing against it on the other, might justly occasion you to hesitate. The proper mean to observe in this case will be to make no change in what is past, but to allow those senators who are already elected, though contrary to law, to keep their seats, to whatever city they may belong ; in all future elections, however, to pursue the directions of the Pompeian law ; for to give it a retrospective operation would necessarily introduce great confusion.

[1] About $210.00.   [2] About $420.00.

204. Misgovernment of Diocletian   A.D. 284–305

Lactantius: *On the Death of the Persecutors*, chapter 7

When Diocletian, that inventor of crimes and deviser of evils, was ruining all things, he could not refrain his hands even from God. He was the man who overturned the whole world, partly by avarice and partly by cowardice. He made three partners in his government, dividing the Empire into four parts, so that armies were multiplied, because each of the four endeavored to have a much greater number of soldiers than former Emperors had when they ruled the State alone. Thus the receivers of taxes began to be more in number than the payers, so that by reason of the consumption of husbandmen's goods by the excess of land-taxes, the farms were left waste and tilled lands turned into forests. In order, too, that all places might be filled with terror the provinces also were cut up into fragments, and many presidents and sundry companies of officials lay heavy on every territory, and indeed almost on every city ; and there were many receivers besides and secretaries and deputies of the prefects. All these very seldom had civil cases before them, only condemnations and continual confiscations and requisitions — I will not say frequent, but unceasing — of every kind of property, and in the levying intolerable wrongs. Even these might be borne if they were intended to provide pay for the soldiers ; but Diocletian in his insatiable avarice would never let his treasures be diminished, but was always heaping up extraordinary aids and benevolences, in order to keep his hoards untouched and inviolate. Again, when by various evil deeds he caused a prodigious scarcity, he essayed by law to fix the prices of goods in the market. Then much blood was shed for trifling and paltry wares, and through fear nothing appeared in the market, so that the scarcity was made much worse, till after the law had ruined multitudes it was of sheer necessity abolished. In addition to this he had an unlimited taste for building, and levied of the provincials as unlimited exactions for the wages of workmen and artificers, and the supplying of wagons and everything else that was wanted for the works in hand. Here were public offices, there a circus, here a mint, there a factory of arms, here a palace for his wife, and there one for his daughter. On a sudden a large part of the city is turned out of doors : they all had to remove with wives and children, as if the city had been taken by enemies. And when the works had been finished, at the cost of ruin to the provinces, " They are not done right," he used to say ; " let them be done another way." So they had to be pulled down and altered, perhaps only to be demolished again. Thus he always played the madman in his endeavor to make Nicomedia equal to imperial Rome. I leave untold how many perished on account of their estates or wealth, for by the custom of evil men this was become frequent and almost lawful. Yet the worst of it was this, that wherever he saw a field more carefully tilled, or a house more elegantly adorned than usual, straightway an accusation and capital sentence was prepared for the owner, as though he could not spoil his neighbor's goods without shedding of blood.

205. Byzantium

Polybius, Book IV, chapter 38

. . . As far as the sea is concerned, Byzantium occupies a position the most secure and in every way the most advantageous of any town in our quarter of the world ; while in regard to the land, its situation is in both respects the most unfavorable. By sea it so completely commands the entrance to the Pontus, that no merchant can sail in or out against its will. The Pontus therefore being rich in what the rest of the world requires for the support of life, the Byzantines are absolute masters of all such things. For those commodities which are the first necessaries of existence, cattle and slaves, are confessedly supplied by the districts round the Pontus in greater profusion, and of better quality, than by any others; and for luxuries, they supply us with honey, wax, and salt fish in great abundance, while they take our superfluous stock of olive oil and every kind of wine. In the matter of corn there is a mutual interchange, they supplying or taking it as it happens to be convenient.

APPENDIX I

BIOGRAPHIES OF AUTHORS QUOTED

[The name or abbreviation placed after each author refers to the translation used; B. L. to *Bohn's Library;* A. N. L., to the *Ante-Nicene Library;* N. L., to the *Nicene and Post-Nicene Library;* and Penn. Repr., to the Pennsylvania *Translations and Reprints.*]

Appian (*fl. c.* 90–100 A.D.). In the preface to his history (paragraph 15) he writes, " I am Appian of Alexandria, having reached the highest place in my native country, and having been, in Rome, a pleader of causes before the Emperors, until they deemed me worthy of being made their procurator." His work on Roman history embraced twenty-four books, of which we possess about one-half, and some of these only in fragments. Appian adopts the ethnographic treatment of history, taking up the individual lands and peoples included in the Roman Empire. The most important part of his work is the five books on the Civil Wars, the only detailed account of this period that we possess. Like all Greeks, who treated of Roman history, Appian was an enthusiastic admirer of Rome and her institutions. His work is marred by a lack of critical investigation and judgment. — H. WHITE.

Augustine, St., *Aurelius Augustinus* (354–430 A.D.). Born at Tagaste, Africa. He studied at Carthage, where, after a rather wild life, he became a member of the Manichæan sect. He was professor of rhetoric at Tagaste and Carthage and later at Rome. Through the influence of St. Ambrose and of his own pious mother he was led to adopt the orthodox Christian faith. He died during the siege of Hippo by the Vandals, 430 A.D. His best known works are the *City of God* and his *Confessions.* — N. L.

Aurelius, Marcus (Emperor, 161–180 A.D.). " The philosopher on the throne" was a diligent student of the works of Epictetus. His *Thoughts,* written during his reign, in leisure moments, and in part even on his military expeditions, are the chief source of our knowledge of his character. — B. L.

Cæsar, Caius Julius (*c.* 100–44 B.C.). Of Cæsar's life little needs to be said here, as for fifteen years the history of Rome was determined largely by his actions. All his writings have been lost except a few brief letters to Cicero, seven books of *Commentaries on the Gallic Wars* published in 51 B.C., and three books of *Commentaries on the Civil Wars,* which were not made public until after his death. The *Commentaries on the Gallic Wars* were written as a defence of his policy and position. They are remarkably accurate, and the excellence of the style is so great that they have passed into general use as a model of Latin prose. The *Commentaries on the Civil Wars*, which were left unfinished, are not as accurate nor as well written. — WM. DUNCAN.

Cassius Dio Cocceianus. Born at Nicæa, in Bithynia, 155 A.D. After an excellent education in rhetoric, philosophy, and history, he entered, at Rome, upon the career of advocate. His ability won for him rapid promotion through all the grades of office, from ædile to consul. He was also pro-consul of the province of Africa, and later of Dalmatia and Upper Pannonia successively. In 229 A.D. Alexander Severus chose him as his colleague in the consulship. We know nothing of his later years.

Dio's first historical work was the history of the reign of Commodus. Encouraged by its success, he decided to write a complete history of Rome (which extends to 229 A.D.), into which was incorporated the shorter history. After spending ten years in painstaking and careful research, and in the collec-tion of material, he was twelve years in planning and composing his great work. It consisted of eighty books, divided into decades. The treatment is rather uneven, and Dio's superstitious nature found pleasure in recording prodigies and miracles of all kinds. Of the eighty books, there are extant Books XXXVII to LIV complete, and considerable fragments of Books XXXVI, LV to LX. Books LXI to LXXX we possess in epitomized form in the compilation of Xiphilin (of the eleventh century), and some small fragments may also be gleaned from the chronicles of Zonaras (of the twelfth century), who frequently quotes Dio. Dio's work is of great value, filling up the gaps in Tacitus' account. Moreover, he judges and analyzes political questions with the keen eye of a statesman. His conception and understanding of the workings of the Roman state and constitution is much clearer and deeper than is·that of Livy, and he is free from the prejudices and insinuations of Tacitus. — SHUCKBURGH.

Cato, M. Porcius (234–149 B.C.). The censor, in contrast to the annalists who wrote in Greek, wrote his seven books of *Origines* in Latin, treating it not in the form of annals, but as a connected narrative. Moreover, his inter-ests were not limited to the city of Rome ; he included in his history valuable accounts of the tribes of Italy, from the earliest period down to his own times (about 149 B.C.). His treatise on agriculture is the only work which has survived. Of his one hundred and fifty speeches, not one is extant.

Cicero, M. Tullius (106–43 B.C.). Cicero brought Latin prose to its high-est standard of excellence, and was a voluminous writer. His works consist of speeches, dialogues, essays, and letters. His fifty or more speeches are judicial, as, *e.g.*, the famous orations against Verres ; and forensic and political in character, as, *e.g.*, the four orations against Catiline and the so-called *Philippics* against M. Antony. The dialogues and essays are derived largely from Greek sources. Among his philosophical treatises may be mentioned the works, *On the Nature of the Gods*, *De Finibus*, and *On Moral Duties;* of a rhetorical and political character are his, *On the Character of the Orator*, *On the Commonwealth*, and *On the Laws*.

The eight hundred or more letters are addressed mainly to T. Pomponius Atticus, his most intimate friend and confidant; others, to friends and re̶la̶- tions (*ad Familiares*), to his brother Quintus, and to Brutus. T̶h̶e̶ ̶c̶o̶l̶l̶e̶c̶- tion also contains letters from Cæsar, Antony, Pompey, a̶n̶d̶ ̶o̶t̶h̶e̶r̶ prominent Romans. These letters, covering the period from 68 B̶.̶C̶.̶ ̶t̶o̶ 43 B.C., are of the greatest value — more so, perhaps, than his spee̶ch̶es — because of the light they throw on the political intrigues and degeneracy of the Roman society during the last half century of the Republic. — B. L. and SHUCKBURGH.

Corpus Inscriptionum Latinarum (C. I. L.). A monumental work in fifteen volumes. It is the most valuable collection of Latin inscriptions which we possess.

Dionysius of Halicarnassus. Went to Rome about 30 B.C. and lived there twenty-two years, studying and collecting materials for his history. His *Archæ- ology* or *Roman Antiquities* narrated the history of Rome from the mythical period to the beginning of the First Punic War. Of the original twenty books, the first nine have been preserved, and almost all of the tenth and eleventh; these extend to 443 B.C. Of the remaining nine, there exist only fragments. His object was to show his Greek countrymen that the Romans were not barbarians, and that their history was worthy of attention. In fact, he had become almost a Roman in his attitude. He had little critical ability, and narrated the fables of the regal and early republican periods at great length and with comparatively few intimations that they were not fully historical.

Ephemeris Epigraphica. A supplement to the *Corpus Inscriptionum Latinarum*.

Epictetus (*fl. c.* 70–100 A.D.). Of Hieropolis, in Phrygia, by birth a slave. He was a respected teacher at Rome of the practical morality of the Stoics. When the philosophers were expelled from the city by Domitian in 89 A.D., he retired to Nicopolis in Epirus. Here he gathered about him a large throng of enthusiastic followers. He died either in the reign of Trajan or of Hadrian. The *Discourses*, *Encheiridion*, and some other fragments have been preserved. — B. L.

Eusebius Pamphili (died 337–340 A.D.). Born in Palestine. During the persecutions of 309 he fled to Egypt. Later he was bishop of Cæsarea, 314– *c.* 340 A.D. Although his works are more of a compilation than the product of a critical study and sifting of the sources, they are of great value for the study of early church history. The most important are a *Life of Constantine*, in four books; a *Church History*, from its earliest beginnings to about the year 324, in ten books; and a *Chronicle*, in two books, one containing an epitome of universal history, the other a series of chronological tables. — N. L.

Gaius (110–180? A.D.). Born in Asia Minor (?) and spent his life at Rome as a teacher and writer. The most famous of his works on civil law are the *Institutes*, in four books, an introduction to the study of jurisprudence. The greater part of this work, which was used extensively as a manual, and on the basis of which were compiled Justinian's *Institutes*, has been preserved to us. — E. POSTE.

Horace, *Q. Horatius Flaccus* (65–8 B.C.). The son of a freedman. Through the efforts of his father (see above, p. 196) he was able to enjoy an excellent education at Rome, and to finish his studies at Athens. Here, after the outbreak of the Civil War, he joined the standard of Brutus, and fought at Philippi as military tribune. The unsuccessful issue of the war cost him his little farm, which was among those assigned as a reward to the soldiers. Returning to Rome, he secured an appointment as clerk in the government service. Winning the friendship of Vergil, he was introduced by him to Mæcenas, and henceforth his future was assured. His works comprise the *Satires and Epistles*, *Odes and Epodes*, the *Art of Poetry*, and the *Secular Hymn*. — B. L. and THEO. MARTIN.

Justinian's Corpus Juris Civilis (528–534 A.D.). The final codification of the Roman law comprised (1) the *Code* proper, a condensed compilation of the imperial or statute law; (2) the *Digest*, or *Pandects*, an abridgment of the jurists; (3) the *Institutes*, a sort of text-book of the main principles of law and jurisprudence; and (4) the *Novellæ*, or *Novels*, imperial edicts and ordinances issued by Justinian after the compilation of the *Corpus*. — J. B. MOYLE.

Juvenal, *D. Junius Juvenalis* (about 60–140? A.D.), of *Aquinum*, spent his early years in the study of rhetoric. Late in life he turned to poetry, and his sixteen *Satires*, divided into five books, depict " in all the glaring colors of rhetoric " the degeneracy and prevalent vices of Roman society under the Empire. His keen criticism and piercing, passionate invective, however, lead him to exaggerate the condition of affairs. — B. L.

Lactantius, L. Cæcilius Firmianus. A pupil of Arnobius and a teacher of rhetoric at Nicomedia; subsequently appointed by Constantine as tutor of his son Crispus. Most of his works are still extant. Among the most valuable for purposes of historical study is his work, *On the Death of the Persecutors* of Christianity from Nero down to Galerius and Maximinus Daza. — A. N. L.

Livy, *Titus Livius* (59 B.C.–17 A.D.). Born at *Patavium* (Padua); little is known of his life, and the only extant work is a portion of his *History of Rome.* This extended from the founding of the city to the death of Drusus, 9 B.C., and was divided into one hundred and forty-two books. Livy published the first book between 29 and 25 B.C. and continued to write for forty years longer. The portions preserved are the first ten books, extending to 294 B.C. and Books 21 to 45 inclusive, embracing the period from 219 to 167 B.C. The *Epitome* of the other books consists of a brief table of contents, drawn up in the fourth century from an abridgment of his work.

Livy was the only great prose writer of the Augustan age. His aim was not to write a critical history, but to tell the accepted story in a clearer and more pleasing narrative. He borrowed freely from his predecessors, and the popularity of his work caused the earlier ones to be forgotten. He was not a partisan, but was not entirely just to the enemies of Rome. He idealized the past and considered his own age sadly degenerate. In spite of its faults, his work is a masterpiece, and the most important source for the early centuries of Roman history. — B. L.

Martial, *M. Valerius Martialis* (43–104 ? A.D.). Born at Bilbilis, Spain, where he received the customary education in grammar and rhetoric. When about twenty-one he went to Rome. Here the way to an official career was open to him; but he preferred the less burdensome life of a client. This relationship brought him into contact with all classes of Roman society, and his fifteen hundred epigrams are invaluable because of the light they throw on Roman life and manners. Shortly after the death of Domitian he returned to his home in Spain, where he passed the rest of his life in retirement on a splendid estate, the generous gift of his old friend, Marcella. — B. L.

Minucius Felix, M. His dialogue *Octavius,* written probably in the reign of M. Aurelius or Hadrian, is the earliest extant work of Latin Christian literature. A man of learning and culture himself, he embodies in this work the ideas of Christianity then prevailing among the educated classes. He grows eloquent in the defence of monotheism and in the refutation of the current prejudices. — A. N. L.

Monumentum Ancyranum. *The Deeds of the Divine Augustus* is an inscription, in both Greek and Latin, found on the walls of a temple to Augustus and Rome at *Ancyra* (Angora) in Asia Minor. It is the most authentic piece of ancient autobiography that has come down to us, being a copy of a document written by Augustus himself, justifying his policy and enumerating his services to the state and the honors he had received. Cf. for a second document, the selection from Tacitus, p. 221. — FAIRLEY, *Penn. Repr.,* V, No. 1.

Ovid, *P. Ovidius Naso* (43 B.C.–17 A.D.). Born at Sulmo, in central Italy. He pursued the study of law, but later turned to poetry. He held several minor offices, until, for some unknown reason, Augustus, in 9 A.D., sent him into exile to Tomi (Kustendje), on the Danube, where, in spite of repeated attempts to obtain his recall, he died in exile. Among his chief works are the *Fasti,* or *Calendar, Metamorphoses,* or *Transformations,* in which he treats of early Roman history and the apotheosis of the Emperor, the *Tristia,* and the four books of *Letters,* written in exile. — B. L.

Oxyrhynchus Papyri. In the excavations at Oxyrhynchus (Egypt), in 1896, a large number of papyri were found in rubbish heaps among the old buildings of the town. The greater part of them are Greek. Of these, about three hundred are literary, and belong for the most part to the first three centuries after Christ. About half of these are Homeric, a few are Byzantine. There are also about two thousand non-literary fragments, belonging to the first seven centuries after Christ. — GRENFELL and HUNT.

Petronius Arbiter. Almost nothing is known of his life, but he is doubtless the same Petronius whom Nero, instigated by the jealous Tigellinus, compelled to commit suicide (see above, p. 154). Of his work, a novel of twenty books or more, based on adventures supposed to have taken place on a journey, we now possess but fragments, of which the story of *Trimalchio's Dinner* is the most considerable. The work is of value for its vivid portrayal of the degenerate manners and debased tastes of the time. — H. T. PECK and PELLISON.

Pliny, *C. Plinius Secundus* (23–79 A.D.). Commonly known as Pliny the Elder, a wealthy citizen of *Comum* in northern Italy. Amid the varied duties of his long career as officer and official under Vespasian, he devoted all his spare moments to study and literary pursuits, in the fields of history, rhetoric, and natural science. His *Natural History,* the only one of his many works still extant, is an inexhaustible mine of information. Pliny met his death at the eruption of Mount Vesuvius, in 79 A.D., "a victim to his zeal for investigation." — B. L.

Pliny, *C. Plinius Cæcilius Secundus* (62–113 ? A.D.). Pliny the Younger, of *Comum,* the nephew and adopted son of Pliny the Elder. He was a pupil of Quintilian, and followed the profession of advocate. Great ability secured for him ready recognition, and he rose through the regular course of offices, until he was made consul, in 100 A.D., by Trajan. In 111 or 112 A.D. he was sent by the Emperor as imperial legate to Bithynia. It was during his governorship that Pliny's correspondence with Trajan (Book X of his *Letters*) — valuable material for the study of the provinces and early Christianity — took place. The first nine books of Pliny's letters, covering the years 97–109 A.D., though written with a view to publication, furnish a valuable corrective to the dark and overdrawn picture of Roman life under the Empire as painted by the satirists Juvenal, Persius, Petronius, and by Tacitus, the friend of Pliny. Of his speeches only the *Panegyricus*, in praise of the Emperor Trajan, is extant. — B. L.

Plutarch (46–120 A.D.). A native of Chæronea, in Bœotia. After completing studies in rhetoric, philosophy, and natural science at Athens, he entered upon an active public career, being employed in diplomatic business by the Roman Emperor. He made several visits to Rome, where he had friends among the higher classes and at the court. Trajan conferred consular honors upon him. Yet he always remained a loyal citizen of his native Chæronea, active in her service, honored and respected throughout Greece. He devoted much time to study and to the instruction and education of his sons and other promising youths. Of the many works of this versatile writer, a large part has been preserved. They may be divided into two classes, — his *Lives*, or historical works, and his philosophical-literary studies, a collection of eighty-three treatises, mostly on ethical subjects, generally known as the *Morals*. Of the parallel biographies of the great men of Greece and Rome, forty-six (twenty-three pairs) are still extant. The twelve from the Gracchi to J. Cæsar are especially valuable. Plutarch was no critical historian, nor did he make a very discriminating use of the sources at hand ; his aim was rather to present character sketches, which should teach a lesson in practical morality. Among his numerous sources may be mentioned Polybius, Dionysius of Halicarnassus, Livy, and Sallust. — A. H. CLOUGH.

Polybius (204–122? B.C.). The son of Lycortas, of Megalopolis, in Arcadia. He was active in the public service, but did not neglect literary studies. After the battle of Pydna, Polybius was one of the one thousand hostages who were sent to Rome. There his literary talents and the friendship of Scipio opened for him the way into the best society of the day. Here, too, in his intercourse with the great men of Rome, he had occasion to observe the workings of that constitution he so much admired. He travelled extensively in Italy, Egypt, Asia Minor, and accompanied Scipio on his campaigns in Gaul, Spain, and Africa. In 146 B.C., after the fall of Corinth, he served his countrymen by settling affairs in the Peloponnese to their entire satisfaction.

The rapid extension of the Roman Empire made a tremendous impression on Polybius. Moreover, it taught him the continuity and unity of history. And out of this splendid material he constructed his " pragmatic " history — " philosophy teaching by example." In his attempt to explain the internal and external development of political history, the cause and the effect, he tries to discover the motives underlying this series of events, with frequent reflections of a moral or political nature. His history covers the period of the

Second Punic War down to 166 B.C., with a brief introduction on the causes and events of the First Punic War. Conscientious and painstaking in the collection and investigation of the documents, the inscriptions, and other sources available, he was equally critical in sifting this material, and made an honest effort at impartiality of treatment. Only about an eighth of the original thirty-nine books is still extant. Livy, Plutarch, and Appian have borrowed largely from Polybius for this period of history. — SHUCKBURGH.

Quintilian, *M. Fabius Quintilianus* (*c.* 35–95 A.D.). His home was Calagurris, in Spain. Educated at Rome, where his father was a rhetorician, he returned to Spain. In the year 68, Galba, after his accession to the throne, took him back to Rome, where he was appointed professor of rhetoric, the first to be paid out of the public treasury. He was also engaged as advocate, but published only one of his speeches. His fame rests on his career as a teacher ; he was appointed the tutor of Domitian's grandchildren, and rewarded by him with the consulship. After twenty years of fruitful labor, he retired to compose his treatise on the causes of the decay in oratory, now lost, and the twelve books on the training of a perfect orator, the *Institutes*, still extant, which embodied the results of his lifelong experience as a teacher. — B. L.

Sallust, *C. Sallustius Crispus* (86–*c.* 33 B.C.). The first real Roman historian of any importance. He was tribune of the people in 52 B.C., and was opposed to Cicero and his policy. After his expulsion from the senate in 50 B.C. for misconduct, he followed the fortunes of Cæsar, who rewarded him with an official career, appointing him governor of Africa in 46 B.C. After Cæsar's death, Sallust retired to a life of leisure and luxury on the wealth he had acquired as governor, and devoted himself to literary pursuits. His two monographs — the *Catiline* and the *Jugurthine War* — are still extant. In both, the rhetorical style and diction are offset by a strong tendency to discover the political motives of historical events, often leading to a perverse interpretation of the facts. They are of great value, however, in that they are the expression of a fit spokesman for the popular party, while most of the Roman literature was and remained in the hands of the nobility, directly or indirectly. Sallust, "severer in his writings than in his conduct," knew little of historical criticism, nor did he take the pains to use the documentary sources which must have been at hand. In consequence, his chronology of events is frequently confused. Moreover, proper discount must be made for the fictitious speeches which he, like most other ancient historians, introduces at opportune points in the narrative. His last work — the *Histories*, in five books, from the death of Sulla in 78 B.C. to 67 B.C. — was the most perfect of all, but only a few fragments have been preserved. — B. L.

Seneca, L. Annæus (4 B.C.–65 A.D.). Was born at *Corduba* (Cordova), Spain. He was a senator under Caligula. In 41 A.D. Claudius sent him into exile, from which he was recalled, eight years afterward, through the influence of Agrippina, and the education of her son Nero was given into his charge. Made consul by Nero, he for a time guided the destinies of the Empire. But in 65 A.D., Nero, tired of his tutor and counsellor, compelled him to commit suicide, charging him with participation in the conspiracy of Piso. Seneca's writings in prose and verse cover a wide range of subjects, — tragedies and epigrams, speeches, works on Egypt and India, philosophical writings founded on the Stoic creed, letters, and researches in natural science. — B. L.

Strabo (*c.* 64 B.C.–19 A.D.) was of a noble Greek family of Amaseia, in the province of Pontus. After devoting his early years to the study of grammar and philosophy, he came to Rome in 29 B.C. Leaving in 24 B.C. for an extensive trip through Egypt, he returned to Rome in 20 B.C. Subsequently he travelled extensively throughout the Roman Empire, gathering material for his geographical-historical writings. His *Historical Commentaries*, which treated of the two periods before and after the period covered by Polybius, down to 27 B.C., is unfortunately lost. The *Geography*, in seventeen books, though unfinished, is the fruit of his many years of study and travel, and is a storehouse of information. — B. L.

Suetonius Tranquillus, C. (about 75–160 A.D.), the friend of Pliny the Younger, was an advocate under Trajan and private secretary for a time to Hadrian. Devoting his later years to literary studies, he published (*c.* 120 A.D.) his eight books on *The Lives of the Twelve Cæsars*, from J. Cæsar to Domitian, which is preserved almost complete. Though drawn from good sources, little selection and critical sifting of material have been done, so that we have in them a combination of much that is valuable with much that is worthless. The chronology is often inexact, and little attention is given to political and military affairs. Of his *Lives of Eminent Grammarians and Rhetoricians*, we possess only fragments. His other works have been lost. — B. L.

Tacitus, Cornelius, was born about 54 A.D. and died about 117 A.D. He was of good family and held various offices, including the consulship, 98 A.D. His writings are: (1) the *Dialogue on Orators*, written between 79 and 81 A.D.; (2) the *Agricola*, written in 98 A.D.; (3) the *Germania*, written about the same time or a little later; (4) the *History* and *Annals*, on which he worked continuously after about 98 A.D. The *Annals* were not published till after 115 A.D.

In the *Dialogue* his object is to explain the cause of the decline of oratory. His republican sympathies are clearly marked. The life of *Agricola*, his father-in-law, is the best biography in ancient literature. The *Germania* furnishes most of our knowledge of the early Germans. The *Annals* and *History* together included originally the account of the eighty-two years from the death of Augustus to the death of Domitian. The portions extant embrace the reign of Tiberius except for a gap of over two years, the seventh year of Claudius to the thirteenth of Nero, and the account of the Civil War, 69–70 A.D.

Of Tacitus' style and excellence no praise is necessary, as he has long been recognized as one of the greatest of historians. But in his story of the Emperors facts must be carefully distinguished from innuendo and rhetoric. His anti-imperialistic bias must be remembered. And, furthermore, it must be kept constantly in mind that he entirely failed to grasp the truth that the provinces were far more important than the city of Rome. To his influence it is due that the history of the Empire has been so often degraded into a series of biographies of the Emperors. — CHURCH AND BRODRIBB.

Tertullian, *Q. Septimius Florens Tertullianus* (*c.* 150–230 A.D.), of Carthage, occupies an important place in early Christian literature. Among his numerous works, mostly of a controversial character, his *Apology* is one of the most important for the study of the legal and political relations of the early Christians with the imperial government. There are extant also several of his more practical, Christian writings, of which the two letters *To his Wife* are of especial value. In his later life he became a follower of the doctrines of Montanus, "with its ecstatic dreams of a millennium and the approaching end of the world and its probation for the same by means of bodily and spiritual mortification." — A. N. L.

Velleius Paterculus, M. The two books of his *Roman Histories*, from the earliest times down to his own day (*c.* 30 A.D.), are still preserved to us, the first book only in part, the second in its entirety. The history of Rome is treated in summary fashion, not objectively, but with the lively interest and enthusiastic admiration of a loyal officer, who, in the long and faithful service of his prince, both in the field of battle and in an official capacity as prefect, has learned to respect and revere him. The *Histories* are, therefore, of value for a correct judgment of the character of Tiberius and constitute an " official version " of the events of his time. — B. L.

APPENDIX II

REMARKS ON ILLUSTRATIONS

FIG. 1. FRONTISPIECE. PONT DU GARD, *near Nîmes.* (*Ancient Nemausus.*) *Schreiber,* pl. 57, fig. 6. A bridge in the valley of Gardon, carrying at present one aqueduct of Nîmes, which in the times of the later Empire brought the water a distance of twenty-one miles to the baths. There are three rows of arches, the lowest arch being sixty-five feet above the water, the middle arch, now repaired to carry a carriage road, being thirty feet higher, and the top row, which carries the channel of the aqueduct, being one hundred and fifty-eight feet above the water. The cover is made of slabs of rock, sometimes eight by ten feet in size. This old Roman bridge is an abiding testimony to the thorough Romanization of the Gallic province and to the character of the work done by the Romans.

FIG. 2. PAGE 10. FARMER'S CALENDAR. (*Schreiber,* pl. 62, fig. 3.) A marble cube, two feet by one foot, of about 31-29 B.C.

FIG. 3. PAGE 16. COOP WITH THE SACRED CHICKENS. (*Schreiber, Atlas of Classical Antiquities,* pl. 19, fig. 13.) Auspices ("observations of birds") were taken from the observation of the regions of the heaven, or from the flight of birds, or from the behavior of the *pulli* or sacred chickens, when corn was thrown to them. If they rushed eagerly out of the coop at the food and some of the corn fell from their beaks, it was considered a most lucky omen; if they refused to leave the coop, or flew away, or refused to eat, the omen was unfavorable. This method, because of its convenience, was generally used on military expeditions. The chickens were carried about in a coop by a special functionary.

FIG. 4. PAGE 21. SUOVETAURILIA. (*Baumeister, Denkmäler,* III, p. 1713, fig. 1799.) A relief of Pentelic marble, six feet long, of the Roman imperial period. The *suovetaurilia* was an old Italian sacrifice of a bull, a ram, and a boar, offered to Mars, to secure purification from sin. This ceremony of lustration (*lustratio;* cf. selections from the *Monum. Ancyr.,* p. 222) was performed at the end of each five years or *lustrum,* after the taking of the census. The victims were led three times around the assembled people in arms, and then sacrificed to Mars. In later classical times, the victims were offered on other great occasions; *e.g.* a triumph, and to "Jupiter and the other Capitoline deities, rather than to Mars."

To the right in the relief are two sacred laurel trees and two fruit-laden altars, crowned with garlands. Before one of them stands the officiating magistrate, his head, according to the Roman ritual, covered with the toga. With his right hand he sprinkles incense on the altar from the incense box which an attendant holds before him, while another attendant behind him carries the ewer with the libation. Then follow a number of attendants, wearing garlands of laurel, among them the sacrificer with the axe, and after them the three victims in the order given in the term *suovetaurilia* — boar, ram, and bull.

Fig. 5. Page 26. A Roman Standard-bearer. (*Schreiber*, pl. 39, fig. 7.) A relief of the first century, on the tomb of one Pintaius, as the inscription below the relief shows. The soldier wears a *tunica* or shirt, a coat of mail, and a leather jerkin with tassels, girt with two belts studded with metal. On the upper girdle, on the left, he wears a sword, on the lower, on the right, a dagger. His half-boots leave the toes uncovered. Covering his helmet is a bearskin which falls over his shoulders, this skin being worn only by standard-bearers and musicians. The standard consists of a spear, on the top of which is a wreath; just below this " a cross-bar with pendant acorns; next to this a metal desk, then Jupiter's eagle, a crescent moon, and an amulet. Lowest of all is a large tassel."

Fig. 6. Page 30. A Roman Camp. (*Marquardt*, Vol. VI, p. 404.) For a detailed description, see the *Histories* of Polybius, Book VI, ch. 27 *et seq.*

Fig. 7. Page 39. A Testudo. *From the Column of Trajan.* (*Baumeister*, I, p. 536, fig. 571.) The name *testudo*, "a tortoise (shell)," was applied " to the covering made by a close body of soldiers, who placed their shields over their heads to secure themselves against the darts of the enemy. The shields fitted so closely together as to present one unbroken surface without any interstices between them, and were also so firm that men could walk upon them and even horses and chariots be driven over them. A *testudo* was formed either in battle to ward off the arrows and other missiles of the enemy, or, more frequently, to form a protection to the soldiers when they advanced to the walls or gates of a town for the purpose of attacking them." (*Harper's Dict. Ant.*)

Fig. 8. Page 69. A Roman Sacrificing. (*Schreiber*, pl. 85, fig. 11.) This statue is of the imperial period, "the first example of a statue in a toga." According to the Roman ritual, the toga is drawn over the head. The toga was the distinctive Roman dress and a mark of citizenship. The young

Romans, upon reaching manhood, usually at the age of sixteen, assumed the "toga virilis," *i.e.* the white toga of the Roman citizen.

FIG. 9. PAGE 94. A ROMAN LITTER. (*Baumeister*, fig. 1602.) "The litter consists of an ordinary couch, to which four posts carrying an arched canopy and a pair of poles have been added. Above the canopy is a rod running lengthwise, to which curtains were fastened by rings. The occupant could hide himself from view by drawing these curtains across the sides." Especially under the empire splendidly ornamented and furnished litters became the fashion. In the city women made more use of them than men. In the country and on journeys, on the other hand, the use of litters was general, it being the common manner of travelling among the wealthy aristocrats who could command a considerable number of slaves.

FIG. 10. PAGE 99. ROMANO-CARTHAGINIAN AQUEDUCT. (*Schreiber*, pl. 58, fig. 6, p. 122.) "In the valley of the Meliana (*Wad el Meliana*) near Tunis. This aqueduct supplied Carthage with water in Roman times."

FIG. 11. PAGE 106. A ROMAN ORATOR. (*Baumeister*, fig. 1921.) This is the earliest form of the toga, which is very scanty as compared with the later form worn in imperial times, shown in fig. 14.

FIG. 12. PAGE 132. GLADIATORS. (*Baumeister*, fig. 2351; *from wall paintings in the amphitheatre of Pompeii*.) An umpire or referee, in a white tunic, is giving directions to a pair of gladiators. On the right is a Samnite in full armor, two attendants carrying his helmet and sword. On the left stands his opponent, a Thracian, wearing long greaves, two other attendants carrying his helmet and round shield. The Thracian is blowing a *tuba*, or curved trumpet, probably as a signal for the beginning of the combat. A Victory, with the crown and palm branch, stands behind each of the combatants.

FIG. 13. PAGE 133. GLADIATORS. (*Baumeister*, fig. 2353, *from a stucco relief on the tomb of Scaurus*.) Beginning on the left are two horsemen, fully armed, fighting with lances. Behind these are a Thracian and a Samnite who is appealing to the people. Next follows a combat between a Thracian and a Samnite, the latter in his defeat raises his hands in appeal. All of the gladiators wear the short apron. The lower half of the relief represents fights with wild beasts (*venatio*), showing lightly clad *bestiarii* in combat with boars, bears, bulls, and stags. The inscription above the gladiators shows that they are all *Juliani*, *i.e.* either his own trained slaves, or belonging to some corporation founded by him. They were probably employed regularly by Ampliatus, the governor of the show, for one of the gladiatorial advertisements in the Basilica at Pompeii (*C.I.L.*, IV, 1183) runs: "The gladiatorial troupe of N. Festus Ampliatus will fight for the second time on the 16th of May.

There will be hunting and awnings." These games lasted down to the fifth century.

FIG. 14. PAGE 145. MONUMENTUM ANCYRANUM. (*Duruy*, Vol. IV, p. 165.) For description see *Appendix of Authors*, page 243.

FIG. 15. PAGE 153. PLAN OF THE HOUSE OF THE TRAGIC POET. (From a photograph.) See Mau : *Pompeii*, ch. 32 and 39; Preston and Dodge: *Private Life of the Romans*, ch. 2. Compare with the following illustration and ask the pupils to describe what the *andron*, etc., were.

FIG. 16. PAGE 161. VIEW OF THE HOUSE OF THE TRAGIC POET. (From a photograph.) This house was built, probably, only a few years before the destruction of Pompeii. The house owes its name to an error made in identifying one of its pictures ; consequently the name has no real meaning. In the *fauces* was found the well-known mosaic picture, *Cave canem*, now in the museum at Naples, as well as several well-preserved wall-paintings. Compare this with the plan and ask the pupils to tell which rooms they can see.

FIG. 17. PAGE 169. INTERIOR OF A HOUSE, LOOKING FROM THE ATRIUM TOWARD THE REAR. (From a photograph.) This gives a good view of the condition in which the Pompeian houses are now. It shows the *atrium* with the *impluvium*, the *tablinum* with its wall-paintings, and the general plan of the building. Compare with the plan and name the rooms.

FIG. 18. PAGE 181. ALTAR OF THE LARES COMPITALES. (*Schreiber*, pl. 18, fig. 4.) Pompeii, at the meeting of four streets. Of the first century, A.D. In addition to the public worship in the temples, the Roman also held private worship in his house, at his *Lararium*, a shrine where the *Lares*, *Penates*, and *Genii* were invoked. "The ancients, who believed in the immortality of the soul, accepted the existence of secondary divinities, intermediaries between heaven, the lower world, and the earth. The *Manes* of the dead, it was thought, haunted their old homes to protect them." Yet all the dead did not become tutelary *Genii*. There were the evil spirits (*Larvæ*) and the souls of those who had not received the rites of burial, the "unquiet ghosts." The spirits of the good were the *Lares*, or *Lemuria* (cf. above, the selection from Ovid, p. 13). "Yet as the truer nature of the dead man could never be known, the purest part of the spirit was included under the name *Manes*, which were honored as demigods, and became the *Lares*, or protectors of the hearth." There were many classes of *Lares :* the *Lares* public, or *Augusti*, the *Genii* of the deified emperors ; *Lares compitales*, the patron deities of the cross-roads ; *Lares rusticii*, and others.

There is a wall-painting behind the altar at Pompeii which represents two *Lares* with serpents at their feet, and on each side a group of men and women (?). The Romans regarded serpents as protecting *Genii*. The pedi-

ment above the painting is filled with an eagle spreading out its wings, perhaps suggesting the apotheosis of a deceased hero.

FIG. 19. PAGE 194. YOUTH READING AT A BOOKCASE. WRITING MATE-
RIALS. (*Seignobos, Hist. Rome*, p. 165.) On the top of the bookcase is a
reading desk. The writing materials (from a wall-painting from Pompeii)
consist of a *diptychon*, or double tablet, in which the holes through which
passes the sealing cord can be readily seen; a letter, probably of papyrus,
bearing the address, "To M. Lucretius, Flamen of Mars, Decurio, Pompeii";
a double inkstand, penknife, and stilus.

FIG. 20. PAGE 200. A BAKER'S MONUMENT, *outside the Porta Maggiore,
Rome*. (*Schreiber*, pl. 67, No. 7 [wrongly for 5].) The inscription reads :
"This is the monument of Marcus Vergilius Eurysaces," and a manuscript
informs us that he was the owner of a large public bakery. The monument
itself, of imperial times, is in the form of a large baker's oven. Running
round the top of it is a frieze, with reliefs showing scenes from the bakery.

FIG. 21. PAGE 205. COLUMBARIUM. (*Lanciani, Ruins and Excavations
of Ancient Rome*, p. 332.) A *columbarium* is a sepulchral chamber, so called
because of its resemblance to a dove-cote. It was generally a subterranean
vault, in which there were several "stories" of niches. In these niches were
stored the urns containing the ashes of the dead. Such *columbaria* were often
built by wealthy families, and by the Emperors, for their slaves and freedmen.
Others were erected by private individuals, who made a business of selling
these niches to the poor. As a general rule, religious societies or "burial
clubs" constructed *columbaria* for their members, each of whom contributed
a stated sum and thereafter contributed his yearly subscription, which insured
him a niche in the vault and therewith the due rites of burial.

"The characteristic of this coöperative tomb, so evident in our illustration,
is a set of marble brackets which project from the walls between the fourth
and fifth row of niches, counting from the floor. They were destined to support the temporary wooden balcony by means of which the relatives and
friends of the deceased could reach the upper tiers of niches on anniversary
days, when the urns were decorated with flowers, libations were offered, and
other ceremonies were performed. . . . Many (who tenanted this sepulchral
chamber) were freedmen of the Julian dynasty from the age of Augustus and
Livia to that of Claudius." (*Lanciani, Ruins and Excavations*, pp. 328–333.)

FIG. 22. PAGE 208. VIEW OF THE INTERIOR OF THE AMPHITHEATRE AT
POMPEII. (From a photograph.) This is the oldest amphitheatre known to
us. It is 444 feet long and 342 feet broad. There are no underground rooms.
The wall about the arena is only a little over six feet high, but it was appar-
ently surrounded by an iron grating to protect the spectators from the attacks

254 SOURCE BOOK OF ROMAN HISTORY

of the wild beasts. There are thirty-five rows of seats which would hold
about twenty thousand people. Awnings were sometimes provided (see above)
to shelter the spectators from the sun.

FIG. 23. PAGE 212. THE AMPHITHEATRE AT POMPEII. (From a photograph.) View of the exterior as seen from the west.

FIG. 24. PAGE 230. APODYTERIUM OF THE STABIAN BATHS, with the ante-
room leading from the Palæstra. (From Mau: *Pompeii*, p. 182.) These baths
take their modern name from their location on the Stabian street. They are
the oldest in Pompeii, built in the second century B.C., but later remodelled.
The *apodyterium* was the dressing room from which the bathers passed into the
tepidarium (warm), the *caldarium* (hot), or *frigidarium* (cold bath). The
niches in the walls are intended for clothes, like modern lockers in a gymnasium. The ceiling is decorated elaborately. See Mau : *Pompeii*, ch. 26.

INDEX

DATE DUE	
10/18/02	
DEC 06 2004	
DEC 11 2009	

GAYLORD   PRINTED IN U.S.A.